Medicines
An A-Z Guide

Medicines
An A-Z Guide

Matthew Elliott

SELECT
EDITIONS

This book is intended to provide reference information to help people understand more about the medical treatment they have been prescribed or have purchased. While every effort has been made to ensure this book is free from error, the knowledge of medicines and healthcare treatment is constantly changing for many reasons, and so it should not be considered as a substitute for personalised advice from a qualified medical practitioner.

The publisher, the editor and their respective employees shall not accept responsibility for injury, loss or damage occasioned to any person acting or refraining from action as a result of material in this book whether or not such injury, loss or damage is in any way due to any negligent act or omission on the part of the publisher, editor or their employees.

This edition printed in 2005

Selectabook Ltd
Folly Road, Roundway, Devizes,
Wiltshire SN10 2HT

Copyright © 2004, Arcturus Publishing Limited
26/27 Bickels Yard, 151–153 Bermondsey Street,
London SE1 3HA

Cover design by Alex Ingr and Steve Flight.
Layout by Metro Media Limited.

ISBN 1-84193-283-3

Printed in India

Contents

Introduction

Medicines have been a major force in the fight against disease for many centuries. Most of us have taken some kind of medicine to treat or ward off illness.

The range of medicines at our disposal has never been greater than it is today. We have access not only to the conventional pills and potions prescribed by doctors, but to a range of alternative, complementary and over-the-counter products which we can buy without medical consultation. While this is undoubtedly a good thing, in that many people do not feel that conventional medicine meets their needs, it also means that the average consumer is faced with a bewildering array of options from which to choose.

This book is designed as a guide to the most common medicines. It is divided into two sections:

Prescription Medicines
A list of over 450 of the most commonly prescribed medicines together with information about their actions, side effects and special precautions.

Over-the-counter Medicines
An A-Z of many of the most commonly used over-the-counter remedies for common complaints.

IMPORTANT
If a problem persists and does not respond to over-the-counter treatment you should consult a medical professional. This book is not intended as a substitute for professional medical, or pharmaceutical advice. For queries regarding prescription medicines consult your doctor or pharmacist. If patients are concerned about medicines they receive from hospital they should visit the consultant in charge of their case.

Prescription Medicines

This section is designed as a quick-reference guide to the medicines most commonly prescribed for people both at home and in hospital. It may be that you have been given information about a prescribed medicine and have forgotten it, or that you want to find out more about a drug which has been prescribed for yourself or a member of your family. Whatever your motive for searching, this chapter offers basic information about each medicine in layman's language.

HOW TO USE THIS SECTION

The medicines are listed in alphabetical order, according to their most commonly used generic name, which is the official name for a medicine and is the name of the active ingredient.

Brand name: These are the names given to the product by a manufacturer. For instance, Aspirin is the generic name for the painkilling drug, while Anadin is one of the many brand names under which it is marketed.

Type of drug: This loosely classifies the drug, either by the type of action it has (eg. anti-inflammatory) or the effect it has (eg. anticancer).

Uses: This section describes the most common uses for the medicine concerned. However this is not an exhaustive list and doctors may prescribe medicines for uses other than those listed here. If patients are concerned about what exactly they are taking medicines for, they are advised to see their doctor or pharmacist.

How it works: Where known, an explanation of how the drug works and what effect it has.

Availability: Either indicated as POM (a prescription only medicine) or if available over-the-counter.

Possible adverse effects: This section gives an overview of the possible adverse effects of a medicine. It also advises on serious adverse effects which may need immediate medical attention. However a full list can be obtained from the information leaflet supplied with the medicine or any pharmacist. Any worrying side effects should be reported to the doctor or pharmacist who supplied it.

Other information: Any other relevant details about the drug. This will also include whether a medicine can be used for children or in pregnancy and breastfeeding. Any specific cautions for children or pregnancy and breastfeeding will be listed in the 'caution' section.

CAUTION
Divided into four key areas covering:

Children: This section will state at what age children can be treated with a particular medicine. If it is suitable for any children this will be stated in 'other information'. If there is no information on children it means that the medicine is either NOT suitable, or should only be used when prescribed by a doctor. If there is concern over whether a medicine can be taken by children, patients should consult their doctor or pharmacist.

Pregnancy and breastfeeding: This will state whether it is safe to use in pregnancy and breastfeeding. If it is suitable to use in pregnancy and breastfeeding this will be stated in 'other information'. If there is no information on pregnancy and breastfeeding it means that the medicine is either NOT suitable, or should only be used when prescribed by a doctor who specialises in treating pregnant and breast-feeding women. If there is concern over whether a medicine can be taken during pregnancy and breastfeeding patients should consult their doctor or pharmacist.

Alcohol: This part sets out special precautions to be taken with regard to alcohol consumption. If there is no information it means there are no special precautions – although alcohol should ideally NOT be consumed when taking any medicine. Direct any concerns to your doctor or pharmacist.

Driving and operating machinery: If there are no special precautions with regard to driving or operating machinery, patients should ensure they are not suffering any detrimental effects before driving or performing any other manual task.

ABBREVIATIONS USED WITH PRESCRIPTION MEDICINES

There are a wide variety of abbreviations used in connection with prescribed medicines; some of the more commonly used ones are listed here. All questions concerning anything written on the labels or boxes of medicines should be directed to the pharmacist who supplied them.

BP/EP/BPC/USP:
These abbreviations mean that the active ingredient of the medicine has reached certain standards. In the pharmaceutical industry these are generally called pharmacopial standards – hence the P in the name. The first letter refers to its origin for example: B=British, E=European, US=United States. BPC is an old British Standard referring to the British Pharmaceutical Codex.

E/C:
This means the tablet or capsule has been 'enteric coated'. This is usually carried out to protect the stomach from the active ingredient inside the medicine.

MR/CR/SR:
These mean that the medicine has been given a coating that releases the drug more slowly, and over a more prolonged period of time in the digestive system. A medicine without these letters dissolves in the stomach straight away.

ACAMPROSATE CALCIUM

Brand name: Campral EC

Type of drug: Used in alcohol dependence

Uses: The treatment of people who are alcohol dependent to maintain abstinence. Usually used in conjunction with counselling, particularly for people who are at risk of using alcohol again.

How it works: It is believed that acamprosate intereferes with signalling in the brain which impedes alcohol dependence.

Availability: POM

Possible adverse effects: Diarrhoea, nausea, vomiting, stomach pain and itchy rash.

Other information: Treatment will usually start as soon as the patient has stopped drinking and continue for around a year. Counselling increases the effectiveness of treatment. This medication should not be taken if the recipient has severe liver or kidney problems.

CAUTION

Alcohol: Should not be consumed whilst taking this medication.

ACARBOSE

Brand name: Glucobay

Type of drug: Antidiabetic

Uses: Adjuvant treatment of non-insulin dependant diabetes.

How it works: Slows down the rate at which sugars and starch are digested, which in turn, reduces blood sugar levels.

Availability: POM

Possible adverse effects: Flatulence and abdominal pain although these tend to decrease with time. This will be minimised if sucrose and starch are reduced, but a qualified medical practitioner should be consulted before changing a diabetic diet.

Other information: Acarbose should be taken with or immediately before meals for maximum effect. Patients should carry glucose with them to allay low blood sugar levels.

ACEBUTOLOL

Brand name: Sectral

Type of drug: Cardiac, beta-blocker
Uses: A treatment for angina, abnormal heart rhythms and high blood pressure. Can also be used as a treatment for anxiety.
How it works: Slowing and steadying heart rate.
Availability: POM
Possible adverse effects: Lethargy and fatigue, cold hands and feet, nausea, vomiting, nightmares. Sometimes a slow pulse may be noticed. A rash and/or breathlessness should always be reported to a doctor.
Other information: Acebutolol should be prescribed with caution for people with asthma or other lung disorders because it can worsen the conditions. It may need to be taken for long periods and should not be discontinued unless advised by a doctor.

ACEMETACIN
Brand name: Emflex
Type of drug: Anti-inflammatory
Uses: Treatment of pain and inflammation associated with rheumatism and other musculoskeletal disorders.
How it works: Reduces pain and inflammation by blocking the production of prostaglandins which are involved in the inflammatory process.
Availability: POM
Possible adverse effects: Stomach and bowel pain, discomfort, headaches, blurred vision and dizziness, tinnitus. Gastrointestinal ulceration and/or bleeding may occur, so if you suffer severe stomach pain, or there is blood in your stools then seek urgent medical advice.
Other information: Patients allergic to aspirin or indomethacin may also be allergic to acemetacin and should not take this medicine without advice from the doctor or pharmacist. Patients on long-term treatment should have regular eye examinations.
CAUTION
Driving and operating machinery: As this drug can cause dizziness and blurred vision, patients receiving this medication should not drive or perform skilled tasks until they are certain they are not experiencing these or any other side effects.

ACETAZOLAMIDE

Brand name: Diamox, Diamox SR

Type of drug: Glaucoma treatment, carbonic anhydrase inhibitor

Uses: Glaucoma, fluid retention (although its use for this is declining) and epilepsy.

How it works: Reduces the formation of excess fluid inside the eye, and so lowers the pressure. For fluid retention this drug causes the kidneys to excrete more water as urine.

Availability: POM

Possible adverse effects: A tingling sensation in the hands and feet, headache, dizziness, fatigue, increased thirst, an increased need to urinate, a loss of appetite, and a strange taste in the mouth. If unexplained bruising or rashes occur, or the patient has a sore throat and fever, medical advice must be sought immediately.

Other information: May affect the levels of potassium in the body, and regular blood tests are carried out for long time use.

CAUTION

Children: It can be used to treat epilepsy in children and specific guidelines have been developed.

Alcohol: Should be avoided when taking this medication because of an increased risk of dehydration associated with the combination.

Driving and operating machinery: As this drug can cause dizziness, patients receiving this medication should not drive or perform skilled tasks until they are certain they are not experiencing this or any other side effects.

ACICLOVIR

Brand name: Zovirax

Type of drug: Antiviral

Uses: Treatment of viral infections caused by herpes, including herpes simplex (cold sores and genital infections), and varicella-zoster (chicken-pox and shingles).

How it works: Stops the multiplication of the virus.

Availability: OTC cream for cold sores, POM tablets, injection and ointment.

Possible adverse effects: The tablet form can cause headaches, nausea, vomiting, diarrhoea and stomach pain. The cream may cause a burning or stinging when applied. The eye ointment may also cause a burning or stinging sensation and produce a redness or rash around the eye.

Other information: Best used in the early stages of infection. For cold sores this means when the affected area starts to tingle. Always complete the full course. This medicine may be prescribed for children.

ACITRETIN

Brand name: Neotigason

Type of drug: Psoriasis treatment, oral retinoid

Uses: The treatment of severe psoriasis and other problematic skin conditions where other treatments have failed.

How it works: Slows down the reproduction of skin cells.

Availability: POM

Possible adverse effects: Eyes, mouth and skin can become very dry, inflamed or red. Dry hair or hair loss. If a severe headache, severe muscle pain, nausea, vomiting or problems with sight occur, a doctor should be consulted immediately.

Other information: Avoid exposure to sunlight and sun lamps. Blood tests will be performed to monitor liver function. Patients will not be allowed to donate blood during treatment or for 1 year after the course is completed.

CAUTION

Pregnancy and breastfeeding: Effective means of contraception are mandatory during, and for 2 years after the treatment ends, as the drug can be harmful to foetuses.

Driving and operating machinery: Problems with night vision may occur so patients should not drive or perform skilled tasks until they are certain they are not experiencing this or any other side effects.

ACRIVASTINE

Brand name: Semprex, Benadryl

Type of drug: Antihistamine

Uses: A short-acting antihistamine used for the treatment of hay fever and allergic skin conditions such as urticaria (hives).

How it works: Blocks the action of histamine – a chemical released by the body in response to allergies – thus stopping symptoms such as runny noses and sneezing.

Availability: OTC

Possible adverse effects: Drowsiness, headache or dry mouth.

CAUTION

Children: This drug may be used in children over 12 years old.

Alcohol: Should be avoided, as it will increase the likelihood of drowsiness.

Driving and operating machinery: Patients should not drive or perform skilled tasks until they are certain they are not experiencing any side effects.

ADENOSINE

Brand name: Adenocor

Type of drug: Cardiac, anti-arrhythmic

Uses: Treatment of some kinds of rapid heartbeat (paroxysmal supraventricular tachycardia).

How it works: Adenosine slows the passage of signals through the heart causing it to return to its normal rhythm

Availability: Intravenous injection in hospital.

Possible adverse effects: Facial flushing, breathing difficulties, chest pain, nausea, dizziness and light-headedness.

Other information: This drug is only administered in hospital.

CAUTION

Driving and operating machinery: As this drug can cause dizziness, patients receiving this medication should not drive or perform skilled tasks until they are certain they are not experiencing this or any other side effects.

ADRENALINE (Epinephrine)

Brand name: Epipen, Anapen

Type of drug: Cardiac, allergy treatment, hormone

Uses: For emergency treatment of anaphylactic shock caused by insect bites, food allergies and other allergies; also used in severe asthma, croup and cardiac arrest.

How it works: Adrenaline causes the blood vessels to narrow, and the heart to beat faster and more forcefully. This stops the patient's blood pressure falling too low, which can occur in a severe allergic reaction. Adrenaline also dilates the airways allowing patients to breathe more easily.

Possible adverse effects: Anxiety, breathlessness, restlessness, rapid heartbeat, dizziness, tremor, higher blood pressure, dry mouth, vomiting, sweating, cold hands and feet.

Availability: Used in emergency situations

Other information: This drug usually comes as an auto-injecting device commonly referred to as a pen. High risk patients may be advised to carry adrenaline with them at all times. After using the device the patient should go to hospital as soon as possible. Special dose syringes are available for children.

CAUTION

Driving and operating machinery: As this drug can cause dizziness, patients receiving this medication should not drive or perform skilled tasks until they are certain they are not experiencing this or any other side effects.

ALENDRONIC ACID

Brand name: Fosamax

Type of drug: Bisphosphonate

Uses: Treatment and prevention of osteoporosis.

How it works: It acts on the rate of bone growth by preventing bone cells from releasing calcium from the bones.

Availability: POM

Possible adverse effects: Abdominal symptoms such as discomfort, nausea, diarrhoea, swelling, wind, headache. Rarely, alendronic acid can lead to irritation of the oesophagus which may cause pain on swallowing, heartburn and chest pain. Any problems should be reported to a doctor immediately.

Other information: May be administered once a day or once a week. For the latter it should be taken on the same day of the week. The tablets should be taken on an empty stomach, at least 30 minutes before breakfast (and any other medication) with a full glass of water.

Certain groups of people are at increased risk of osteoporosis including post-menopausal women and those receiving particular drugs and treatments. In addition to medication, it is important to have a balanced diet.

ALFACALCIDOL

Brand name: One-Alpha

Type of drug: Similar to Vitamin D

Uses: The prevention or treatment of bone disease caused by either kidney malfunction or vitamin D deficiency (rickets and osteomalacia).

How it works: Vitamin D helps to regulate the amount of calcium and phosphate in the blood. Thus Alfacalcidol works similarly to regulate the amount of calcium available in the blood, the bones and the teeth.

Availability: POM

Possible adverse effects: If the calcium level becomes too high this can cause nausea, vomiting, feeling thirsty, constipation and the need to pass urine more frequently.

Other information: Blood tests will be carried out to monitor the calcium levels. This medicine may be prescribed for children.

ALIMENAZINE

(Formerly known as trimeprazine)

Brand name: Vallergan

Type of drug: Antihistamine

Uses: To help relieve itching of the skin.

How it works: Blocks the action of histamine – a chemical produced by the body in response to allergies – so stopping runny nose and itching.

Availability: POM

Possible adverse effects: Drowsiness, dizziness, headache, dry mouth and blocked nose. Report any sign of sore throat, raised temperature, or feeling generally unwell to the doctor immediately.

Other information: Patients should avoid direct sunlight and using sunlamps. Sunscreen should be worn during treatment because this medicine may cause the body to react badly to the sun.

CAUTION

Children: This medicine may be used in children over 2 years of age.

Alcohol: Avoid while taking this medicine.

Driving or operating machinery: This medicine causes drowsiness, which will affect the ability to drive or perform skilled tasks. It is recommended that patients do not drive or perform such tasks during the first few days of treatment. After this time they should ensure that they are not affected before driving or operating machinery.

ALLOPURINOL
Brand name: Zyloric
Type of drug: Gout prevention
Uses: Prevents attacks of gout; also used with chemotherapy.
How it works: High levels of uric acid in the body can lead to uric acid crystals being deposited in the joints, causing pain and inflammation characteristic of gout. The crystals can also cause damage to the kidney. Allopurinol stops an enzyme in the body called xanthine oxidase from breaking down waste products of the body into uric acid.
Availability: POM
Possible adverse effects: The most commonly reported side effect is a skin rash. If this occurs it should be reported to the doctor. Nausea, vomiting and headaches may also occur.
Other information: Allopurinol is taken to prevent further attacks of gout and during some types of chemotherapy. It is advisable to drink plenty of fluids while taking this medication. This medicine may be prescribed for children in certain circumstances.
CAUTION
Alcohol: As alcohol may precipitate an attack of gout, it is recommended that it is only consumed in moderation.
Driving and operating machinery: Although rare, problems with vision may occur, so patients should not drive or perform skilled tasks until they are certain they are not experiencing this or any other side effects.

ALPROSTADIL
Brand name: Caverject
Type of drug: Increases blood flow
Uses: Treatment of impotence.

How it works: It increases the blood flow to the penis and makes an erection easier to achieve.

Availability: POM as an injection.

Possible adverse effects: Pain in the penis following the injection, bruising at the injection site, although this may become less problematic with practice, and the area injected may also become red and swollen. An erection may become painful. These adverse effects should be reported to your doctor. However if an erection lasts more than 4 hours seek urgent medical advice.

Other information: Qualified medical staff will teach the correct injection technique. The drug should not be used more than once in 24 hours or more than 3 times a week.

ALTEPLASE

Brand name: Actilyse

Type of drug: Clot buster

Uses: Treatment of heart attack, some types of stroke and clots in the lungs.

How it works: If administered early enough, it works to dissolve clots that cause the above conditions, thus restoring the blood flow to the heart, brain or lungs. It is also used to unblock central venous lines.

Availability: POM

Possible adverse effects: Bleeding, nausea and vomiting. Allergic symptoms can occur such as a rash, wheezing or a low blood pressure.

Other information: Administered as emergency treatment in hospitals.

ALUMINIUM HYDROXIDE

Brand name: Alu-Cap, Aludrox

Type of drug: Antacid and a phosphate binding agent

Uses: Treatment of indigestion and heartburn, and of high levels of phosphate in the blood of some patients with kidney disease.

How it works: When used as an antacid it neutralises the acid produced by the stomach, relieving the symptoms of indigestion and heartburn. When used as a phosphate binder it prevents the absorption of phosphate from the gut.

Availability: Available in many over-the-counter preparations.

Possible adverse effects: Constipation is the most common side effect.

Other information: For patients receiving long-term treatment, blood tests will be carried out to monitor the phosphate levels.

AMANTADINE

Brand name: Symmetrel, Lysovir

Type of drug: Parkinsonism and antiviral treatment

Uses: Alleviates the symptoms of Parkinson's disease.

How it works: Amantadine increases the amount of a chemical messenger called dopamine in the brain, which is reduced in Parkinson's disease. This allows the patient to lead a more normal daily life. It is also sometimes used to treat certain viral infections including influenza and some herpes infections.

Availability: POM

Possible adverse effects: Swelling of the ankles is a commonly reported side effect. Nervousness, agitation, confusion, disorientation, blurred vision and dry mouth can occur. If dizziness, fainting or fits occur, stop the medication and seek urgent medical advice.

Other information: It is important to continue taking this medication as directed by your doctor, as suddenly halting treatment may make the condition worse. This medication may become less effective with time.

CAUTION

Alcohol: Should be avoided because of an increased risk of confusion associated with the combination.

Driving and operating machinery: As this drug may cause agitation and confusion, patients should not drive or perform skilled tasks until they are certain they are not experiencing these or any other side effects.

AMILORIDE

Brand name: Amilamont, Amilospare, Berkamil, Midamor

Type of drug: Diuretic

Uses: Helps the body reduce excess fluid. Unlike most other diuretics amiloride does not cause the body to lose potassium.

How it works: Excess fluid in the body can lead to high blood pressure, swollen ankles and breathlessness. Amiloride acts on the kidney to increase the amount of urine passed, which in turn reduces excess fluid in the body. It also has an effect of different salts in the body.

Availability: POM

Possible adverse effects: Side effects are uncommon but can include nausea, abdominal pain, constipation, flatulence and a mild skin rash.

Other information: This medication is best taken in the morning or afternoon to avoid interrupting sleep due to frequent visits to the toilet. Foods high in potassium, such as bananas, should be avoided. Blood tests may be carried out to monitor kidney function.

CAUTION

Alcohol: May increase the likelihood of dehydration and low blood pressure. It is therefore advised that alcohol is either not consumed or in moderation.

AMINOGLUTETHIMIDE

Brand name: Orimeten

Type of drug: Hormone antagonist

Uses: Treatment of advanced stages of breast cancer and prostate cancer.

How it works: It prevents an enzyme called aromatase, from working. This enzyme acts on hormones to convert testosterone to oestrogen. Many types of breast and prostate cancer require hormones to grow, so lack of the hormones prevents growth of the cancer.

Availability: POM

Possible adverse effects: Side effects usually occur within 2 weeks of treatment and include loss of appetite, nausea, vomiting, drowsiness and tiredness. These side effects usually lessen with continued use. Fever may also occur.

Other information: Patients may receive other medication with this drug as part of the chemotherapy regimen.

CAUTION

Alcohol: Should be avoided because of an increased risk of drowsiness associated with the combination.

Driving and operating machinery: As this drug may cause drowsiness, patients receiving this medication should not drive or perform skilled tasks until they are certain they are not experiencing this or any other side effect.

AMINOPHYLLINE

Brand name: Phyllocontin Continus
Type of drug: Bronchodilator
Uses: Treatment of reversible airways obstruction and severe asthma attacks.
How it works: Causes the airways to open, allowing the patient to breathe more easily.
Availability: POM
Possible adverse effects: Rapid heart beat, palpitations, nausea, stomach discomfort, dizziness and headaches may occur.
Other information: Blood tests may be carried out to monitor the drug and potassium levels. The tablets should be swallowed whole not crushed or chewed.

CAUTION

Children: This medicine may be prescribed for children over 3 years of age.
Alcohol: May increase the likelihood of palpitations and nausea.
Driving and operating machinery: As this drug may cause dizziness and palpitations, patients receiving this medication should not drive or perform skilled tasks until they are certain they are not experiencing these or any other side effects.

AMIODARONE

Brand name: Cordarone
Type of drug: Cardiac, anti-arrhythmic
Uses: Prevention and treatment of a range of abnormal heart rhythms such as Wolff-Parkinson-White syndrome, atrial fibrillation and ventricular fibrillation.
How it works: It slows the messages sent to the heart muscle with the result that the heartbeat is slowed and steadied.
Availability: POM
Possible adverse effects: Amiodarone can affect a number of organs. In

the eyes, it may cause night glare (when it takes the eyes a long time to recover from a bright light, especially at night). It can affect the liver, causing jaundice. It also can make a thyroid gland underactive or overactive, leading to tiredness, constipation and weight gain, or anxiety, restlessness and weight loss. It may cause inflammation within the lungs causing breathlessness. It makes the skin more sensitive to the effects of the sun. Patients receiving this medication are monitored for these side effects.

Other information: A total sun block should be used to protect the skin, and sunglasses should be worn to protect the eyes. Sunlamps should be avoided. This medicine is generally started by a doctor experienced in treating heart disorders, who will oversee and monitor treatment. Blood and other tests will be performed to monitor the side effects of amiodarone.

CAUTION

Alcohol: Patients should only drink alcohol in moderation, as it may make any effects on the liver worse.

Driving and operating machinery: As this drug may cause problems with vision, patients receiving this medication should not drive or perform skilled tasks until they are certain they are not experiencing this, or any other side effects.

AMITRIPTYLINE

Brand name: Domical, Elavil, Tryptizol

Type of drug: Antidepressant, atypical painkiller

Uses: The treatment of depression, when there is also a need for a sedative effect. Also used to treat atypical pain. Occasionally used in the treatment of bed-wetting in children.

How it works: Inhibits the re-uptake of chemical messengers in the brain, resulting in a heightening of mood. It also encourages appetite and enables users to lead a more normal daily life. The sedative effect is also useful for people who have difficulty sleeping at nights.

Availability: POM

Possible adverse effects: Dry mouth, blurred vision, drowsiness, changes in appetite, impaired memory, light headedness (especially on standing up), muscle weakness, interrupted sleep and insomnia, weight gain, rapid beating of the heart, constipation, skin rash and a loss of libido. These side effects usually lessen with continued use.

Other information: It may take between 2 and 4 weeks to feel the beneficial effects of this medication. This drug can have a 'hangover' effect – a feeling of tiredness, disorientation and sedation when waking in the morning. It is advisable to take this drug prior to going to sleep at night in order to avoid daytime sleepiness.

CAUTION

Children: This medicine may be prescribed for children over 6 years of age for bed-wetting.

Alcohol: Should be avoided whilst taking this medicine because the combination may worsen the side effects.

Driving and operating machinery: As this drug can cause drowsiness, patients should not drive or perform skilled tasks until they are certain they are not experiencing this or any other side effects.

AMLODIPINE

Brand name: Istin

Type of drug: Cardiac

Uses: Treatment of high blood pressure and angina.

How it works: Relaxes the blood vessels in the circulatory system allowing blood to flow more easily, so therefore reducing blood pressure. For angina it relaxes the blood vessels of the heart and allows more blood and oxygen to reach the heart muscle. This allows it to pump more effectively and relieves pain.

Availability: POM

Possible adverse effects: Headache and dizziness may occur due to a fall in blood pressure. Rashes, leg or ankle swelling and facial flushing can also occur.

Other information: Amlodipine should not be discontinued unless advised by a doctor, but any side effects should be reported. Do not take this medication with grapefruit juice.

CAUTION

Alcohol: May increase the likelihood of experiencing side effects and so should only be consumed in moderation.

AMOXICILLIN

Brand name: Amoxil

Type of drug: Antibiotic

Uses: Treatment of a wide range of infections that occur in the chest, ears, skin, teeth, urinary tract and sinuses.

How it works: Penicillin and related drugs treat infections caused by bacteria by damaging the outer, protective layer of bacteria, which leads to its death.

Availability: POM

Possible adverse effects: The most common side effects are nausea, vomiting and diarrhoea. If allergic symptoms such as an itchy rash, wheezing or swelling of the face occur, the patient should stop taking the medication and seek urgent medical advice.

Other information: Patients allergic to penicillin may also be allergic to amoxicillin and should not take this medicine without advice from the doctor or pharmacist. The course of antibiotics should always be completed and taken regularly. Amoxicillin may also reduce thr effectiveness of the contraceptive pill, so other methods of contraception should be used whilst taking this medicine, and for at least 7 days after finishing. It is commonly prescribed for children. This medicine is safe for use in pregnant women.

AMPHOTERICIN

Brand name: Fungilin

Type of drug: Anti-fungal

Uses: Treatment of fungal infection.

How it works: Treats infections caused by a fungus by damaging the outer, protective layer of the fungus, which leads to its death.

Availability: POM

Possible adverse effects: Stomach symptoms such as nausea and diarrhoea when taken by mouth. Following injection nausea, vomiting, stomach pain, headache, muscle and joint pain, rash, fever and renal problems can occur. Severe allergic symptoms such as difficulty in breathing and low blood pressure may also occur, but when given by injection this is only in hospital under the supervision of a experienced doctor.

Other information: This medicine is prescribed for children.

ANASTROZOLE

Brand name: Arimidex

Type of drug: Hormone antagonist

Uses: Treatment of breast cancer.

How it works: It prevents an enzyme called aromatase from working. This enzyme acts on hormones to convert testosterone to oestrogen. Many types of breast cancer require hormones to grow, so lack of the hormones prevents growth of the cancer.

Availability: POM

Possible adverse effects: Headache, hot flushes, sweating, thinning of the hair, vaginal irritation, joint pain and stiffness, drowsiness, nausea and diarrhoea.

Other information: This medicine is only given in hospital under the supervision of a doctor experienced in treating cancer. Patients may receive other medication with this drug as part of the chemotherapy regimen.

CAUTION

Alcohol: Should be avoided because of an increased risk of drowsiness associated with the combination.

Driving and operating machinery: As this drug can cause drowsiness, patients receiving this medication should not drive or perform skilled tasks until they are certain they are not experiencing this, and any other side effects.

ANTAZOLIN

Brand name: Otrivine-Antistin

Type of drug: Antihistamine

Uses: Treatment of mild allergic reactions and hay fever.

How it works: Blocks the action of histamine – a chemical released by the body in response to allergies, stopping symptoms such as runny nose and sneezing.

Availability: OTC

Possible adverse effects: These are rare, but a rapid heart beat can occur.

CAUTION

Children: This drug can be used in children over 5 years of age.

APOMORPHINE HYDROCHLORIDE

Brand name: APO-go, Uprima

Type of drug: Treatment drug used in Parkinson's disease, and erectile dysfunction

Uses: Control of some of the symptoms of Parkinsonism in patients for whom the effects of other drugs are no longer sufficient. Apomorphine is also used to treat problems with obtaining and maintaining an erection in men.

How it works: Apomorphine acts like dopamine, a chemical messenger in the brain, which is reduced in Parkinson's disease, allowing the patient to lead a more normal daily life. It also acts on a specific area of the brain involved in the process of obtaining and maintaining an erection.

Availability: POM

Possible adverse effects: Nausea, vomiting, dizziness, confusion, headache, sleepiness, a strange taste in the mouth, sweating, runny nose and involuntary movements can occur. Following injection there may be skin reactions such as a rash, redness, swelling or lumps under the skin which can form ulcers.

Other information: Apomorphine is not related to morphine.

For the treatment of Parkinson's disease, this medicine is only given in hospital under the supervision of an experienced doctor. Patients or their carers will then be taught to administer the injection.

When used for erectile dysfunction the tablets should be allowed to dissolve under the tongue.

CAUTION

Alcohol: Should be avoided because of an increased risk of confusion associated with the combination.

Driving and operating machinery: As this drug can cause sleepiness and dizziness, patients receiving this medication should not drive or perform skilled tasks until they are certain they are not experiencing these or any other side effects.

APRACLONIDINE

Brand name: Iopidine

Type of drug: Glaucoma treatment

Uses: This drug is available as eye drops of different strengths. The 1%

solution is used to prevent a rise in the internal pressure of the eye after laser surgery. The 0.5% solution is used together with other medicines for short-term treatment of glaucoma.

How it works: Stops the production of fluid found inside the eye. A reduction in the production of this fluid reduces the pressure inside the eye.

Availability: POM

Possible adverse effects: Dry mouth, a strange taste in the mouth, eye discomfort and headache. Although not taken by mouth, the drug can be absorbed into the body and causes sleepiness and unwanted effects in the heart including high blood pressure.

CAUTION

Alcohol: Should be avoided because of an increased risk of drowsiness associated with the combination.

Driving and operating machinery: As this drug can cause drowsiness, patients receiving this medication should not drive or perform skilled tasks until they are certain they are not experiencing this or any other side effect.

ASPIRIN

Brand name: Nu-Seals Aspirin

Type of drug: Anti-inflammatory, painkiller and reduces fevers

Uses: Treatment of a wide variety of mild to moderate pain, including menstrual pain, headache and toothache. It relieves the inflammation present in conditions such as arthritis. It is also useful in controlling the symptoms of colds and flu, and is an effective way of treating a fever. Aspirin is used in the treatment of some types of heart disease and is also used to reduce the risk of blood clots in patients who have circulation and heart problems.

How it works: Reduces pain and inflammation by blocking the production of prostaglandins, that are involved in the inflammatory process. To reduce temperature aspirin acts in a part of the brain called the hypothalamus which contains the body's thermostat. Aspirin also reduces the effectiveness of platelets which normally helps the blood to clot, making them work less well.

Availability: OTC

Possible adverse effects: Stomach and bowel pain or discomfort, allergic reactions and breathlessness. Gastrointestinal ulceration and/or bleeding may occur, so if you suffer severe stomach pain, or there is blood in your stools then seek urgent medical advice. If allergic symptoms such as wheezing or swelling of the face occur, the patient should stop taking the medication and seek urgent medical advice. In patients with asthma, aspirin can sometimes make these symptoms worse.

Other information: Additional medication may be prescribed to reduce stomach irritation and should be taken with food or milk to help protect the stomach.

CAUTION

Children: This drug should not be used for children under 16 years old unless under medical supervision as, rarely, it can cause Reye's syndrome, a severe condition affecting the brain and liver.

ATENOLOL
Brand name: Tenormin

Type of drug: Cardiac, beta-blocker

Uses: A treatment for angina, abnormal heart rhythms and high blood pressure. If administered soon after a heart attack it can be effective at reducing heart damage. It can also be used as a treatment for anxiety.

How it works: Atenolol slows the rate at which the heart beats. This reduces its workload and makes it more efficient.

Availability: POM

Possible adverse effects: Tiredness and fatigue, cold hands and feet, nausea, vomiting, headaches and nightmares may occur. Sometimes a slow pulse may be noticed. A rash and/or breathlessness should always be reported to a doctor.

Other information: Atenolol should only be prescribed with caution for people with asthma or other lung disorders because it can worsen the conditions.

ATORVASTATIN
Brand name: Lipitor

Type of drug: Reduces cholesterol, HMG-CoA Reductase inhibitor

Uses: Atorvastatin is used to treat high cholesterol and to prevent heart disease.

How it works: Atorvastatin stops an enzyme in the liver, called HMG-CoA Reductase, from producing cholesterol.

Availability: POM

Possible adverse effects: Constipation, flatulence, indigestion, headache, nausea, vomiting, diarrhoea, and insomnia may occur. In some patients HMG-CoA Reductase inhibitors may cause muscle pain, tenderness, or weakness, which should be reported to your doctor, or pharmacist. Also this drug can cause liver abnormalities. These symptoms generally improve on stopping the drug.

Other information: Blood tests may be performed to check liver function.

CAUTION

Pregnancy: Atorvastatin is usually stopped 1 month prior to pregnancy, and patients should inform the doctor if they are considering becoming pregnant.

ATROPINE

Brand name: Available as a generic preparation

Type of drug: Increases the size of the pupil of the eye

Uses: Atropine eye drops are used to treat inflammation of part of the eye, and to dilate the pupil so it is ready for examination or other procedures. It is also for emergency treatment in cardiac arrests, to increase the heart rate after heart attacks and to reduce the production of saliva.

How it works: It stops the transmission of signals to the muscles in the eye that make the pupil smaller. It also works on many other nerves in the body causing both desirable and unwanted effects.

Availability: POM

Possible adverse effects: Blurred vision, dry mouth, skin flushing, dry skin, constipation, fast heartbeat and thirst may occur. If eye pain or palpitations occur, stop taking the medication and seek medical advice.

CAUTION

Driving and operating machinery: As this drug affects the eye and can cause blurred vision, patients receiving this medication should not drive or perform skilled tasks until they are certain they are not experiencing this or any other side effect.

AURANOFIN

Brand name: Ridaura
Type of drug: Anti-inflammatory drug
Uses: The treatment of severe rheumatoid arthritis.
How it works: Auranofin is derived from gold. The precise actions of auranofin are unknown at present, but it is believed to act on the immune system to reduce inflammation in the affected joints.
Availability: POM
Possible adverse effects: Diarrhoea is the main side effect of oral therapy and a rash may also occur. It may affect blood cells and cause problems with the kidneys, eyes and lungs. A doctor should be informed at once if there are any signs of sore throat, fever, infection, mouth ulcers or bleeding and bruising.
Other information: This medicine is only given in hospital under the supervision of a doctor experienced in treating rheumatic diseases. Regular blood tests and examinations are required to monitor the effects. It may take several weeks or months to see the beneficial effects of this medication. Women should use effective means of contraception during treatment and for 6 months following it. The tablets should be taken with or after meals.

AZAPROPAZONE

Brand name: Rheumox
Type of drug: Anti-inflammatory, painkiller
Uses: Reduce inflammation and associated pain in conditions such as rheumatoid arthritis, ankylosing spondylitis, and acute gout where other medication has not worked.
How it works: Reduces pain and inflammation by blocking the production of prostaglandins involved in the inflammatory process.
Availability: POM
Possible adverse effects: Stomach and bowel pain or discomfort, headaches, breathlessness, dizziness, sensitivity of the skin to sunlight, ringing in the ears, problems with hearing and kidney problems.

Gastrointestinal ulceration and/or bleeding may occur. If you suffer severe stomach pain or there is blood in your stools then seek urgent medical advice.

Other information: Patients allergic to aspirin or indomethacin may also be allergic to azopropazone and should not take it without advice from the doctor or pharmacist. This medicine is only given in hospital under the supervision of a doctor experienced in treating rheumatic diseases. Do not take aspirin or similar drugs whilst on this medication as this will increase the risk of stomach irritation. This medication can be taken after meals to minimise the risk of stomach problems. An effective sun block must be used and exposure to sunlamps must also be avoided.

AZATHIOPRINE

Brand name: Imuran

Type of drug: Immunosuppressant

Uses: Treatment of a variety of inflammatory and auto-immune conditions including rheumatoid arthritis. It is also used after some types of transplants.

How it works: Stops the production of cells within the immune system, which means that they cannot attack the joints in rheumatoid arthritis, and other organs or cells.

Availability: POM

Possible adverse effects: Vomiting, diarrhoea, headache, dizziness can occur should be reported to the doctor or pharmacist. It can increase the patient's risk of getting infections through its effect on the immune system. It can also cause changes in the blood cells, hair loss and liver problems.

Other information: This medicine is only given in hospital under the supervision of a doctor experienced in looking after rheumatic diseases, and other autoimmune conditions. They will oversee and monitor treatment. Regular blood tests are required to assess the effects. Any sign of infection, such as a sore throat, unexplained bleeding or bruising, generally feeling unwell or high temperature should be reported to the doctor immediately. This drug is used for some conditions in children.

CAUTION

Pregnancy: Patients should not become pregnant whilst taking this medicine. Effective contraceptive measures should be used before, during, and for 6 weeks after usage.

AZITHROMYCIN
Brand name: Zithromax
Type of drug: Antibiotic
Uses: The treatment of a wide range of infections that occur in the chest, skin, ears and tonsils. Often used for people allergic to penicillin.
How it works: Azithromycin treats infections caused by bacteria by interfering with the actions of proteins that the bacteria need to survive.
Availability: POM
Possible adverse effects: Stomach upsets such as nausea, vomiting and diarrhoea are commonly reported side effects. If allergic symptoms occur such as an itchy, red skin rash, the patient should stop taking the medication and inform the doctor or pharmacist.
Other information: Should be taken an hour before food or on an empty stomach. Indigestion remedies should not be taken at the same time as this medicine – but if required take 1 hour before or 2 hours after azithromycin. It is important to take as prescribed, and to complete the whole course. It may make the contraceptive pill less effective, and other means of contraception should be used throughout the treatment course, and for 7 days after completing it. It is used to treat infections in children.

BACLOFEN
Brand name: Lioresal, Baclospas
Type of drug: Muscle relaxant
Uses: A muscle relaxant that relieves painful spasms that occur in conditions such as multiple sclerosis, cerebral palsy, stroke and following brain or spinal injuries.
How it works: Baclofen acts in the spinal cord. It prevents the transmission of signals to the muscles, which makes them relax so spasms are reduced.
Availability: POM
Possible adverse effects: Dizziness, drowsiness, nausea, diarrhoea, headache, confusion, mood changes, muscle weakness and liver problems can occur. These effects are more likely to occur at the start of treatment,

and if you are over 40 years of age.

Other information: It may take between 2 and 4 weeks to see the beneficial effects of this medication however if there is no obvious improvement after 6 weeks the medication is often gradually reduced, then stopped. It should not be stopped suddenly. Baclofen may interfere with a diabetic's blood sugar levels.

CAUTION

Children: This medicine may be prescribed for children over 12 months of age with strict guidance.

Alcohol: Should be avoided because of an increased risk of drowsiness associated with the combination.

Driving and operating machinery: As this drug may cause dizziness and drowsiness, patients receiving this medication should not drive or perform skilled tasks until they are certain they are not experiencing these, or any other side effects.

BECLOMETASONE

(Formerly known as: beclomethasone)

Brand name: Becloforte, Becotide, Aerobec, Becodisks, Beconase, Propaderm

Type of drug: Steroid, antiinflammatory, immunosupressant

Uses: Used to prevent asthma attacks, to reduce the symptoms of hay fever and to treat skin conditions such as eczema.

How it works: When inhaled into the lungs, it reduces inflammation of the airways making it easier to breathe. With long term use it can reduce the number of asthma attacks that the patient has. It also reduces inflammation in the nose which reduces nasal congestion and makes it easier to breathe.

Availability: Some preparations are available over-the-counter.

Possible adverse effects: Occasionally fungal infections can occur in the mouth due to its effects on the immune system, but gargling with water after inhaling will prevent this in most cases. Nasal discomfort and a sore throat may occur. Occasionally wheezing can become worse after use of the inhaler. If this occurs seek urgent medical advice. Creams and ointments can cause thinning of the skin, increased hair growth, increased or decreased colouration of the skin, and can make infections worse.

Other information: With creams and ointments rubbed into the skin, the least amount necessary should be used. For inhalers, it may take up to 2 weeks to see the beneficial effects of this medication, and they need to be taken regularly for maximum effect. Asthmatics often describe this inhaler as 'the brown one' or the 'preventer'. This medication is commonly prescribed for children with asthma.

BENDROFLUMETHIAZIDE

(Formerly known as: bendrofluazide)

Brand name: Neo-NaClex

Type of drug: Diuretic

Uses: Treatment of high blood pressure.

How it works: This drug acts on the kidneys to increase the amount of urine passed, which in turn, reduces excess fluid in the body. Fluid in the wrong places can cause high blood pressure, breathlessness and swollen ankles. In addition to water, salts are also lost from the body into the urine.

Availability: POM

Possible adverse effects: Nausea, and feeling light-headed when standing may occur. Also abnormalities of salts in the body can occur and symptoms such as muscle cramps, tiredness and nausea can arise if potassium levels are reduced,.

Other information: Blood tests may be performed to monitor the potassium levels and sometimes potassium supplements may be required.

CAUTION

Alcohol: Can increase the likelihood of dehydration and low blood pressure. It is therefore advised that alcohol is not consumed, or only consumed in moderation.

BENZOYL PEROXIDE

Brand name: Panoxyl

Type of drug: Acne treatment

Uses: Used mainly to treat moderate acne.

How it works: Benzoyl peroxide kills the bacteria associated with acne, and acts to unblock the pores of the skin.

Availability: Available as an ingredient in preparations that can be bought without a prescription.

Possible adverse effects: Drying, leading to stinging or redness on the skin, which may feel uncomfortable. If the skin starts to peel, the drug should be applied less frequently. If this fails to control the peeling then discontinuing use for a few days and then restarting may help.

Other information: Available as a cream, lotion or gel. Benzoyl peroxide may bleach clothing. Avoid contact with the eyes and mouth. It should not be used for more than 6 weeks at a time unless under medical supervision. This medication is considered suitable for use in pregnancy and breastfeeding.

CAUTION

Children: This drug is not usually used in children before puberty.

BETAHISTINE

Brand name: Serc

Type of drug: Treatment of Meniere's disease

Uses: Used to control the nausea, vertigo and ringing in the ears that are characteristic of Meniere's disease. It can also be used to control the ringing in the ears and dizziness caused by other conditions.

How it works: Thought to improve the blood flow through the small blood vessels in the ear, with the result that the pressure in the inner ear is reduced.

Availability: POM

Possible adverse effects: Nausea, headache, indigestion and occasionally a rash.

Other information: Should be taken with or after meals.

BETAMETHASONE

Brand name: Betnesol, Betnovate

Type of drug: Steroid, anti-inflammatory, immunosuppressant

Uses: Mainly applied to the skin, eyes, ears, or nose to reduce inflammation. Sometimes given orally to treat a variety of inflammatory and autoimmune conditions including rheumatoid arthritis.

How it works: Steroids work by suppressing the production of cells, chemicals and enzymes involved in inflammation, which in turn reduces pain and swelling.

Availability: POM

Possible adverse effects: Creams and ointments can cause thinning of the skin, increased hair growth, increased or decreased colouration of the skin, and can make infections worse – this is usually only with long-term treatment. When used on the eyes, ears or nose, this drug can cause irritation making the area red, inflamed and/or painful. When using the drops in the eye, blurred vision can occur. When taken by mouth, the drug has more side effects, including swelling and high blood pressure due to excess fluid, muscle weakness, interference with growth in children, increased risk of infection due to its effects on the immune system and irritation of the stomach. Gastrointestinal ulceration and/or bleeding may occur, so if you suffer severe stomach pain, or there is blood in your stools then seek urgent medical advice. It may cause a decrease in hormone production leading to irregular or suppressed menstrual periods, weight gain and hair loss.

Other information: With creams rubbed into the skin, the least amount necessary should be used. When taking the tablet form, you will usually be given a steroid card so that appropriate action can be taken if you should become unwell. If drops are to be used in the eye it is recommended that patients do not wear soft contact lenses as the drops may damage the lens.

CAUTION

Children: Amounts used are limited.

Driving and operating machinery: As the eye drops can cause blurred vision, patients receiving this medication should not drive or perform skilled tasks until they are certain they are not experiencing this or any other side effects.

BETHANECHOL CHLORIDE

Brand name: Myotonine

Type of drug: Muscle stimulant

Uses: The treatment of people who are unable to pass urine and when catheterisation (the passing of a tube into the bladder) is not an option.

How it works: Stimulates the nerves in the bladder, which in turn helps the bladder to contract and urine to be passed.

Availability: POM
Possible adverse effects: Nausea, vomiting, sweating, blurred vision, slowed pulse and intestinal discomfort.
Other information: The tablets should be taken between 30 minutes and 1 hour before food.
CAUTION
Driving and operating machinery: As the eye drops can cause blurred vision, patients receiving this medication should not drive or perform skilled tasks until they are certain they are not experiencing these or any other side effects.

BETAXOLOL
Brand name: Betoptic
Type of drug: Glaucoma treatment, beta-blocker
Uses: Betaxolol is used in the treatment of glaucoma.
How it works: Stops the production of fluid found in the eye. This reduces internal pressure in the eye, alleviating symptoms of glaucoma.
Availability: POM
Possible adverse effects: Discomfort of the eye on application and tears may occur when using these drops.
Other information: Although this drug is only applied to the eyes some of the drug may be absorbed into the body. Remove soft contact lenses before putting the drops in, and wait at least 15 minutes before putting them back in.
CAUTION
Betaxolol should be prescribed with caution for people with asthma because it can make the condition worse. It can also slow the heart rate so should be prescribed with caution in people with heart disease.

BEZAFIBRATE
Brand name: Bezalip
Type of drug: Reduces fats such as triglycerides in the blood, fibrate
Uses: To lower the level of fats (lipids) in the blood, which are thought to contribute to coronary heart disease, angina, heart attacks and stroke.
How it works: It causes a lower level of lipids in the blood by inhibiting an enzyme that produces them, and promoting lipid breakdown.

Availability: POM

Possible adverse effects: Nausea, loss of appetite, headache, stomach discomfort and a feeling of fullness may occur. These side effects usually lessen with continued use. However it can cause muscle pain, tenderness or weakness that should be reported to your doctor, or pharmacist. These symptoms generally improve on stopping the drug.

Other information: Should be taken in conjunction with a low fat diet. Blood tests may be performed to monitor its effect on the level of lipids in the blood. These tablets should be taken with or after food.

BICALUTAMIDE

Brand name: Casodex

Type of drug: Hormone antagonist

Uses: The treatment of advanced prostate cancer.

How it works: It prevents the normal male hormones called androgens from working. Many types of prostate cancer require hormones to grow, so lack of the hormones prevents growth of the cancer.

Availability: POM

Possible adverse effects: Nausea, vomiting, breast enlargement, hot flushes, diarrhoea, weight gain, hair loss, reduced sex drive, muscle weakness, skin rash, dry skin, liver problems and itching may occur.

Other information: Patients may receive other medication with this drug as part of the chemotherapy regimen.

CAUTION

Alcohol: Can increase the likelihood of experiencing side effects and so should only be consumed in moderation.

BISOPROLOL

Brand name: Cardicor

Type of drug: Cardiac, beta-blocker

Uses: For the treatment of high blood pressure and heart failure.

How it works: Bisoprolol slows the rate at which the heart beats. This reduces its workload and makes it more efficient. It also improves the ease of blood flow around the body, which also reduces blood pressure.

Availability: POM

Possible adverse effects: Coldness and numbness of the hands and feet, nausea, vomiting, diarrhoea and constipation. Tiredness, exhaustion, dizziness and headache can occur at the start of the treatment, but usually lessen within 1 to 2 weeks. Sometimes a slow pulse may be noticed. A rash and/or breathlessness should always be reported to a doctor.

Other information: Bisoprolol should only be prescribed with caution for people with asthma or other lung disorders because it can make the conditions worse. It should not be discontinued unless advised by a doctor but any side effects should be reported to your doctor or pharmacist.

CAUTION

Driving and operating machinery: As this drug may cause dizziness and tiredness, patients should not drive or perform skilled tasks until they are certain they are not experiencing these or any other side effects.

BRIMONIDINE

Brand name: Alphagan

Type of drug: Glaucoma treatment

Uses: Brimonidine is used to treat glaucoma.

How it works: Reduces the production of fluid in the eye, which leads to reduced pressure within the eye, so alleviating the symptoms of glaucoma.

Availability: POM

Possible adverse effects: Irritation of the eye and surrounding skin after putting the drops in, blurred vision, a feeling of dryness of the eye, headache, dry mouth, dizziness, and drowsiness.

Other information: Remove soft contact lenses before putting the drops in, and wait at least 15 minutes before putting them back in.

CAUTION

Driving and operating machinery: As this medicine may cause dizziness, drowsiness, and blurred vision, patients receiving this medication should not drive or perform any skilled tasks until they are certain they are not experiencing these, or any other side effects.

BRINZOLAMIDE

Brand name: Azopt

Type of drug: Glaucoma treatment

Uses: This medicine is used in the treatment of glaucoma.

How it works: Reduces the production of fluid in the eye, which leads to reduced pressure within the eye, and alleviation of the symptoms of glaucoma.

Availability: POM

Possible adverse effects: A strange taste, blurred vision which may last for a few minutes after putting the drops into the eye, irritation of the eye, increased production of tears, dizziness, chest pain, nausea and headache may occur.

Other information: Remove soft contact lenses before putting the drops in, and wait at least 15 minutes before putting them back in.

CAUTION

Driving and operating machinery: May cause dizziness and blurred vision, patients receiving this medication should not drive or perform skilled tasks until they are certain they are not experiencing these or any other side effects.

BROMOCRIPTINE

Brand name: Parlodel

Type of drug: Fertility and Parkinsonism

Uses: The treatment of both male and female infertility and a variety of menstruation problems. It can be used to stop breast milk production. It is also effective for some people who are in the later stages of Parkinsonism and is also used to treat tumours of the pituitary gland.

How it works: It prevents the pituitary gland from producing a hormone, prolactin, which causes women to produce breast milk. It also acts like dopamine, a chemical messenger in the brain, which is reduced in Parkinson's disease, allowing the patient to lead a more normal daily life.

Availability: POM

Possible adverse effects: Nausea, vomiting, headache, constipation, dizziness, light-headness when you stand up, drowsiness, suddenly falling asleep, hallucinations, dry mouth, leg cramps, and difficulty in moving may occur. If allergic symptoms such as wheezing occur seek urgent medical advice.

Other information: This medicine is only given in hospital under the supervision of a doctor experienced in treating endocrine diseases or

Parkinson's disease, who will oversee and monitor treatment. Regular blood and other tests are performed to assess the effectiveness of the drug. It should be taken with meals to help prevent, or alleviate side effects.

CAUTION

Children: It may be prescribed for children over 15 years of age.

Alcohol: Alcohol can increase the likelihood of experiencing side effects and so should be avoided or consumed in moderation.

Driving and operating machinery: As this drug may cause drowsiness, patients should not drive or perform skilled tasks until they are certain they are not experiencing this or any other side effects.

BUDESONIDE

Brand name: Pulmicort, Entocort

Type of drug: Steroid, anti-inflammatory, immunosuppressant

Uses: Prescribed to control the symptoms of asthma. When taken as a capsule or enema it is used to treat inflammatory bowel disease.

How it works: When inhaled into the lungs it reduces inflammation of the airways making it easier to breathe. With long-term use it can reduce the number of asthma attacks that the patient has.

When used as an enema it stops the production of cells, chemicals and enzymes that cause bowel inflammation, and so relieves the pain and diarrhoea characteristic of the condition.

Availability: Preparations for use in hay fever are available over-the-counter.

Possible adverse effects: Occasionally fungal infections can occur in the mouth due to its effects on the immune system, but gargling with water after each inhalation will prevent this in most cases. Nasal discomfort and a sore throat may occur. Occasionally wheezing can become worse after use of the inhaler, if this occurs seek urgent medical advice. When taken by mouth, the drug has more side effects, including swelling and high blood pressure due to excess fluid, muscle weakness, slight rounding of the face, acne, heartburn, indigestion, nausea, vomiting, an increased risk of infection due to its effects on the immune system and irritation of the stomach. Gastrointestinal ulceration and/or bleeding may occur, so if you suffer severe stomach pain, or there is blood in your stools then seek urgent medical advice. Budesonide may cause a decrease in hormone production leading to irregular or suppressed menstrual periods, weight gain and hair loss.

Other information: When taking the tablet form, you will usually be given a steroid card so that appropriate action can be taken if you become unwell. It can be prescribed as nebules for more severe cases of asthma and other lung diseases. For inhalers, it may take up to 2 weeks to feel the beneficial effects of this medication, and they need to be taken regularly for maximum effect. When taking capsules, indigestion remedies should not be taken for at least 1 to 2 hours afterwards. Capsules should be taken half to 1 hour before food and should be swallowed whole with a glass of water. This medicine may be prescribed for children to treat asthma and other lung conditions.

BUMETANIDE

Brand name: Burinex

Type of drug: Diuretic

Uses: Treatment of high blood pressure, heart failure, and other conditions associated with fluid retention, such as cirrhosis of the liver.

How it works: This drug acts on the kidneys to increase the amount of urine passed, which in turn, reduces excess fluid in the body. Fluid in the wrong places can cause high blood pressure, breathlessness and swollen ankles. In addition to water, salts are also lost from the body into the urine with this drug.

Availability: POM

Possible adverse effects: Abdominal pain, nausea, vomiting, headache, muscle pain and feeling light headed when standing may occur. Also abnormalities of salts in the body can occur and symptoms can occur if potassium levels are reduced, such as muscle cramps, tiredness and nausea.

Other information: Blood tests may be performed to monitor the potassium levels.

CAUTION

Alcohol: Can increase the likelihood of dehydration and low blood pressure. It is therefore advised that alcohol is not consumed, or only consumed in moderation.

BUPRENORPHINE

Brand name: Temgesic

Type of drug: Painkiller, opioid analgesic

Uses: Treatment of moderate to severe pain.

How it works: This drug stops the transmission of pain messages through the spinal cord to the brain.

Availability: POM

Possible adverse effects: Nausea, vomiting, dizziness, constipation, hiccoughs, drowsiness, lower blood pressure and sweating may occur. Skin reactions including redness and itching can occur with patches that are applied to the skin.

Other information: It is usually prescribed as a tablet that needs to be dissolved under the tongue. Do not swallow these tablets.

CAUTION

Children: This medication may be prescribed to treat pain in children over 6 months of age.

Alcohol: Can increase the likelihood of experiencing side effects and so should only be consumed in moderation.

Driving and operating machinery: As this drug may cause drowsiness and dizziness, patients should not drive or perform skilled tasks until they are certain they are not experiencing these or any other side effects.

BUSERELIN

Brand name: Suprefact

Type of drug: Hormone analogue

Uses: The treatment of prostate cancer. Also used to treat endometriosis.

How it works: It reduces both hormone production of both androgens and oestrogens. Many types of prostate cancer require hormones to grow, so lack of the hormones prevents growth of the cancer. For endometriosis, it blocks the production of hormones by the ovaries.

Availability: POM

Possible adverse effects: Nausea, vomiting, breast enlargement and soreness, hot flushes, diarrhoea, dizziness, weight gain, excess fluid causing swelling of the feet and ankles, changes in appetite, hair loss, mood changes, reduced sex drive, and muscle pain may occur. With the nasal spray, nasal irritation and nosebleeds can occur. If allergic symptoms occur such as a skin rash or swelling of the tongue or mouth, the patient should stop taking the medication and seek urgent medical advice.

Other information: Patients may receive other medication with this drug as part of a chemotherapy regimen for prostate cancer. Barrier methods of contraception should be used during treatment to prevent unwanted pregnancy.

Other information: Nasal decongestants should not be used for a minimum of 30 minutes before using the nasal spray.

CAUTION

Pregnancy and breastfeeding: Contraception must be used, but if you become pregnant while on this medicine, inform your doctor as soon as possible.

Alcohol: Can increase the likelihood of experiencing side effects and so should only be consumed in moderation.

Driving and operating machinery: As this drug may cause dizziness, patients receiving this medication should not drive or perform skilled tasks until they are certain they are not experiencing this or any other side effects.

CABERGOLINE

Brand name: Cabaser, Dostinex

Type of drug: Treatment of Parkinson's disease

Uses: Can be used to stop breast milk production. It is also effective for some people who are in the later stages of Parkinsonism.

How it works: Prevents the pituitary gland, which is within the brain, from producing a hormone, prolactin, which causes women to produce breast milk. It also acts like dopamine, a chemical messenger in the brain, which is reduced in Parkinson's disease, allowing the patient to lead a more normal daily life.

Availability: POM

Possible adverse effects: Nausea, vomiting, stomach pain, heartburn, headache, constipation, dizziness, light-headedness when you stand up, drowsiness, suddenly falling asleep, dry mouth, breast pain, difficulty in moving and chest problems may occur. If breathlessness, a persistent cough, and chest pain occur, inform your doctor or pharmacist.

Other information: This medicine is only given in hospital under the supervision of a doctor experienced in treating endocrine diseases or Parkinson's disease, who will oversee and monitor treatment. Regular blood and other tests are performed to assess effectiveness. Should be taken with meals to help prevent, or alleviate side effects.

CAUTION

Driving and operating machinery: As this drug may cause dizziness and drowsiness, patients should not drive or perform skilled tasks until they are certain they are not experiencing these or any other side effects.

CALCIPOTRIOL

Brand name: Dovonex

Type of drug: Similar to Vitamin D

Uses: Treatment of moderate to severe psoriasis.

How it works: Reduces the production of skin cells that cause the symptoms of skin thickening and scaling associated with psoriasis.

Availability: POM

Possible adverse effects: Irritation of the skin when the cream or ointment is first applied which lessens with continued use. If the psoriasis appears to be getting worse, inform your doctor or pharmacist. A decrease in levels of calcium in the blood can occur.

Other information: Hands should be washed before and after applying the cream, ointment, or lotion. Calcipotriol should only be applied to the affected areas of the skin, which should be well moisturised before the cream or ointment is applied. Avoid applying to the face.

CAUTION

Children: It may be prescribed for children over 6 years of age.

CALCITONIN

Brand name: Miacalcic

Type of drug: Hormone

Uses: Treatment of osteoporosis in women who have been through the menopause. Also to used to reduce high levels of calcium in the blood.

How it works: Calcitonin acts on the rate of bone growth by preventing cells from releasing calcium from the bones which is a contributing factor in the development of osteoporosis. It can also reduce bone pain.

Availability: POM

Possible adverse effects: A runny nose, nasal congestion, sneezing, irritation and swelling of the nose can occur with the nasal spray. Nausea, vomiting, diarrhoea, abdominal pain, dizziness, and a strange taste in the mouth may also occur. If allergic symptoms occur such as an itchy rash or swelling of the mouth or tongue, the patient should stop taking the medication and seek urgent medical advice.

CAUTION

Driving and operating machinery: As this drug may cause dizziness, patients receiving this medication should not drive or perform skilled tasks until they are certain they are not experiencing this or any other side effects.

CALCIUM POLYSTYRENE SULFONATE

Brand name: Calcium Resonium

Type of drug: Ion exchange resin

Uses: To treat increased potassium in the blood.

How it works: Once in the gut, it encourages calcium to be kept in the body in exchange for potassium which is excreted, reducing potassium levels in the blood.

Availability: POM

Possible adverse effects: Stomach pain, nausea, vomiting, constipation or diarrhoea and irritation of the rectum may occur. Side effects can also occur if too much calcium is absorbed, such as irritability, confusion, muscle weakness, nausea, vomiting and stomach pain.

Other information: Regular blood tests will be done to monitor the effect of the drug. It should not be used in people who have serious bowel problems. Foods rich in potassium such as bananas should also be avoided.

CAPTOPRIL

Brand name: Capoten

Type of drug: ACE inhibitor

Uses: To treat high blood pressure and heart failure. It can also be used to treat the kidney problems associated with diabetes.

How it works: It enables the blood vessels to relax, which allows them to increase in size. This reduces the pressure of the blood flowing through them that lowers blood pressure, increases the effectiveness of the heart and improves blood flow to the kidney.

Availability: POM

Possible adverse effects: Dizziness, low blood pressure, a strange taste in the mouth, chest pain, nausea, indigestion, abdominal pains, headache, a dry cough (which usually subsides over time), and skin rashes. If allergic symptoms such as wheezing or swelling of the mouth or tongue occur, the patient should stop taking the medication and seek urgent medical advice.

Other information: This drug should be used with caution in patients with kidney problems. Blood tests are usually carried out to monitor the levels of potassium. Patients should avoid salt substitutes containing potassium, and should take care in hot weather, or if taking exercise, to avoid over-heating and dehydration.

The first dose should be taken while lying down as there is a risk of falling due to the sudden drop in blood pressure. This drug can be used in children.

CAUTION

Alcohol: Should only be consumed in strict moderation whilst taking this medicine because the combination may cause a large fall in blood pressure.

Driving and operating machinery: As this drug may cause dizziness, patients receiving this medication should not drive or perform such tasks until they are certain they are not experiencing this, or any other side effecs.

CARBAMAZEPINE

Brand name: Tegretol

Type of drug: Antiepileptic, atypical painkiller

Uses: Treatment of epilepsy. It is also used for nerve pain.

How it works: An epileptic fit (or seizure) is thought to occur when the brain receives too many or abnormal signals. Carbamazepine acts by reducing the number of signals that the brain receives. How it works to prevent nerve pain is less well understood.

Availability: POM

Possible adverse effects: Headache, dizziness, confusion, double and blurred vision, dry mouth, nausea, vomiting, tiredness, may occur. It can also affect the blood cells and cause liver problems. If fever, sore throat, a skin rash, mouth ulcers, bruising or bleeding develop, medical attention should be sought immediately

Other information: Do not stop taking this medication unless advised to do so by your doctor. Tablets should be swallowed whole and not crushed or chewed. This drug is suitable for use in children.

CAUTION

Alcohol: Should be avoided if possible or taken in moderation whilst taking this medication because it may enhance the side effects of the drug and increase the tendency to have a fit.

Driving and operating machinery: As this drug may cause dizziness and problems with vision, patients receiving this medication should not drive or perform such tasks until they are certain they are not experiencing these or any other side effects.

CARBARYL

Brand name: Carylderm

Type of drug: Anti parasite

Uses: Used in the eradication of head lice.

How it works: It acts by interfering with the nervous system of the lice, causing their death through paralysis.

Availability: POM

Possible adverse effects: Skin irritations are the mostly likely side effect, so it should not be used more than once a week, and for 3 weeks only.

Other information: This medicine should not be used for long periods of time.

CAUTION

Children: Can be used in children over 6 months of age.

CARBIMAZOLE

Brand name: Neo-Mercazole

Type of drug: Anti-thyroid

Uses: Used for people with an overactive thyroid and before thyroid surgery.

How it works: It reduces the production of thyroid hormones.

Availability: POM

Possible adverse effects: Nausea, headaches, joint pain, stomach pain, a skin rash and liver problems may occur. It can also affect blood cells so if a sore throat, mouth ulcers, fever, or unexplained bleeding and bruising occur, seek urgent medical advice.

Other information: This drug will either be used alone or in combination with other drugs. Regular blood tests are required to assess the effects.

CAUTION

Children: This drug is prescribed for children but this should only occur in hospital under the supervision of a doctor experienced in treating children with this condition.

CARNITINE

Brand name: Carnitor

Type of drug: Essential dietary component

Uses: To treat a deficiency of carnitine, a chemical which is vital in the process of changing fat to energy. Carnitine deficiency can occur due to a genetic defect or kidney dialysis.

How it works: It helps to move fats and glucose into cells, where they are used to produce energy.

Availability: POM

Possible adverse effects: Nausea, vomiting, stomach pain and diarrhoea.

Other information: This medicine may be prescribed for children.

CARVEDILOL

Brand name: Eucardic

Type of drug: Cardiac, alpha- and beta-blocker

Uses: Treatment of high blood pressure, heart failure and angina.

How it works: Reduces blood pressure by allowing the blood vessels of the body and heart muscle to relax. This increases the diameter and therefore decreases the blood pressure. It also slows the heart and gives it a more regular rhythm – improving its efficiency at pumping blood around the body.

Availability: POM

Possible adverse effects: Tiredness and fatigue, coldness or pain in the hands and feet, dry eyes, dizziness, headache, tiredness, headache, stomach upsets and light-headedness on standing may occur. Sometimes a slow pulse may be noticed. A rash and/or breathlessness should always be reported to a doctor.

This medication can affect the level of glucose in the blood, so diabetics should monitor their blood sugars closely.

Other information: Carvedilol should only be prescribed with caution for people with asthma or other lung disorders because it can make the conditions worse. It is likely that you will need to take this drug for a long period of time and it should not be discontinued unless advised by a doctor. Contact lens wearers may experience problems from dry eyes.

CAUTION

Alcohol: Can increase the likelihood of experiencing side effects and so should only be consumed in moderation.

Driving and operating machinery: As this drug can cause dizziness, patients receiving this medication should not drive or perform skilled tasks until they are certain they are not experiencing this or any other side effects.

CEFACLOR

Brand name: Distaclor

Type of drug: Antibiotic

Uses: Treatment of a wide variety of bacterial infections that occur in the chest, sinuses, skin, ear and urinary tract.

How it works: Cefaclor treats infections caused by bacteria by damaging the outer, protective layer of the bacteria, which leads to its death.

Availability: POM

Possible adverse effects: Diarrhoea is the most common side effect. If it is severe then the drug should be stopped and medical advice sought as little benefit will be obtained from the antibiotic. Nausea and vomiting may also occur. If allergic symptoms occur such as an itchy rash or swelling of the face, the patient should stop taking the medication and seek urgent medical advice.

Other information: The course of antibiotics should always be completed and taken regularly. The suspension should be kept in the fridge until the course is complete. The tablet must not be crushed or chewed, but swallowed whole. Take with or after meals. It may reduce the effectiveness of the contraceptive pill and alternative measures should be taken during, and for at least 7 days after finishing the course. Approximately 20% of patients allergic to penicillins will also be allergic to cepahalosporins such as cefaclor.

CAUTION

Children: It may be prescribed for children over 1 month of age.

CEFALEXIN

(Formerly known as: cephalexin)

Brand name: Keflex

Type of drug: Antibiotic

Uses: Antibiotic most commonly used for treatment of chest infections, bladder infections and some skin infections.

How it works: Treats bacterial infections caused by damaging the outer protective layer of the bacteria, which leads to its death.

Availability: POM

Possible adverse effects: Diarrhoea, stomach and abdominal pain, nausea and vomiting may occur. If allergic symptoms occur such as an itchy rash or swelling of the face, the patient should stop taking the medication and seek urgent medical advice.

Other information: The course of antibiotics should always be completed and taken regularly. It may reduce the effectiveness of the contraceptive pill and alternative measures should be taken during, and for at least 7 days after finishing the course. Approximately 20% of patients allergic to penicillins will also be allergic to cepahlosporins, such as cefalexin. This medicine is prescribed for children.

CEFRADINE

(Formerly known as: cephradine)

Brand name: Velosef

Type of drug: Antibiotic

Uses: Treatment of infections of the urinary tract, chest, ears, sinuses, skin and soft tissue.It is sometimes used to prevent infection during surgery.

How it works: Cefradine treats infections caused by bacteria by damaging the outer, protective layer of the bacteria, which leads to its death.

Availability: POM

Possible adverse effects: Diarrhoea, stomach and abdominal pain, nausea and vomiting may occur. If allergic symptoms occur such as an itchy rash or swelling of the face, the patient should stop taking the medication and seek urgent medical advice.

Other information: The course of antibiotics should always be completed and taken regularly. It may reduce the effectiveness of the contraceptive pill and alternative measures should be taken during, and for at least 7 days after finishing the course. Approximately 20% of patients allergic to penicillins will also be allergic to cepahlosporins, such as cefradine. It is used to treat infections in children.

CELECOXIB

Brand name: Celebrex

Type of drug: Anti-inflammatory, painkiller

Uses: Used for relief from the symptoms of rheumatoid, and osteoarthritis.

How it works: Reduces pain and inflammation by blocking the production of prostaglandins, that are involved in the inflammatory process.

Availability: POM

Possible adverse effects: Sinusitis, difficulty sleeping, indigestion, flatulence, and constipation may occur. Gastrointestinal ulceration and/or bleeding may occur, so if you suffer severe stomach pain, or there is blood in your stools then seek urgent medical advice. If allergic symptoms occur, such as an itchy skin rash or swelling of the mouth or tongue, the patient should stop taking the medication and seek urgent medical advice

Other information: Patients allergic to aspirin may also be allergic to celecoxib and should not take this medicine without advice from the doctor or pharmacist.

CAUTION

Driving and operating machinery: As this drug can cause difficulty sleeping resulting in tiredness, patients should not drive or perform skilled tasks until they are certain they are not experiencing this or any other side effects.

CETIRIZINE
Brand name: Zirtek
Type of drug: Antihistamine
Uses: The treatment of hay fever and other allergies.
How it works: Blocks the action of histamine – a chemical released by the body in response to allergies – so stopping symptoms such as runny nose and sneezing.
Availability: Available in some over-the-counter preparations.
Possible adverse effects: Drowsiness, dizziness, headaches and stomach pain, agitation and a dry mouth may occur.
Other information: If side effects are noticed the dose can be split into two, so taking half a tablet in the morning, and half a tablet at night. Although this is supposed to be a non-drowsy drug, it can still cause drowsiness in some people.

CAUTION
Children: Cetirizine may be prescribed for children over 6 years old.
Alcohol: Should be avoided because of an increased risk of drowsiness associated with the combination.
Driving and operating machinery: As this drug may cause dizziness and drowsiness, patients receiving this medication should not drive or perform skilled tasks until they are certain they are not experiencing these or any other side effects.

CLOMETHIAZOLE
(Formerly known as: clormethiazole)
Brand name: Heminevrin
Type of drug: Sleep inducing
Uses: This drug is used for the elderly and in alcohol withdrawal in younger adults.
How it works: Clormethiazole is a sedative, but the precise way in which it works is not known at the present time.
Availability: POM
Possible adverse effects: The most common is nasal congestion, accompanied by sneezing, which occurs 15-20 minutes after taking the drug. Nausea, headache, confusion and stomach pain may also occur.

Drowsiness that persists into the next day is not uncommon with this drug.

Other information: This is not suitable for people who are dependent on alcohol, who should not be drinking but who continue to drink.

CAUTION

Alcohol: Should not be consumed.

Driving and operating machinery: As this drug may cause drowsiness and tiredness – that may persist into the next day – it can impair the ability to drive or perform skilled tasks.

CHLORAL HYDRATE

Brand name: Welldorm

Type of drug: Sleep inducing

Uses: For short-term treatment when unable to sleep. Used to produce sleepiness in children for certain medical tests.

How it works: Acts on the brain to induce drowsiness.

Availability: POM

Possible adverse effects: Headache, unsteadiness on the feet, nausea, vomiting, dizziness, drowsiness, nightmares, flatulence and irritation of the stomach.

Other information: If taking the drug for longer than 4 weeks, a gradual reduction in dosage is recommended rather than stopping suddenly. It should be taken with plenty of water. This medicine may be prescribed for children

CAUTION

Alcohol: Should be avoided because of an increased risk of drowsiness associated with the combination.

Driving and operating machinery: As this drug may cause drowsiness and unsteadiness, patients should not drive or perform skilled tasks until they are certain they are not experiencing these or any other side effects.

CLOPIDOGREL

Brand name: Plavix

Type of drug: Anti-platelet

Uses: It is used to stop the formation of blood clots in patients who are at risk of a heart attack or stroke.

How it works: Clopidogrel thins the blood by making one of the blood's constituents, platelets, less effective. Platelets are involved in the formation of blood clots.

Availability: POM

Possible adverse effects: Bleeding, indigestion, heartburn, abdominal pain and diarrhoea. If bleeding or bruising occur, seek urgent medical advice.

Other information: Clopidogrel is sometimes used with aspirin which also increases the risk of bleeding.

CHLORAMBUCIL

Brand name: Leukeran

Type of drug: Chemotherapy

Uses: Used for the treatment of various forms of leukaemia and lymphoma, in particular leukaemia and Hodgkin's disease.

How it works: It causes permanent damage to the DNA of cancer cells, which in turn stops the cancer cell from multiplying and leads to its death.

Availability: POM

Possible adverse effects: Nausea, vomiting, diarrhoea and rashes may occur. This drug causes a temporary reduction in the numbers of blood cells produced. Any sign of infection, such as a sore throat, unexplained bleeding or bruising, high temperature or generally feeling unwell should be reported to the doctor immediately. If allergic symptoms occur such as an itchy rash or swelling of the mouth or tongue, the patient should stop taking the medication and seek urgent medical advice.

Other information: This medicine is only given in hospital under the supervision of a doctor experienced in treating cancer. Regular blood tests are required to assess the effects. It may be used alone or with other chemotherapy drugs. Patients are often given additional drugs to prevent some of the side effects of this drug.

CAUTION

Children: This drug is used to treat Hodgkins disease in children.

Pregnancy: A barrier method of contraception (such as a condom) is recommended, but if you become pregnant while on this medicine inform your doctor as soon as possible.

CHLORAMPHENICOL
Brand name: Chloromycetin
Type of drug: Antibiotic
Uses: This is a broad spectrum antibiotic. Used topically to treat ear and eye infections. Also used occasionally to treat more serious infections such as meningitis, typhoid or pneumonia.
How it works: Chloramphenicol does not kill bacteria, but it stops them multiplying which then allows the body's immune system to destroy the bacteria.
Availability: POM
Possible adverse effects: When used for the ears and eyes, the drops or ointment may cause irritation and the area becomes red, stings, burns, or itches, and vision may be blurred. Extremely rarely can cause a reduction in the numbers of blood cells produced by the bone marrow which is permanent and can be fatal. This medicine should be used at regular intervals and the prescribed course be completed. The eye drops should be stored in the fridge.
CAUTION
Children: Prescribed for children with eye infections.
Driving and operating machinery: As this drug can cause blurred vision, patients receiving this medication should not drive or perform skilled tasks until they are certain they are not experiencing this or any other side effects.

CHLORDIAZEPOXIDE
Brand name: Librium
Type of drug: Anxiolytic
Uses: Treating anxiety and encouraging sleep. It can also be used to treat the symptoms of alcohol withdrawal, and for reducing muscle spasms.
How it works: Feelings of anxiety are in part due to increases in hormones in the brain, such as adrenaline, noradrenaline and GABA. Anxiety is believed to be caused by an increase in the transmission of signals through nerves in particular parts of the brain. Chlordiazepoxide reduces the signals transmitted to and from certain parts of the brain and relieves anxiety.
Availability: POM
Possible adverse effects: Drowsiness, confusion, light-headedness,

nausea and constipation may occur. Drowsiness can still be present the next day, this is called the 'hangover effect'. Sometimes this drug can have the opposite effect and make the person more anxious.

Other information: Not suitable to be used long term as the drug can be habit-forming and dependence can occur. Treatment is usually limited to 2 weeks.

CAUTION

Alcohol: This should be avoided because of an increased risk of drowsiness associated with the combination.

Driving and operating machinery: As this drug can cause drowsiness, which may persist into the next day, it may impair the ability to drive or perform skilled tasks.

CHLOROQUINE

Brand name: Avloclor

Type of drug: Antimalarial, immunosuppressant

Uses: For prevention and treatment of malaria. It is also used to treat severe rheumatoid arthritis.

How it works: The drug kills the malaria parasite before it can multiply. How it works in rheumatoid arthritis is less well understood.

Availability: OTC

Possible adverse effects: Nausea, vomiting, diarrhoea, abdominal pain, headache, convulsions or fitting, anxiety, changes in mood, problems with vision. If allergic symptoms such as wheezing occur or an itchy skin rash, the patient should stop taking the medication and seek urgent medical advice. This drug can also reduce the number of blood cells, and can cause anaemia in individuals with G6PD deficiency.

Other information: Malarial strains that are resistant to chloroquine are not uncommon, so it is important to discuss the most effective prevention of malaria before travelling abroad. This medicine is usually started a week before entering the malaria zone to allow the drug to reach effective levels in the blood before the person is exposed to the malaria parasite and should be continued for 4 weeks after returning from a malarial area. In addition to medication, it is important to take precautions against being bitten by mosquitoes, as this is how malaria is transmitted. Other recommendations include using mosquito repellents, wearing long sleeves and trousers after dusk, avoiding swamps and marshy areas where possible and using mosquito nets around the bed.

In rheumatoid arthritis chloroquine is only given in hospital under the supervision of a doctor experienced in treating rheumatic diseases. Regular blood tests and examinations are required to monitor the effects. It may take several weeks or months to see the beneficial effects of this medication. Prolonged use of the drug can lead to serious damage of the retina, which could progress to blindness. Regular eye checks should be carried out, especially for patients on the drug for arthritis. Indigestion remedies should not be taken at the same time of day as chloroquine.

CAUTION

Children: For prevention of malaria this drug is prescribed for children.

Driving and operating machinery: As this drug can cause problems with vision it may impair the ability to drive or perform skilled tasks.

CHLORPHENAMINE

Brand name: Piriton

Type of drug: Antihistamine

Uses: To help treat the symptoms of hay fever, allergic conjunctivitis and hives. It is also used in emergency situations when a severe allergic reaction has occurred.

How it works: Blocks the action of histamine – a chemical produced by the body in response to something you are allergic to – so stopping symptoms such as a runny nose, sneezing, itching, wheezing, breathlessness and swelling of the mouth or face.

Availability: Chlorpheniramine is available as an ingredient in many over-the-counter preparations.

Common adverse effects: Drowsiness – from a slight feeling of tiredness to a deep sleep, excitability in children, indigestion, nausea, vomiting, diarrhoea, dizziness, headaches, blurred vision and rashes.

Other information: Tablets should be swallowed whole not crushed or chewed.

CAUTION

Children: Used in children over 1 year of age.

Alcohol: Should not be consumed whilst taking this medicine because it may increase the effect of drowsiness.

Driving and operating machinery: As this drug can cause drowsiness, patients receiving this medication should not drive or perform skilled tasks until they are certain they are not experiencing this or any other side effects.

CHLORPROMAZINE

Brand name: Largactil

Type of drug: Antipsychotic

Uses: Used to treat schizophrenia, mania and other conditions that result in confused or abnormal behaviour. It is also used to suppress hiccoughs and can be used to prevent nausea and vomiting.

How it works: Schizophrenia and related disorders are thought to be due to an excessive amount of one of the chemical messengers, called dopamine, in the brain. Chlorpromazine reduces dopamine levels; it also has effects upon other messengers in the brain.

Availability: POM

Possible adverse effects: Sedation is common and may be a desired effect in agitated patients. Dizziness, drowsiness, dry mouth, constipation, anxiety, a rash that develops when skin is exposed to sunlight, stomach upsets and weight gain may occur. Dizziness and light-headedness can occur when standing up. It may also cause a change in the perception of the body's temperature so you feel hotter, or colder than normal. Unwanted effects include abnormal, involuntary movements, stiffness, restlessness and condition that is like Parkinson's disease.

Other information: Sunlight should be avoided, especially between the hours of 11:00 and 14:00 when the sun is strongest. Sensible precautions to prevent this skin reaction to sunlight would include; to apply a total sun block, cover the arms and legs in long clothes, wear a wide brimmed hat and sunglasses, and not using sunlamps.

Handle the tablets as little as possible as they can make the skin irritated and sensitive. The drug should be taken exactly as prescribed.

CAUTION

Children: Can be used in children over 1 year of age.

Alcohol: This should be avoided by patients taking this medication because of an increased risk of drowsiness associated with the combination.

Driving and operating machinery: As this drug can cause dizziness and drowsiness, patients receiving this medication should not drive or perform such tasks until they are certain they are not experiencing any side effects.

CICLOSPORIN

(Formerly known as: cyclosporine)

Brand name: Neoral

Type of drug: Immunosuppressant

Uses: Used to prevent organ rejection following transplants. It is also prescribed in a variety of inflammatory and autoimmune conditions such as severe cases of eczema and psoriasis and rheumatoid arthritis where other drugs have failed to help.

How it works: Stops the production of cells within the immune system, that cause inflammation and damage in autoimmune and inflammatory diseases; these cells are responsible for organ rejection after transplant surgery.

Availability: POM

Possible adverse effects: Nausea, headaches, confusion, overgrowth of gums, muscle weakness, cramp, fatigue, tremor, increased hair growth, diarrhoea, excess fluid, weight gain, high blood pressure, and anaemia may occur. It can also cause damage to the liver and kidneys. This medication can increase the patient's risk of getting infections through its effect on the immune system. Any sign of infection, such as a sore throat, high temperature or generally feeling unwell should be reported to the doctor immediately.

Other information: This medicine is only given in hospital under the supervision of a doctor experienced in looking after transplant patients, rheumatic diseases, and other autoimmune conditions. Regular blood tests are required to monitor the level of the drug in the blood and to assess the effects. It is usually taken twice a day. Grapefruit juice should be avoided for at least 1 hour before the ciclosporin is taken. The liquid may be mixed with any other fruit juice to mask its taste. The syringe provided with the ciclosporin liquid should not be used for any other medication, and must not be allowed to come into contact with any other fluids. This drug is used for some conditions in children.

CAUTION

Pregnancy: Patients should not become pregnant whilst taking this medicine. Effective contraceptive measures should be used.

Driving and operating machinery: This drug can impair the ability to drive or perform skilled tasks.

CHORIONIC GONADOTROPHIN

(Human Chorionic Gonadotrophin)

Brand name: Pregnyl, Choragon

Type of drug: Hormone treatment

Uses: The treatment of female infertility where the problem is due to an inability to ovulate as long as the ovaries, uterus and Fallopian tubes are normal. It is also sometimes used when puberty fails to occur in boys and to treat sterility in men.

How it works: This drug acts like a hormone that is produced by both sexes called leuteinizing hormone. In women this leads to the production of oestrogen and progesterone, which permits ovulation. In males it leads to an increased production of testosterone which leads to increased sperm production.

Availability: POM

Possible adverse effects: Abdominal pain, headache, mood changes or swelling may occur but this should pass soon after treatment.

Other information: Patients offered this treatment should be aware of the increased likelihood of multiple births as several eggs may be released at once.

CILAZAPRIL

Brand name: Vascace

Type of drug: ACE inhibitor

Uses: To treat high blood pressure and heart failure.

How it works: It enables the blood vessels to relax, which allows them to increase in size. This reduces the pressure of the blood flowing through them.

Availability: POM

Possible adverse effects: Chest pain, nausea, indigestion, abdominal pains, headache, dizziness and tiredness may occur. A dry cough can occur when first taking this medicine, but this side effect usually lessens with continued use. Persistent cough should be reported to the doctor or pharmacist.

Other information: The first dose should be taken when sitting or lying down because the fall in blood pressure can be quite considerable and lead to dizziness or fainting. This drug should be used with caution in patients with kidney problems. Blood tests are usually carried out to monitor the levels of potassium. Patients should avoid salt substitutes containing potassium, and should take care in hot weather, or if taking exercise, to avoid over-heating and dehydration.

CAUTION

Alcohol: Should only be consumed in strict moderation whilst taking this medicine because the combination may cause a large fall in blood pressure.

Driving and operating machinery: As this drug can cause dizziness and sedation, patients receiving this medication should not drive or perform such tasks until they are certain they are not experiencing any side effects.

CIMETIDINE
Brand name: Tagamet
Type of drug: Ulcer treatment
Uses: To treat ulcers of the stomach and duodenum, and heartburn.
How it works: This drug reduces the secretion of gastric acid, and pepsin – an enzyme that helps in the digestion of protein, in the stomach. This prevents irritation of the stomach or oesophagus by acid and promotes healing of the stomach or gut where the ulcers occur.
Availability: OTC
Possible adverse effects: Headache, diarrhoea, dizziness, and a rash may occur. Rarely it can cause breast enlargement and sexual problems in men.
Other information: Cimetidine may alter the effectiveness of many other medicines. So always tell your doctor and pharmacist all the medicines that you are taking.

CAUTION

Children: This drug is used in children over 1 year of age.

Driving and operating machinery: As this drug can cause dizziness and sedation, patients receiving this medication should not drive or perform such tasks until they are certain they are not experiencing any side effects.

CINNARIZINE

Brand name: Stugeron

Type of drug: Antihistamine

Uses: To control travel sickness, dizziness, ringing in the ears, and other symptoms associated with Ménière's disease.

How it works: Stops the contractions of muscles in the stomach and elsewhere in the body that cause the sensations associated with feeling sick.

Availability: OTC

Possible adverse effects: Drowsiness, low blood pressure and stomach pains may occur. If allergic symptoms occur such as an itchy skin rash, the patient should stop taking the medication and discuss with their doctor or pharmacist.

CAUTION

Children: Used in children over 5 years old.

Alcohol: Should be avoided whilst taking this medicine because alcohol increases the amount of drowsiness that may be experienced.

Driving and operating machinery: As this drug can cause drowsiness, patients receiving this medication should not drive or perform skilled tasks until they are certain they are not experiencing this, or any other side effects.

CIPROFIBRATE

Brand name: Modalim

Type of drug: Reduces fats such as triglycerides in the blood

Uses: To lower the level of fats (lipids) in the blood, which are thought to contribute to coronary heart disease, angina, heart attacks and stroke.

How it works: Ciprofibrate causes a lower level of lipids in the blood by inhibiting an enzyme that produces them, and promoting lipid breakdown.

Availability: POM

Possible adverse effects: Nausea, loss of appetite, headache, stomach discomfort and a feeling of fullness may occur. These side effects usually lessen with continued use. However it can cause muscle pain, tenderness or weakness that should be reported to your doctor, or pharmacist.

Other information: Should be taken in conjunction with a low fat diet. Blood tests may be performed to monitor its effect on the level of lipids in the blood. These tablets should be taken with, or after food.

CIPROFLOXACIN

Brand name: Ciproxin

Type of drug: Antibiotic

Uses: To treat infections of the chest, gut and urinary tract. It is also used as a single dose treatment for gonorrhoea.

How it works: It acts on the DNA of the bacteria to stop them multiplying.

Availability: POM

Possible adverse effects: Headache, dizziness, nausea, vomiting, diarrhoea, heartburn, ringing in the ears, abdominal and joint pain are the most commonly reported side effects. This drug may increase the chances of a seizure in epileptic patients.

Other information: Patients are advised to drink plenty of fluids while taking this drug. Tablets should be swallowed whole, and not crushed or chewed. Do not take at the same time as indigestion remedies, milk and medicines containing iron or zinc. It should be taken at regular intervals until the prescribed course is completed.

CAUTION

Alcohol: Should be avoided whilst taking this medicine because alcohol increases the amount of drowsiness that may be experienced.

Driving and operating machinery: As this drug can cause dizziness, patients receiving this medication should not drive or perform skilled tasks until they are certain they are not experiencing this or any other side effects.

CISPLATIN

Brand name: Only available as a generic medicine

Type of drug: Platinum compound

Uses: Treatment for cancers of the bladder, head, neck, lung, bone, ovaries and testicles.

How it works: Attacks the DNA of cancer cells to prevent them from multiplying.

Availability: POM

Possible adverse effects: Severe nausea and vomiting, impairment of kidney function. Also tinnitus and damage to hearing.

Other information: This medicine is only given in hospital under the supervision of a doctor experienced in treating cancer. Regular blood tests are required to assess the effects. Any sign of infection, such as a sore throat, unexplained bleeding or bruising, generally feeling unwell or high temperature should be reported to the doctor immediately. Anti-sickness drugs and other medications are often given at the same time.

CAUTION

Children: This drug is used for some conditions in children.

Pregnancy: Should be avoided.

Driving and operating machinery: This drug can impair the ability to drive or perform skilled tasks.

CITALOPRAM

Brand name: Cipramil

Type of drug: Antidepressant

Uses: To treat depression and anxiety.

How it works: It increases the length of time that a specific chemical messenger in brain, called serotonin, is effective for. This leads to an increase in mood and reverses depression.

Availability: POM

Possible adverse effects: Citalopram can have some effect on the gut; notably nausea, vomiting, stomach upsets and diarrhoea. This drug may also cause appetite and weight changes, changes in mood, insomnia, confusion, impaired concentration, dizziness and drowsiness, sweating, and tremor.

Other information: This drug may take between 2 and 4 weeks to take effect. There may be some side effects when treatment is stopped including; dizziness, headache, anxiety, and nausea, so the drug is reduced gradually.

CAUTION

Alcohol: Should be avoided whilst taking citalopram as it may reverse the effects of the drug, or stop it working as effectively.

Driving and operating machinery: As this drug can cause dizziness and drowsiness, patients receiving this medication should not drive or perform skilled tasks until they are certain they are not experiencing these or any other side effects.

CLARITHROMYCIN

Brand name: Klaricid

Type of drug: Antibiotic

Uses: Clarithromycin is used to treat a wide range of infections that occur in the chest, skin, ears and tonsils. Often used for people allergic to penicillin. It is also used to treat *H. Pylori* infection of the stomach.

How it works: Binds to enzymes within the bacterial cell that produce chemicals essential for the bacteria to survive. Without these chemicals the bacteria cannot survive and die.

Availability: POM

Possible adverse effects: Stomach upsets such as nausea, vomiting and diarrhoea are commonly reported side effects. Joint pain and discolouration of the tongue may also occur. If allergic symptoms occur such as an itchy, red skin rash, the patient should stop taking the medication and inform the doctor or pharmacist.

Other information: Should be taken an hour before food or on an empty stomach. Indigestion remedies should not be taken at the same time as this medicine – but if required take 1 hour before or 2 hours after clarithromycin. It is important to take as prescribed, and to complete the whole course. It may make the contraceptive pill less effective, and other means of contraception should be used throughout the treatment course and for 7 days after completing it. This medicine is used to treat infections in children.

CLINDAMYCIN

Brand name: Dalacin C

Type of drug: Antibiotic

Uses: Treatment of severe joint and bone infections such as osteomyelitis. Also used on the skin to treat acne, and as a cream to cure vaginal thrush.

How it works: Binds to enzymes within the bacterial cell that produce chemicals essential for the bacteria to survive. Without these chemicals the bacteria cannot multiply, and this allows the body's immune system to overcome the infection.

Availability: POM

Possible adverse effects: Abdominal discomfort, nausea, rash and vomiting may occur. It can cause liver problems and reduced blood cells. If severe diarrhoea occurs stop taking it immediately and seek urgent medical attention. This particular side effect may occur weeks after first taking this drug.

Other information: Capsules should be taken with a full glass of water and should be taken at regular intervals throughout the prescribed course. The cream or lotion should never be applied to the eyes.

CAUTION

Children: Used to treat serious infections in children.

CLOBETASOL

Brand name: Dermovate

Type of drug: Steroid, anti-inflammatory

Uses: Used to treat eczema, psoriasis and other disorders of the skin.

How it works: This drug has two major effects; the first is to make blood vessels narrower, which stops inflammatory cells and chemicals from reaching the affected area. The second is to stop the production of chemicals that cause inflammation.

Availability: POM

Possible adverse effects: If used correctly there are generally no problems. However a worsening of the skin condition, thinning of the skin, skin discolouration and stretch marks may all occur if too much is used or it is used for too long. It can also make some skin infections worse.

Other information: Water-based creams are usually prescribed for moist or weeping eczema; an ointment is more likely for dry and scaly patches. Apply thinly over the affected area. Do not use dressings over the cream/ointment unless told to do so by the doctor or pharmacist – this includes nappies for children.

CAUTION
Children: Used in children over 1 year of age.

CLOBETASONE
Brand name: Eumovate
Type of drug: Corticosteroid
Uses: Used to treat eczema, psoriasis and other skin conditions.
How it works: Stops the production of cells, and chemicals that produce inflammation.
Availability: Available as an ingredient in some preparations that are available over-the-counter.
Possible adverse effects: Worsening of the skin condition, thinning of the skin, skin discolouration and stretch marks may all occur if too much is used or it is used for too long. It can also make skin infections worse.
Other information: Water-based creams are usually prescribed for moist or weeping eczema; an ointment is more likely for dry and scaly patches. Apply thinly over the affected area. Do not use dressings over the cream/ointment unless told to do so by the doctor or pharmacist – this includes nappies for children.
CAUTION
Children: Used in children over 1 year of age.

CLOMIFENE
(Formerly known as: clomiphene)
Brand name: Clomid
Type of drug: Infertility treatment
Uses: Treatment of infertility in women where ovulation is not taking place due to inadequate levels of the necessary hormones.
How it works: Although it blocks the effects of oestrogens, this leads to increased production of hormones necessary for egg release, or ovulation as long as the ovaries, uterus and fallopian tubes are normal.
Availability: POM
Possible adverse effects: Hot flushes and abdominal discomfort, headaches, insomnia and depression. Visual impairment is possible but rare.

Other information: Patients offered this treatment should be aware of the increased likelihood of multiple births as several eggs may be released at once. This drug is given in cycles corresponding to a woman's menstrual cycle. This drug will not usually be used for longer than 6 treatment cycles. It is only given in hospital under the supervision of a doctor experienced in treating infertility, who will oversee and monitor treatment. Regular tests are required to see whether pregnancy has been achieved and to assess the side effects.

CAUTION

Driving and operating machinery: As this drug can cause blurred vision, patients receiving this medication should not drive or perform skilled tasks until they are certain they are not experiencing this or any other side effects.

CLOMIPRAMINE
Brand name: Anafranil
Type of drug: Antidepressant
Uses: Long term treatment of depression, irrational fears and obsessive behaviour.
How it works: It inhibits the re-uptake of brain chemicals, which results in a heightening of mood. It also encourages appetite and enables users to lead a more normal daily life. Its sedative effect is also useful for people who find difficulty in sleeping at nights.
Availability: POM
Possible adverse effects: Dry mouth, constipation, drowsiness and dizziness (especially when standing up), hot flushes, blurring of vision, tiredness, increased appetite, disorientation, anxiety, problems sleeping and nightmares, problems with memory and concentration, tremor, nausea, decreased libido, strange taste in the mouth and problems with hearing.
Other information: Avoid using over-the-counter medications that contain antihistamines and decongestants. Always inform your doctor or pharmacist so that appropriate treatments can be selected.
CAUTION
Alcohol: Should not be consumed whilst taking this medication because it

can cause an increase in drowsiness, and may reduce its effectiveness.

Driving and operating machinery: As this drug can cause blurred vision, and drowsiness, patients receiving this medication should not drive or perform skilled tasks until they are certain they are not experiencing these or any other side effects.

CLONAZEPAM

Brand name: Rivotril

Type of drug: Antiepileptic, sedative

Uses: Prevention and treatment of epileptic fits, particularly in children.

How it works: An epileptic fit (or seizure) is thought to occur when the brain receives too many signals via the nervous system. Clonazepam reduces the signals transmitted to and from certain parts of the brain by blocker a chemical messenger in the brain known as GABA, this reduces the likelihood of a seizure occurring.

Availability: POM

Possible adverse effects: Tiredness, drowsiness and dizziness, reduced co-ordination of movement, light-headedness, limbs that appear to be 'floppy' are the most commonly seen side effects. They usually only occur during the early part of treatment and are reduced, if not avoided, by gradually increasing the amount taken.

Other information: The anticonvulsant effect tends to lessen after several months of use. It is possible to become physically dependant on clonazepam, and the drug will be withdrawn very slowly to stop any ill effects. Dependence is usually only associated with treatment for a long period of time. Do not stop taking this medication unless advised to do so by your doctor. This medication can be given to children of all ages.

CAUTION

Alcohol: Should not be consumed whilst taking this medicine as it can increase the effect of any drowsiness.

Driving and operating machinery: As this drug can cause dizziness and drowsiness, patients receiving this medication should not drive or perform skilled tasks until they are certain they are not experiencing these or any other side effects.

CLONIDINE
Brand name: Dixarit, Captapres
Type of drug: Antihypertensive
Uses: To help prevent migraine attacks. It is also used for controlling menopausal flushing and for high blood pressure.
How it works: Stops production of signals from the brain that cause blood vessels to narrow. This causes them to widen, which improves blood flow and reduces blood pressure. This drug also causes the heart rate to slow down, further reducing the blood pressure. It has a similar effect on blood vessels in the brain, which reduces attacks of migraine.
Availability: POM
Possible adverse effects: Drowsiness, dizziness, cold hands and feet, fatigue, excess fluid, nausea and dry mouth may occur but lessen with time. A slow heart rate may also occur.
Other information: Report any excessive weight gain. Do not stop taking this drug suddenly except on medical advice. The tablets should be swallowed whole and not crushed or chewed.

CAUTION
Children: Can be used in children over 12 years of age.
Alcohol: In strict moderation whilst taking clonidine as it can cause an excessive drop in blood pressure and exacerbate drowsiness.
Driving and operating machinery: As this drug can cause dizziness and drowsiness, patients receiving this medication should not drive or perform skilled tasks until they are certain they are not experiencing these or any other side effects.

CLOTRIMAZOLE
Brand name: Canesten
Type of drug: Antifungal
Uses: Used to treat ringworm, and thrush of the mouth, vagina or penis. It is also used to control fungal skin and outer ear infections.
How it works: Clotrimazole stops the production and repair of the fungal cell membrane.
Availability: Clotrimazole is available as an ingredient in some over-the-counter products.

Possible adverse effects: The skin may become irritated, inflamed and sore, but this rarely requires the treatment to be discontinued.

Other information: Can be used in pregnancy.

CLOZAPINE

Brand name: Clozaril

Type of drug: Antipsychotic

Uses: To treat people with schizophrenia who have not responded to other treatments.

How it works: Schizophrenia and related disorders are thought to be caused by an excess of one of the chemical messengers, called dopamine, in the brain. Clozapine reduces dopamine levels; it also has effects upon other messengers in the brain.

Availability: POM

Possible adverse effects: Drowsiness, dizziness, confusion, fatigue, dry mouth, increased saliva production, weight gain, constipation, blurred vision, possible rigidity and difficulty with movement, tremor and nausea. This drug can also cause hyperthermia or a feeling of warmth. During the first stages of treatment dizziness on standing may occur, but this will improve as treatment progresses.

Other information: This medicine is only given in hospital under the supervision of an experienced psychiatrist. Regular blood tests are required to assess the effects. Any sign of infection, such as a sore throat, unexplained bleeding or bruising, generally feeling unwell or high temperature should be reported to the doctor immediately because this drug can produce a life-threatening fall in white blood cells. You will be registered with an organisation called the Clozapine Patient Monitoring Service (CPMS) who are responsible for carrying out the necessary blood tests. It can take up to three weeks for the benefits of this drug to be felt.

CAUTION

Children: This drug is only used in children above the age of 16 years old.

Pregnancy and breastfeeding: It is recommended that contraception should be used, but if you become pregnant while on this medicine, inform your doctor as soon as possible.

Alcohol: Alcohol should not be consumed in any form whilst taking this medication as it can lead to dizziness and an increase in drowsiness.

Driving and operating machinery: As this drug can cause dizziness and drowsiness, patients receiving this medication should not drive or perform skilled tasks until they are certain they are not experiencing these or any other side effects.

CO-AMILOFRUSE

Brand name: Frumil

Type of drug: Combination of 2 diuretics; frusemide and amiloride

Uses: It is used to reduce the number of tablets a patient has to take for fluid retention associated with heart failure, and high blood pressure.

How it works: Both drugs act together to reduce excess fluid in the body. See the individual drugs for more details on how they work.

Availability: POM

Possible adverse effects: Nausea, stomach and bowel upsets, gout, tiredness and dry mouth. Any rashes should be reported to a doctor.

Other information: Blood tests may be carried out to measure the level of potassium in the blood. Frusemide starts to work within an hour and the effects last for up to 6 hours.

CAUTION

Alcohol: This should only be consumed in moderation whilst taking this medication as it may increase the risk of dehydration and cause a greater than expected drop in blood pressure.

CO-AMILOZIDE

Brand name: Moduretic

Type of drug: Co-Amilozide is a combination of two diuretics, amiloride and hydrochlorthiazide.

Uses: It is used to reduce the number of tablets a patient has to take for fluid retention associated with heart failure, liver failure, and some other conditions.

How it works: The two ingredients act together to reduce excess fluid in the body. See the individual drugs for more details on how they work.

Common adverse effects: Headache, tiredness, chest and back pain, nausea, vomiting, diarrhoea or constipation, thirst, and may also precipitate attacks of gout, joint and muscle pain, dizziness, insomnia, unusual taste in the mouth, and problems with vision.

Other information: The effects will be noticed within 1 to 2 hours of taking this medicine, and may last for 12 hours or more.

CAUTION

Alcohol: Should only be consumed in moderation whilst taking this medication as it may increase the risk of dehydration and cause a greater than expected drop in blood pressure.

CO-AMOXICLAV

Brand name: Augmentin

Type of drug: Antibiotic

Uses: Used to treat infections of the respiratory tract, genito-urinary, abdominal infections, severe dental infection and animal bites.

How it works: This is a combination of amoxycillin and clavulanic acid. Amoxicillin stops the production and repair of the bacteria's cell wall, causing the bacteria to die. However some bacteria can break down amoxicillin, so adding clavulanic acid makes it more effective.

Availability: POM

Possible adverse effects: Nausea, vomiting, diarrhoea, and rashes are the most commonly reported adverse effects. If a rash or jaundice – a yellowing and itching of the skin – develop, then a doctor or pharmacist should be consulted. If allergic symptoms occur such as wheezing or swelling of the face, the patient should stop taking the medication and seek urgent medical advice.

Other information: Patients allergic to penicillin may also be allergic to amoxycillin. It is not usually used for more than 2 weeks at a time. Take at regular intervals and complete the prescribed course. The dispersible tablets should be dissolved in water before use. It should be taken at the start of meals if the gut side effects are troublesome. This medicine is used in children of all ages. This medicine can be used during breastfeeding.

CO-BENELDOPA

Brand name: Madopar

Type of drug: A combination of levodopa and benserazide.

Uses: Treats the symptoms of Parkinson's disease.

How it works: Levodopa increases the amount of a chemical messenger called dopamine in the brain which is reduced in Parkinson's disease, and this allows the symptoms of the disease to be alleviated. However dopamine is broken down in the body – before it gets to the brain – by an enzyme called dopa-decarboxylase. Benserazide stops this enzyme breaking down dopamine, and so increases the effectiveness of the levodopa.

Availability: POM

Possible adverse effects: Weight loss, nausea, vomiting, dizziness on standing, rapid heart rate and diarrhoea are common when starting this medication. Mood changes, drowsiness, insomnia, involuntary movements and facial flushing are also felt, but lessen with time. If urine is red in colour, this is no cause for concern.

Other information: This medicine should be taken with or after food to relieve some of the problems associated with the gut such as nausea and diarrhoea. The amount taken usually needs adjusting by a doctor over a period of time. It is only usually used for patients over 25 years old.

CAUTION

Alcohol: Alcohol should be avoided because of an increased risk of drowsiness associated with the combination.

Driving and operating machinery: The drug is known to cause sudden sleepiness. If this occurs do not drive or undertake other skilled tasks.

CO-CARELDOPA

Brand name: Madopar

Type of drug: A combination of levodopa and carbidopa

Uses: Levodopa increases the amount of a chemical messenger called dopamine in the brain which is reduced in Parkinson's disease, and this allows the symptoms of the disease to be alleviated. However dopamine is broken down in the body – before it gets to the brain – by an enzyme called dopa-decarboxylase. Carbidopa stops this enzyme breaking down dopamine, and so increases the effectiveness of the levodopa.

Possible adverse effects: Nausea, muscle twitching, problems with movement, and involuntary movements. Dizziness, changes in mood, drowsiness, insomnia, vomiting, dark saliva, sweating, dry mouth, weight loss, indigestion, flushing of the face and blurred vision.

Other information: This medicine should be taken with or after food to relieve some of the problems associated with the gut such as nausea and diarrhoea. The severity of the adverse effects decreases with time. Tablets should be swallowed whole, and not chewed or crushed. The amount taken usually needs adjusting by a doctor over a period of time. This medication is only usually prescribed for over 18 year olds.

CAUTION

Driving and operating machinery: This drug is known to cause sudden sleepliness. If this occurs do not drive or undertake other skilled tasks.

CO-CODAMOL

Brand name: Solpadol, Tylex

Type of drug: Painkiller, a combination of paracetamol and the opioid analgesic codeine.

Uses: Treatment of moderate pain.

How it works: The sensation we attribute to pain is only felt once signals from the body reach the brain. Codeine stops those signals reaching the brain by blocking their transmission through the spinal cord. Paracetamol works by making the nerves less responsive to painful signals.

Availability: 2 preparations are available; medicines containing 8mg of codeine are available over-the-counter, and those containing 30mg are only available on prescription.

Possible adverse effects: Light-headedness, nausea, vomiting, drowsiness, constipation, and shortness of breath. Some of these side effects may be alleviated by lying down.

Other information: A maximum of 2 tablets should be taken at any one time up to a maximum of 4 times a day. A maximum of 8 tablets can be taken within one 24-hour period. Do not exceed this amount as paracetamol overdosage can lead to potentially fatal liver damage. If too many tablets are taken, seek urgent medical attention. Do not take any other products containing paracetamol while taking this medication. In case of uncertainty about whether a particular product is suitable to take with co-codamol the advice of a pharmacist should be sought.

CAUTION

Children: Usually only used in children over the age of 12 years old.

Alcohol: Should not be consumed because it will increase the effects of drowsiness and dizziness.

Driving and operating machinery: As this drug can cause dizziness and drowsiness, patients should not drive or perform skilled tasks until they are certain they are not experiencing these or any other side effects.

CO-DANTHRAMER

Brand name: Co-Danthramer

Type of drug: Laxative, a combination of dantron and poloxamer '188'

Uses: Laxative for use in terminally ill patients.

How it works: Dantron acts to stimulate the nerves in the gut to contract and expel faeces. Poloxamer '188' acts to draw more water into the faeces making the stool softer and easier for the gut to pass out.

Availability: POM

Possible adverse effects: The urine and skin around the anus may turn red or pink. This resolves after treatment has ended. Prolonged use may change the colour of the large intestine and possibly any material passed out.

Other information: This is not usually the first treatment for constipation as dantron has been associated with a possible risk of cancer. It is only usually used for constipation in terminally ill patients.

CO-DANTHRUSATE

Brand name: Normax

Type of drug: Laxative containing dantron and docusate

Uses: Laxative for use in terminally ill patients.

How it works: Dantron acts to stimulate the nerves in the gut to contract and expel faeces. Docusate acts to draw more water into the faeces making the stool softer and easier for the gut to pass out.

Availability: POM

Posssible adverse effects: The urine may turn orange during use.

Other information: Not usually the first treatment for constipation as dantron has been associated with a possible risk of cancer. It is only usually used for constipation in terminally ill patients.

CO-DYDRAMOL

Brand name: Remedeine

Type of drug: A combination of paracetamol, and the opioid analgesic dihydrocodeine

Uses: Treatment of moderate pain.

How it works: The sensation that we attribute to pain is only felt once signals from the body reach the brain. Dihyrocodeine stops those signals from reaching the brain by blocking their transmission through the spinal cord. Paracetamol works by making the nerves less responsive to painful signals.

Availability: Two preparations are available; medicines containing 7.46mg of dihydrocodeine are available over-the-counter, and those containing 10mg are only available on prescription.

Possible adverse effects: Light-headedness, nausea, vomiting, drowsiness, constipation, and shortness of breath. Some of these side effects may be alleviated by lying down.

Other information: A maximum of 2 tablets should be taken at any one time up to a maximum of 4 times a day. A maximum of 8 tablets can be taken within one 24-hour period. Do not exceed this amount as paracetamol overdosage can lead to potentially fatal liver damage. If too many tablets are taken, seek urgent medical attention. Do not take any other products containing paracetamol whilst taking this medication. In case of uncertainty about whether a particular product is suitable to take with co-dydramol the advice of a pharmacist should be sought.

CAUTION

Children: Co-dydramol is usually only used in children over the age of 12 years old.

Alcohol: Should not be consumed whilst taking this medicine because it will increase the effects of drowsiness and dizziness.

Driving and operating machinery: As this drug can cause dizziness and drowsiness, patients receiving this medication should not drive or perform skilled tasks until they are certain they are not experiencing these or any other side effects.

CO-PHENOTROPE

Brand name: Lomotil

Type of drug: A combination of diphenoxylate hydrochloride and atropine

Uses: It is used to stop acute attacks of diarrhoea.

How it works: Both atropine and diphenoxylate affect gut movement. They act in slightly different ways on the nerves of the gut to slow it down and therefore stop diarrhoea.

Possible adverse effects: Nausea, vomiting and drowsiness are the most common adverse effects.

CAUTION

Children: It can be used to treat children over 4 years of age.

Driving and operating machinery: As this drug can cause dizziness and drowsiness, patients receiving this medication should not drive or perform skilled tasks until they are certain they are not experiencing these, or any other side effects.

CO-PROXAMOL

Brand name: Distalgesic

Type of drug: Painkiller, a combination of two painkillers; paracetamol and an opioid called dextropropoxyphene.

Uses: Painkiller used to relieve mild to moderate pain.

How it works: The sensation we attribute to pain is only felt once signals from the body reach the brain. Co-proxamol stops those signals reaching the brain by blocking their transmission through the spinal cord. Paracetamol works by making the nerves less responsive to painful signals.

Availability: POM

Possible adverse effects: Side effects are uncommon and usually relate to the dextropropoxyphene. The most commonly reported are nausea, vomiting, and drowsiness or dizziness. This drug can be habit forming if taken for long periods of time.

Other information: A maximum of 2 tablets should be taken at any one time up to a maximum of 4 times a day. A maximum of 8 tablets can be taken within one 24-hour period. Do not exceed this amount as paracetamol overdosage can lead to potentially fatal liver damage. If too many tablets are taken, seek urgent medical attention. Do not take any other products containing paracetamol whilst taking this medication. In case of uncertainty about whether a particular product is suitable to take with co-proxamol the advice of a pharmacist should be sought.

CAUTION

Alcohol: Should not be consumed whilst taking this medicine because it will increase the effect of drowsiness and dizziness.

Driving and operating machinery: As this drug can cause dizziness and drowsiness, patients receiving this medication should not drive or perform skilled tasks until they are certain they are not experiencing these or any other side effects.

CO-TRIMOXAZOLE

Brand name: Septrin

Type of drug: Combination of two antibiotics: sulphamethoxazole and trimethoprim.

Uses: The treatment of chest and urinary tract infections

How it works: Both of the drugs in co-trimoxazole prevent bacteria producing folic acid which is essential for their survival.

Availability: POM

Possible adverse effects: Nausea, vomiting and rashes are the commonly reported side effects. If allergic symptoms such as wheezing, an itchy rash or swelling of the face occur, the patient should stop taking the medication and seek urgent medical advice. It may also cause reduced production of white blood cells.

Other information: Long term use of this drug could lead to folic acid deficiency, so a supplement may be required. It is also important to drink plenty of fluids. Blood tests will be taken to monitor for any changes in the levels of white cells in the blood. It should be taken regularly throughout the prescribed course. Co-trimoxazole can be taken with, or before, meals to minimise any adverse effects associated with the digestive tract.

CAUTION

Children: It can be used for children over 6 weeks old.

Driving and operating machinery: This drug can impair the ability to drive or perform skilled tasks.

CODEINE

Brand name: Only available as a generic medicine

Type of drug: Opioid analgesic

Uses: Painkiller for treatment of mild to moderate pain, treatment of diarrhoea, and occasionally to prevent coughing.

How it works: The sensation we attribute to pain is only felt once signals from the body reach the brain. Codeine stops those signals reaching the brain by blocking their transmission through the spinal cord.

Availability: As an ingredient in some over-the-counter preparations.

Possible adverse effects: Light-headedness, nausea, vomiting, constipation, drowsiness and shortness of breath. Lying down may alleviate some of these side effects. If allergic symptoms occur such as wheezing or swelling of the face, the patient should stop taking the medication and seek urgent medical advice.

Other information: A maximum of 2 tablets should be taken at any one time up to a maximum of 4 times a day. A maximum of 8 tablets can be taken within one 24-hour period. Can be habit forming if taken for long periods; usually only prescribed for short-term relief.

CAUTION

Alcohol: Should not be consumed while taking this medication as it may exacerbate the effects of drowsiness, or cause blood pressure to fall.

Driving and operating machinery: As this drug can cause drowsiness, patients receiving this medication should not drive or perform skilled tasks until they are certain they are not experiencing any side effects.

COLCHICINE

Brand name: Only available as a generic medicine

Type of drug: Gout treatment

Uses: Used to relieve joint pain and inflammation during attacks of gout.

How it works: High levels of uric acid in the body can lead to uric acid crystals being deposited in the joints causing pain and inflammation which are characteristic of gout. The crystals can also cause damage to the kidney.

Colchicine has anti-inflammatory properties and provides pain relief by reducing inflammation that causes pain.

Availability: POM

Possible adverse effects: Nausea, vomiting and abdominal pain are common side effects of this drug. Profuse diarrhoea is also a possible side effect and should be reported to a doctor or pharmacist as soon as possible.

Other information: This drug is most effective when taken at the first sign of an attack.

CAUTION

Alcohol: May precipitate an attack of gout, so therefore should be consumed in moderation while taking this medication.

COLESTYRAMINE

(Formerly known as: cholestyramine)

Brand name: Questran

Type of drug: Reduces cholesterol

Uses: To treat people who have high levels of cholesterol in their blood, and who are at risk from heart disease. It is also used to treat persistent itching and severe diarrhoea.

How it works: Colestyramine binds the bile acids whixh are required to digest foods. The body makes more bile acids from cholesterol, which reduces the amount of cholesterol in the blood. Raised cholesterol can lead to heart disease. Persistent itching may be due to bile salts in the skin. By reducing the amount of bile acids in the body colestyramine can reduce itchiness.

Availability: POM

Possible adverse effects: This treatment commonly causes constipation, nausea, and general abdominal discomfort. These effects lessen with continued use.

Other information: Supplements of the fat soluble vitamins A, D, E and K may be required. No other medicines should be taken 2 hours before cholestyramine, and between 4 and 6 hours after. This medicine will come as a powder that must be reconstituted with about 200ml of fluid such as water, milk or thin soup.

CAUTION
Children: Can be used in children over 6 years old.

CONJUGATED OESTROGENS
Brand name: Premarin
Type of drug: Hormone
Uses: This medicine is used to relieve the symptoms of the menopause and to prevent osteoporosis in postmenopausal women.
How it works: When given by mouth, this medicine raises the level of oestrogen in the blood, and eases the symptoms of the menopause.
Availability: POM
Possible adverse effects: Nausea, sore breasts, breakthrough vaginal bleeding and spotting, dizziness, migraine, leg cramps, fluid retention, high blood pressure and weight changes. This medication is also associated with an increased risk of clots in the legs and lungs, and raised lipids in the blood.
Other information: There has been an increased risk of breast and endometrial cancer associated with the use of Hormone Replacement Therapies. The risk is small, but does increase in proportion to the length of time it is taken.

CYCLOPENTHIAZIDE
Brand name: Navidrex
Type of drug: Diuretic
Uses: This drug acts on the kidneys to increase the amount of urine passed, which in turn, reduces excess fluid in the body. Fluid in the wrong places can cause high blood pressure, swollen ankles and breathlessness. In addition to water, salts are also lost from the body into the urine with this drug.
Availability: POM
Possible adverse effects: Nausea, vomiting, tiredness, chest discomfort or pain, and feeling light headed when standing may occur. Also abnormalities of salts in the body can occur and symptoms can occur if potassium levels are reduced, such as muscle cramps, tiredness and nausea. Rarely muscle cramps may also occur.
Other information: Blood tests may be performed to monitor the potassium levels and potassium supplements may be required. Rarely,

cramps, lethargy and nausea may also occur. Eating foods rich in potassium may help to replace the potassium lost from the body. This drug is not available as a single drug but comes in tablet combined with amiloride.

CAUTION

Alcohol: Should only be consumed in moderation as the combination may cause a fall in blood pressure.

CYCLOPENTOLATE

Brand name: Mydrilate

Type of drug: Increases the size of the pupil of the eye

Uses: Cyclopentolate eye drops are used to treat inflammation of part of the eye, and to dilate the pupil so it is ready for examination or other procedures.

How it works: This drug stops the transmission of signals to the muscles in the eye that would make it smaller, thus making the pupil larger.

Availability: POM

Possible adverse effects: Stinging and irritation of the eye and possibly conjunctivitis.

Other information: Darker coloured eyes may not respond as well. However do not exceed the prescribed amount as this might result in significant absorption of the drug from the eye into the bloodstream, causing more widespread side effects. There are no commonly reported problems associated with prescribing this medication for children.

CAUTION

Driving and operating machinery: As this drug affects the eye and can cause blurred vision, patients receiving this medication should not drive or perform skilled tasks until they are certain they are not experiencing this side effect. It is not recommended that you drive or operate machinery for at least 2 hours after administration, or until the effects have worn off, whichever is longer.

CYCLOPHOSPHAMIDE

Brand name: Endoxana

Type of drug: Chemotherapy, immunosuppressant

Uses: Used for treating cancers, in particular leukaemia, lymphomas and tumours. It is also used in some autoimmune diseases.

How it works: Cyclphosphamide is activated in the liver and then circulates in the blood until it comes into contact with the tumour. Once inside the tumour it permanently damages the DNA of cancer cells. This stops the cancer cell from multiplying and destroys it.

Availability: POM

Possible adverse effects: Nausea, vomiting, diarrhoea, abdominal pain, reversible hair loss and possible anorexia are common side effects. Cyclophosphamide also reduces the production of blood cells and suppresses the immune system increasing the risk of infection. Any sign of infection, such as sore throat, unexplained bleeding or bruising, generally feeling unwell or high temperature should be reported to the doctor immediately. A by-product of the activation of cyclophosphamide in the liver is a chemical called acreolin, this may cause severe bleeding from the bladder. If there is blood in the urine medical attention should be sought immediately.

Other information: This medicine is only given in hospital under the supervision of a doctor experienced in treating cancer. Regular blood tests are required to assess the effects. Additional medicines to combat side effects may be prescribed. Tablets should be swallowed with plenty of water. It is advised to increase the fluid intake for 24 to 48 hours after taking the tablets to help alleviate some of the side effects.

Only the person taking the drug – because of the serious effects – should handle cyclophosphamide tablets. Keep them in the container that you received them in.

CAUTION

Pregnancy: A barrier method of contraception is recommended during treatment to prevent pregnancy, but if you become pregnant while on this medicine, inform your doctor as soon as possible.

CYCLOSERINE

Brand name: Seromycin

Type of drug: Antibiotic

Uses: Used to treat tuberculosis that is resistant to other drugs. It is usually given in combination with other drugs.

How it works: Stops the production of the bacterial cell wall, without which the bacteria die.

Availability: POM

Possible adverse effects: Headache, dizziness, drowsiness, confusion, and depression. A rash should be reported to a doctor or pharmacist.

Other information: Treatment is likely to be continued for a long period of time, up to 2 years. It should be taken after meals to minimise irritation of the stomach and should be taken regularly throughout the prescribed course. This can be prescribed for children.

CAUTION

Alcohol: Should be avoided whilst taking this medicine because of the increased risk of epileptic seizures that the combination poses.

Driving and operating machinery: This drug cause confusion, dizziness and drowsiness, so patients should not drive or perform skilled tasks until they are certain they are not experiencing these or any other side effects.

CYPROTERONE

Brand name: Cyprostat, Androcur

Type of drug: Anti-androgen

Uses: When the body produces too much testosterone, and in prostate cancer. In women it is used to stop hirsutism (facial hair growth).

How it works: Cyproterone prevents the action of testosterone on the body, and also partially stops its production. This has several effects in men such as stopping production of sperm and causing reversible sterility. Many types of prostate cancer require testosterone to grow, so lack of the hormone prevents growth of the cancer. In women it stops testosterone production, which is responsible for facial hair.

Availability: POM

Possible adverse effects: Reduction in sperm counts, production of abnormal sperm, weight changes, tiredness, breast enlargement or tenderness and occasionally milk production. It may also cause liver problems.

Other information: Usually started under specialist supervision.

CAUTION

Driving and operating machinery: As this drug may cause a general fatigue it can impair the ability to drive or perform skilled tasks.

CYTARABINE

Brand name: Cytosar

Type of drug: Chemotherapy

Uses: Used to treat several types of acute leukaemia.

How it works: Prevents the cancer cells from multiplying, which leads to the cell's death.

Availability: POM

Possible adverse effects: Nausea, vomiting, diarrhoea, mouth ulcers, raised temperature, drowsiness and skin rashes can occur. Additional medication is often given to prevent these effects. Due to its effect on the production of blood cells and immune system, the body's ability to fight infection is reduced. Any sign of infection, such as a sore throat, unexplained bleeding or bruising, generally feeling unwell or high temperature should be reported to the doctor immediately. Eye problems can occur when high doses are used and so eye ointment will also be given.

Other information: This medicine is only given in hospital under the supervision of a doctor experienced in treating cancer, who will oversee and monitor treatment. Regular blood tests are required to assess the effects.

CAUTION

Children: Children can be treated with this medicine.

Pregnancy: Contraception must be used. If you become pregnant while on this medicine, inform your doctor as soon as possible.

Driving and operating machinery: This drug can impair the ability to drive or perform skilled tasks.

DACARBAZINE

Brand name: DTIC-Dome

Type of drug: Chemotherapy

Uses: Treatment of malignant melanomas, Hodgkin's disease and other forms of cancer.

How it works: Attacks the DNA of cancer cells to prevent them from multiplying.

Availability: POM

Possible adverse effects: Severe nausea and vomiting, together with a loss of appetite are relatively common. A flu-like illness may occur a week after treatment and last between 1 and 3 weeks. This drug may decrease the body's ability to fight infection, and any signs of a fever or sore throat should be reported to a doctor immediately. Hair loss has been recorded, but this will grow back after treatment. Any sign of bleeding should also be reported immediately.

Other information: This medicine is only given in hospital under the supervision of a doctor experienced in treating cancer. Regular blood tests are required to assess the effects. Anti-sickness drugs and other medications are often given at the same time. This drug can be used to treat children.

CAUTION

Pregnancy: Patients should not become pregnant whilst taking this medicine, and effective contraceptive measures should be used.

Driving and operating machinery: This drug can impair the ability to drive or perform skilled tasks.

DALTEPARIN SODIUM

Brand name: Fragmin

Type of drug: Low molecular weight heparin

Uses: Used to prevent the formation of blood clots in the veins of patients undergoing surgery who have been identified as being at high risk. It is also used to treat clots if they do form. It can also be used in the treatment of angina.

How it works: Alters the clotting mechanism of the blood to make the formation of clots less likely.

Availability: POM

Possible adverse effects: Rashes are common. Unusual bruising may occur which can indicate bleeding and should be reported immediately. Any bleeding should also be reported to the doctor.

Other information: Avoid any products containing aspirin or other anti-inflammatory drugs.

DANAZOL

Brand name: Danol

Type of drug: Hormone

Uses: Treatment of endometriosis and breast pain.

How it works: It reduces production of the female hormones oestrogens and progesterones and increases the production of testosterone, which in turn reduces the growth of abnormal breast and uterine tissue. Thus relieving the symptoms of breast pain and endometriosis.

Availability: POM

Possible adverse effects: These mainly occur when high doses are prescribed and include: swelling of the feet and ankles, weight gain, back pain, acne, and in women, unusual hair growth and voice changes. Nausea, rash, dizziness and flushing may also occur. Menstrual periods will usually be disrupted or halted. It may increase the chances of seizures in epileptic patients.

CAUTION

Pregnancy: Contraception must be used, but if you become pregnant while on this medicine, inform your doctor as soon as possible.

Alcohol: Should be avoided whilst taking this medication because of the risk of nausea and breathlessness that the combination brings.

DANTROLENE

Brand name: Dantrium

Type of drug: Muscle relaxant

Uses: A muscle relaxant that relieves painful spasms that occur in conditions such as multiple sclerosis, cerebral palsy, stroke and following brain or spinal injuries.

Availability: POM

Possible adverse effects: Dizziness, drowsiness, nausea, diarrhoea, headache, confusion, mood changes, muscle weakness and liver problems can occur. These effects are more likely to occur at the start of treatment, or if you are over 40 years of age.

Other information: It may take between 2 and 4 weeks to see the beneficial effects of this medication. However if there is no obvious improvement after 6 weeks the medication is often gradually reduced then stopped. It should not be stopped suddenly. It may interfere with a diabetic's blood sugar levels.

CAUTION

Alcohol: Should not be consumed whilst taking this medication as it will increase the severity of drowsiness produced by dantrolene.

Driving and operating machinery: As this drug can cause dizziness and drowsiness, patients receiving this medication should not drive or perform skilled tasks until they are certain they are not experiencing these or any other side effects.

DARBEPOETIN ALFA

Brand name: Aranesp

Type of drug: Kidney hormone

Uses: Treatment of anaemia due to kidney failure, and some types of cancer.

How it works: For people who have suffered kidney failure, darbepoetin alfa stimulates the body to produce more red blood cells.

Availability: POM

Possible adverse effects: Headache, raised blood pressure and pain where the drug is injected into the body.

Other information: Iron supplements may also be prescribed to help treat anaemia. Check the syringes before injection to ensure there are no visible particles. Blood pressure will usually be monitored. Blood tests will usually be carried out to ensure that the medication is working.

CAUTION

Children: May be prescribed for children over 3 months of age.

DESFERRIOXAMINE

Brand name: Desferal

Type of drug: Iron reducing medication, chelating agent

Uses: Treatment of iron poisoning, usually due to multiple blood transfusions. Also when there is too much aluminium in the body due to kidney dialysis.

How it works: The drug binds, or chelates, iron in the blood, and both the iron and deferrioxamine are then excreted in the urine.

Availability: POM

Possible adverse effects: Abdominal, joint, and muscle pain, diarrhoea, shock and a drop in blood pressure, dizziness and allergic skin reactions. Vision and hearing problems can occur; regular examinations are advised.
Other information: Treatment should be stopped if the patient develops an infection, and medical advice sought. This medicine can be used in the treatment of children.

CAUTION
Driving and operating machinery: As this drug can cause dizziness and possible problems with vision, patients receiving this medication should not drive or perform skilled tasks until they are certain they are not experiencing these or any other side effects.

DESLORATADINE
Brand name: NeoClarityn
Type of drug: Antihistamine
Uses: This medicine is used in the treatment of hay fever, urticaria, or hives.
How it works: Blocks the action of histamine – a chemical produced by the body in response to allergies – so stopping symptoms such as runny nose and sneezing.
Availability: POM
Possible adverse effects: Drowsiness, dizziness, headaches and stomach pain, agitation and dry mouth may occur.
Other information: If side effects are noticed the dose can be split into 2, so taking half a tablet in the morning, and half a tablet at night. Although this is supposed to be a non-drowsy drug, it can still cause sleepiness in some people.

CAUTION
Children: It may be prescribed for children over 3 months of age.
Driving and operating machinery: As this drug can cause drowsiness in a small minority of patients it may impair the ability to drive or perform skilled tasks.

DESMOPRESSIN
Brand name: DDAVP, Desmospray, Desmotabs

Type of drug: Hormone

Uses: Treatment of diabetes insipidus and nocturnal bed-wetting (enuresis) in children.

How it works: Desmopressin is a synthetic version of the naturally occurring antidiuretic hormone (ADH). ADH controls the amount of urine produced by the body.

Possible adverse effects: Fluid retention, headache, nausea, vomiting and stomach pain.

Other information: Fluid intake must be strictly observed as convulsions can occur. It may be given to mothers who are breastfeeding.

CAUTION

Children: It is used to treat bed-wetting in children over 5 years old.

DEXAMETHASONE

Brand name: Decadron

Type of drug: Corticosteroid, antiinflammatory, immunosuppressant

Uses: To treat rheumatic, allergic and inflammatory disorders such as rheumatoid arthritis asthma and emphysema. It also may be used to treat some types of cancers such as multiple myeloma. It is also used to reduce brain swelling. Drops are used to treat inflammation of the eye.

How it works: Steroids work by suppressing the production of cells, chemicals and enzymes involved in inflammation, which in turn reduces pain and swelling caused by inflammation.

Availability: POM

Possible adverse effects: When taken as a tablet, dexamethasone has different effects. It can cause indigestion, stomach, abdominal and muscle pain, osteoporosis, alteration to the menstrual cycle, rounding of the face, facial hair growth for women (hirsuitism), weight gain, changes in mood, insomnia, unusual bruising, and thinning of the skin. These effects are all minimised when both the amount taken, and the length of treatment, are kept as slow as possible. The effect of insomnia may be counteracted by taking the drug in the morning, and if not then, before 6pm in the evening. Gastrointestinal ulceration and/or bleeding may occur, so if you suffer severe stomach pain, or there is any blood in your stools then seek urgent medical advice. Any sign of infection, such as a sore throat, unexplained bleeding or bruising, generally feeling unwell or high temperature should be reported to the doctor immediately. There is an increased risk of infection due to its effects on the immune system.

Other information: When taking the tablet form, you should be given a steroid card so that appropriate action can be taken if you become unwell. If drops are to be used in the eye it is recommended that patients do not wear soft contact lenses as they may damage the lens.

CAUTION

Children: This medicine is used in children usually at the minimal dose or alternate days to minimise any effects on growth and development.

DEXAMFETAMINE

(Formerly known as: dexamphetamine)

Brand name: Dexedrine

Type of drug: Stimulant

Uses: Used to treat narcolepsy – an uncontrollable tendency to fall asleep.

How it works: Has a stimulant effect on the nervous system in adults, increasing alertness. However, this drug can have a sedative effect on children, so it is sometimes used to calm hyperactive children.

Availability: POM

Possible adverse effects: Insomnia, restlessness, irritability, dizziness, headache, tremor, mood changes, dry mouth, stomach upset, high blood pressure and sweating have been reported as side effects of dexamfetamine.

Other information: Dependence may occur if the medication is taken for extended periods. Tolerance to the medicine, where the body becomes used to the effects of the drug can occur, and higher doses are required to achieve the same effect.

CAUTION

Children: May be used in children over 3 years old only. However regular checks should be made on their growth and development to make sure they are not being adversely affected.

Driving: Patients with narcolepsy should not drive.

DIAMORPHINE

Brand name: Only available as a generic medicine

Type of drug: Opioid analgesic

Uses: Diamorphine is used to relieve severe pain related to heart attacks, surgical procedures and the terminally ill.

How it works: This drug stops the transmission of pain messages through the spinal cord to the brain.

Availability: POM

Possible adverse effects: Drowsiness, nausea, vomiting, constipation and sweating. This drug may also cause reduced breathing, or respiratory rate. If allergic symptoms occur such as wheezing or swelling of the face, the patient should stop taking the medication and seek urgent medical advice

Other information: It is only available as an injection, so patients will be trained in how to administer it. It is usually administered in combination with a drug to stop the feeling of nausea, which is associated with this medicine. Repeated long term administration of diamorphine can lead to dependence, and a condition known as tolerance. This is where larger amounts of drug need to be given to achieve the same pain relieving effect. To counter this, the amount of diamorphine used in long-term care may gradually increase over time. This drug may be prescribed for children.

CAUTION

Alcohol: This should be avoided because of an increased risk of drowsiness associated with the combination.

Driving and operating machinery: As this drug can cause drowsiness, patients receiving this medication should not drive or perform skilled tasks until they are certain they are not experiencing this or any other side effects.

DIAZEPAM

Brand name: Diazemuls, Valium

Type of drug: Benzodiazepine, antiepileptic, sedative, muscle relaxant

Uses: To treat nervousness and insomnia. Also used to treat epileptic fits.

How it works: Feelings of anxiety are in part due to increases in hormones in the brain, such as adrenaline, noradrenaline and GABA. Anxiety is believed to be due to an increase in the transmission of signals through nerves in particular parts of the brain. Diazepam reduces the signals transmitted to and from certain parts of the brain and relieves anxiety. Anxiety is believed to be due to an increase in the transmission of signals through nerves in particular parts of the brain. Diazepam acts on these nerves to stop the signals going any farther. This has the effect of relieving anxiety and encouraging sleep. It works in the same way for epilepsy, as an epileptic fit occurs when signal are sent through the brain in bursts of uncontrolled or uncoordinated signals.

Availability: POM

Possible adverse effects: Drowsiness, confusion, light-headedness, nausea, and constipation may occur. Drowsiness can still be present the next day, as a 'hangover effect'. Sometimes this drug can have the opposite effect and can make the person more anxious.

Other information: Not suitable to be used as a long-term solution as the drug can be habit-forming and dependence can occur. Treatment is usually limited to 2 weeks.

CAUTION

Children: This drug is used to treat epileptic and feverish fits in children.

Alcohol: Should be avoided whilst taking this medicine because it can increase the severity of any side effects experienced.

Driving and operating machinery: This drug will affect your ability to drive and perform skilled tasks. It is therefore recommended that patients do not drive or undertake such tasks whilst taking diazepam.

DICLOFENAC

Brand name: Voltarol

Type of drug: Non-steroidal painkiller, anti-inflammatory drug (NSAID)

Uses: Used to treat the mild to moderate pain in muscles and joints, also used in rheumatoid arthritis and osteoarthritis, gout, menstrual pain and post-operative pain.

How it works: Inhibits the actions of an enzyme called cyclo-oxygenase. This enzyme produces chemical messengers that start, and continue the inflammatory process.

Availability: POM

Possible adverse effects: Irritation of the stomach, nausea, dizziness, vomiting, abdominal cramps, drowsiness, irritability, headache, insomnia and rashes. Gastrointestinal ulceration and/or bleeding may occur, so if you suffer severe stomach pain or there is blood in your stools seek urgent medical advice. It can also lead to kidney problems if taken in excess. In patients with asthma, diclofenac can make these symptoms worse.

Other information: Salt intake should be restricted during treatment. Any bleeding in stools should be reported to the doctor immediately. Additional medication may be prescribed to reduce stomach irritation. Should be taken with food or milk to help protect the stomach.

CAUTION

Children: Children over the age of 1 year old can be treated with diclofenac.

Driving and operating machinery: As this drug can cause dizziness and drowsiness, patients receiving this medication should not drive or perform skilled tasks until they are certain they are not experiencing these, or any other side effects.

DICYCLOVERINE

(Formerly known as: dicyclomine)

Brand name: Merbentyl

Type of drug: Antispasmodic, antimuscarinic

Uses: To relieve the symptoms of irritable bowel syndrome.

How it works: Relaxes the muscles in order to relieve painful abdominal cramps.

Availability: POM

Possible adverse effects: Dry mouth and skin, blurred vision, palpitations, thirst, and giddiness.

Other information: This medication is usually taken in conjunction with other drugs and non-drug remedies such as dietary changes.

CAUTION

Children: Children over 6 months of age can be treated with this medicine.

Driving and operating machinery: As this drug affects the eye and can cause blurred vision, patients receiving this medication should not drive or perform skilled tasks until they are certain they are not experiencing these or any other side effects.

DIDANOSINE (ddI)

Brand name: Videx

Type of drug: Antiretroviral

Uses: Used in the treatment of HIV infection.

How it works: Once inside the cells of the body, didanosine is converted into the active form of the drug, which prevents the virus from multiplying.

Availability: POM

Possible adverse effects: Headaches, nausea, vomiting, diarrhoea, abdominal pain, tingling or numbness in the hands or feet. Fatigue is also common. Like most drugs used to fight HIV infection this may cause an increase in the levels of lipids (or fats) in the blood. There may also be a redistribution of fat about the body. Rarely this drug can cause life threatening liver problems.

Other information: This medicine is only given in hospital under the supervision of a doctor experienced in treating HIV. Regular blood tests are required to assess the effects. Videx is used together with other antiretroviral drugs. The EC capsules should be taken at least 2 hours before or after food, unless being taken with tenofovir when both may be given with food. Tablets should be chewed thoroughly, or crushed and dissolved in water or clear apple juice.

CAUTION

Children: Children over 3 months old can be treated with this medicine.

Alcohol: Because of its effects on the liver, alcohol should be taken in moderation.

DIFLUNISAL

Brand name: Dolobid

Type of drug: Analgesic, nonsteroidal anti-inflammatory

Uses: To alleviate the symptoms of rheumatic diseases and menstrual pain.

How it works: Diflunisal works by inhibiting the actions of an enzyme called prostaglandin synthetase. This enzyme produces chemical messengers that start, and continue, the inflammatory process.

Availability: POM

Possible adverse effects: Stomach and bowel pain or discomfort, allergic reactions and breathlessness. Gastrointestinal ulceration and/or bleeding may occur, so if you severe stomach pain is experienced, or there is blood in the stools then seek urgent medical advice. If allergic symptoms such as wheezing or swelling of the face occur, the patient should stop taking the medication and seek urgent medical advice. In patients with asthma, diflunisal can sometimes make these symptoms worse.

Other information: The tablets should be swallowed whole and not crushed or chewed and be taken with food or milk to help to protect the stomach.

DIGOXIN
Brand name: Lanoxin
Type of drug: Cardiac glycoside
Uses: To treat some conditions associated with abnormal heart rhythm.
How it works: This drug slows down the passage of signals through the heart which make it beat more slowly, so that it pumps blood more effectively.
Availability: POM
Possible adverse effects: Side effects are usually caused by excessive dosage and include nausea, vomiting, diarrhoea, abdominal pain, headache, visual disturbances, fatigue and drowsiness. Any palpitations should be reported immediately.
Other information: Blood tests may be carried out to monitor the level of the drug and potassium levels. Low potassium levels increase the risk of side effects. In case of an accidental overdose, seek medical advice immediately. Digoxin can be used to treat heart problems in children of all ages. It can be used when breastfeeding.

DIHYDROCODEINE
Brand name: DF 118
Type of drug: Analgesic
Uses: To relieve mild to moderate pain.
How it works: The sensation we attribute to pain is only felt once signals from the body reach the brain. It stops those signals reaching the brain by blocking their transmission through the spinal cord. Paracetamol works by making the nerves less responsive to painful signals.

Availability: Dihydrocodeine is available as an ingredient in some over the counter medicines.

Possible adverse effects: Light-headedness, nausea, constipation, vomiting, drowsiness and shortness of breath. Lying down may alleviate some of these side effects. If allergic symptoms occur such as wheezing or swelling of the face, the patient should stop taking the medication and seek urgent medical advice.

Other information: A maximum of 2 tablets should be taken at any one time up to a maximum of 4 times a day. A maximum of 8 tablets can be taken within one 24-hour period. Can be habit forming if taken for long periods; usually only prescribed for short-term relief.

CAUTION

Alcohol: Should not be consumed whilst taking this medication because it may exacerbate the effects of drowsiness, or cause blood pressure to fall.

Driving and operating machinery: As this drug can cause dizziness and drowsiness, patients receiving this medication should not drive or perform skilled tasks until they are certain they are not experiencing these or any other side effects.

DILTIAZEM

Brand names: Tildiem, Adizem, Angitil, Calcicard, Dilcardia, Dilzem, Slozem, Viazem, Zemtard

Type of drug: Cardiac

Uses: Treatment of high blood pressure and angina.

How it works: Relaxes the blood vessels in the circulatory system allowing blood to flow more easily, so therefore reducing blood pressure. For angina it relaxes the blood vessels of the heart and allows more blood and oxygen to reach the heart muscle. This allows it to pump more effectively and relieves the pain associated with angina.

Availability: POM

Possible adverse effects: Headache and dizziness may occur due to a fall in blood pressure. Rashes, leg or ankle swelling, slowed heartbeat and facial flushing can also occur.

Other information: Amlodipine should not be discontinued unless advised by a doctor, but any side effects should be reported. The tablets should be swallowed whole, and not chewed or crushed. Do not take this medication with grapefruit juice.

CAUTION

Alcohol: Can increase the likelihood of experiencing side effects and so should only be consumed in moderation.

Driving and operating machinery: As this drug can cause dizziness, patients receiving this medication should not drive or perform skilled tasks until they are certain they are not experiencing this or any other side effects.

DIPIPANONE

Brand name: Diconal

Type of drug: Analgesic

Uses: Relief of moderate to severe pain.

How it works: The sensation we attribute to pain is only felt once signals from the body reach the brain. Dipipanone stops those signals reaching the brain by blocking their transmission through the spinal cord.

Availability: POM.

Possible adverse effects: Light-headedness, nausea, vomiting, constipation, drowsiness, rash, facial flushing and shortness of breath. If allergic symptoms occur such as wheezing or swelling of the face the patient should stop taking the medication and seek urgent medical advice.

Other information: Dependence may occur if the drug is taken for long periods. It causes less drowsiness than other opioid analgesics. Diconal contains both dipipanone and cyclizine, an anti-sickness drug.

CAUTION

Alcohol: Should not be consumed whilst taking this medication because it may exacerbate the effects of drowsiness.

Driving and operating machinery: This drug can cause drowsiness; patients receiving this medication should not drive or perform skilled tasks until they are certain they are not experiencing this or any other side effects.

DIPIVEFRINE

Brand name: Propine

Type of drug: Sympathomimetic

Uses: To treat open-angle glaucoma.

How it works: Dipivefrine is converted, inside the eye, to adrenaline. This reduces the production of fluid inside the eye, and so reduces the pressure.

Availability: POM

Possible adverse effects: A burning or stinging in the eye when the drug is used.

Other information: Do not wear soft contact lenses while using this medicine.

CAUTION

Driving and operating machinery: As it can cause visual problems, patients receiving this medication should not drive or perform skilled tasks until they are certain they are not experiencing this or any other side effects.

DIPYRIDAMOLE

Brand name: Persantin

Type of drug: Anti-platelet

Uses: To prevent thrombosis (the formation of blood clots) in patients who have had heart valve surgery, or those at risk of transient ischaemic attacks (or mini-strokes) and strokes.

How it works: Dipyridamole thins the blood by making one of the blood's constituents, platelets, less effective. Platelets are involved in blood clot formation.

Availability: POM

Possible adverse effects: Bleeding, indigestion, heartburn, abdominal pain and diarrhoea may occur. The number of the platelets in the blood can also fall. If bleeding or bruising occurs, seek urgent medical advice. If allergic symptoms occur such as wheezing or swelling of the face, the patient should stop taking the medication and seek urgent medical advice

Other information: Dipyridamole is sometimes used with aspirin, which also increases the risk of bleeding. Patient may have to take the drug for several months. Take 30 minutes to 1 hour before food. If capsules have been prescribed they should be kept in their original container and any remaining capsules discarded 6 weeks after opening.

DISODIUM PAMIDRONATE

Brand name: Aredia

Type of drug: Bisphosphonate

Uses: The treatment of Paget's disease. It also reduces the bone pain associated with breast cancer or multiple myeloma, and reduces high calcium levels in the blood .

How it works: It acts on the rate of bone growth and prevents cells from releasing calcium from the bones.

Availability: POM

Possible adverse effects: Nausea, diarrhoea, constipation, muscle and joint pains, flu-like symptoms, changes in the levels of cells in the blood, and conjunctivitis. A raised temperature may also occur, but this usually goes away within 48 hours without the need for treatment. Redness, swelling and pain may occur at the injection site.

Other information: It can be given between once a week to once every 6 weeks.

CAUTION

Driving and operating machinery: This drug may impair the ability to drive or perform skilled tasks.

DISULFIRAM

Brand name: Antabuse

Type of drug: Drug used for treatment of alcohol abuse

Uses: To encourage abstinence in alcohol dependent people.

How it works: This drug causes the conversion of alcohol into a toxic compound called acetaldehyde, which causes severe vomiting.

Availability: POM

Possible adverse effects: Without alcohol: drowsiness, fatigue, nausea and vomiting and a reduced libido. With alcohol: facial flushing, throbbing headache, increased heart rate, nausea and vomiting. If large quantities of alcohol are consumed the reaction are more severe and may be fatal.

Other information: This reaction does not only occur in response to alcoholic beverages, but also when alcohol is found in other products such as deodorant, shampoo, perfume and other medicines. It is advised that a card is carried warning of the effects of this drug. Consult with a pharmacist before using any other products with this medication.

CAUTION

Alcohol: For the reasons stated above alcohol should not be consumed in any form, 24 hours before, during and after taking this medicine.

Driving and operating machinery: As this drug can cause drowsiness, patients receiving this medication should not drive or perform skilled tasks until they are certain they are not experiencing this side effect.

DOCUSATE SODIUM

Brand name: Dioctyl, Docusol

Type of drug: Laxative

Uses: Treatment of constipation

How it works: Docusate acts to draw more water into the faeces making the stool softer and easier for the gut to pass out.

Availability: Docusate is available in some over-the-counter preparations

Possible adverse effects: It may cause abdominal cramps.

Other information: You should increase the amount of water you drink whilst taking this drug. This allows the medication to work better and prevents dehydration.

DOMPERIDONE

Brand name: Motilium

Type of drug: Anti-emetic

Uses: Treatment of nausea and vomiting caused by gastrointestinal problems or as side effects from other medication.

How it works: It acts on an area in the brain associated with vomiting to reduce its activity.

Availability: As an ingredient in some over-the-counter medicines.

Possible adverse effects: This drug has few side effects. It can cause an increase in prolactin one of the hormones from the pituitary gland.

Other information: Treatment will initially be prescribed for approximately 4 weeks, and then reviewed to see if it is still required. It is best taken before meals, because if it taken after meals its absorption from the gut will be delayed. This drug can also be prescribed for children.

DORNASE ALFA
Brand name: Pulmozyme
Type of drug: Mucolytic enzyme
Uses: To treat the symptoms of cystic fibrosis.
How it works: This enzyme helps to breakdown and remove the sticky secretions of the lungs in patients with cystic fibrosis. This allows the patient to breathe more easily.
Availability: POM
Possible adverse effects: Side effects to this medicine are rare, but can include chest pain, conjunctivitis, hoarseness and runny nose.
Other information: The drug is administered through inhalation using a jet-nebuliser. Always follow the manufacturer's instructions for usage.
CAUTION
Children: This medicine is used to treat the symptoms of cystic fibrosis in children over 5 years of age.

DORZOLAMIDE
Brand name: Trusopt
Type of drug: Anti-glaucoma
Uses: Treatment of raised pressure in the eyes in open-angled glaucoma.
How it works: Reduces the formation of excess fluid inside the eye, and so lowers the pressure.
Availability: POM
Possible adverse effects: Stinging and sore eyes, blurred vision, and headache. If allergic symptoms occur such as wheezing or swelling of the face, the patient should stop taking the medication and seek urgent medical advice
Other information: Do not wear soft contact lenses.
CAUTION
Driving and operating machinery: As this drug can cause blurred vision, patients should not drive or perform skilled tasks until they are certain they are not experiencing these or any other side effects.

DOSULEPIN
(Formerly known as: dothiepin)

Brand name: Prothiaden

Type of drug: Tricyclic antidepressant

Uses: Treatment of depression when there is also a need for a sedative effect.

How it works: It inhibits the re-uptake of chemical messengers in the brain, which results in a heightening of mood. It also encourages appetite and enables users to lead a more normal daily life. Its sedative effect is also useful for people who have difficulty sleeping at nights.

Availability: POM

Possible adverse effects: Dry mouth, blurred vision, drowsiness, changes in appetite, impaired memory, light-headedness especially on standing up, muscle weakness, interrupted sleep and insomnia, weight gain, rapid beating of the heart, constipation, skin rash and a loss of libido. These side effects usually lessen with continued use.

Other information: It may take between 2 and 4 weeks to see the beneficial effects of this medication. This drug can have a 'hangover' effect, causing a feeling of tiredness, disorientation and sedation when waking in the morning, so it is advisable to take this drug prior to going to sleep at night in order to avoid daytime sleepiness. It should not be discontinued unless advised by a doctor, when it will gradually be reduced.

CAUTION

Alcohol: Should not be consumed whilst taking dosulepin because it can reduce its effectiveness

Driving and operating machinery: This drug can cause drowsiness; patients receiving this medication should not drive or perform skilled tasks until they are certain they are not experiencing this or any other side effects.

DOXAZOSIN

Brand name: Cardura

Type of drug: Alpha adrenoceptor blocker

Uses: To treat high blood pressure. It is also used in the treatment of an enlarged prostate gland.

How it works: Relaxes blood vessels causing them to widen, improving blood flow and decreasing blood pressure.

Availability: POM

Possible adverse effects: Dizziness on standing up, headache, nausea and general fatigue.

Other information: The first few tablets taken can cause a marked drop in blood pressure, which can make the patient feel faint and dizzy. If prescribed a modified release form of this medicine, the tablets should be swallowed whole, and not crushed or chewed. The tablet shell may appear in the faeces.

CAUTION

Alcohol: Should only be consumed in moderation whilst taking this medicine, as the combination can cause a greater than expected drop in blood pressure.

Driving and operating machinery: Patients receiving this medication should not drive or perform skilled tasks until they are certain they are not experiencing these or any other side effects.

DOXORUBICIN

Brand name: Generic only or special lipid base Caelyx

Type of drug: Chemotherapy

Uses: Treatment of many types of leukaemia, Hodgkin's disease and other cancers.

How it works: Doxorubicin inserts itself into the strands of DNA of the cancer, which permanently damages the DNA, preventing the cancer cell from multiplying. This eventually causes the death of the cancer cells.

Availability: POM

Possible adverse effects: Nausea, vomiting, diarrhoea, abdominal pain, a burning sensation of the hands and feet (which usually gets better within 4 weeks), hair loss and loss of appetite are common side effects. Doxorubicin can also cause damage to the heart. It reduces the production of blood cells and suppresses the immune system, increasing the risk of infection. Any sign of infection, such as sore throat, unexplained bleeding or bruising, generally feeling unwell or high temperature should be reported to the doctor immediately. The urine may be stained red.

Other information: This medicine is only given in hospital under the supervision of a doctor experienced in treating cancer. Regular blood tests are required to assess the effects. Additional medicines to combat side effects may be prescribed.

CAUTION

Pregnancy: A barrier method of contraception is recommended during treatment to prevent pregnancy. however fertility is often also reduced by chemotherapy.

Driving and operating machinery: This drug can impair the ability to drive or perform skilled tasks.

DOXYCYCLINE

(May be referred to as doxycycline hyclate)

Brand name: Vibramycin

Type of drug: Tetracycline

Uses: Treatment of urinary, chest, eye, gut infections and sexually transmitted diseases. Occasionally used for malaria and acne.

How it works: It stops the production of a protein, which is essential for the cell to multiply. This allows the immune system to overcome the infection.

Availability: POM

Possible adverse effects: Nausea, vomiting, diarrhoea, pain when swallowing and discolouration of the teeth. This medicine also makes the body more sensitive to the sun, resulting in a rash on the skin. Avoid direct sunlight and do not use sunlamps.

Other information: Capsules should be taken at regular intervals and always be swallowed whole with a full glass of water and taken with meals. The capsules should be taken whilst sitting or standing and the patient should not lie down for at least 30 minutes after taking the medicine. The course of antibiotics should always be completed and taken regularly.

Tetracyclines may reduce effectiveness of the contraceptive pill, so other methods of contraception should be used whilst taking this medicine, and for at least 7 days after finishing the course.

CAUTION

Children: This drug may be used to treat children over 12 years old.

DYDROGESTERONE

Brand name: Duphaston, Duphaston HRT

Type of drug: Sex hormone, progestogen

Uses: This drug is used to treat a range of disorders related to the menstrual cycle, including endometriosis and recurrent miscarriages. It is also used in hormone replacement therapy (HRT).

How it works: Mimics the action of the female sex hormone, progesterone, the lack of which is thought to be a factor in some menstrual disorders and some cases of recurrent miscarriages.

Availability: POM

Possible adverse effects: Side effects include mood changes, depression, dizziness, headache, growth of facial hair, hair loss, nausea, indigestion, fluid retention, weight changes, changes in breast size, and breast tenderness. It may cause irregular periods and bleeding between periods. Use of this drug may increase the risk of blood clots in the leg veins or lungs. If chest pain, or leg pain and swelling occur that cannot be explained then seek urgent medical advice.

Other information: There has been an increased risk of endometrial cancer associated with the use of Hormone Replacement Therapies. This drug may also be used to treat menstrual problems.

CAUTION

Pregnancy: A pregnancy test is usually carried out before starting this medicine to ensure the patient is not pregnant. If the patient becomes, or suspects she has become pregnant the doctor should be informed.

ECONAZOLE

Brand name: Ecostatin

Type of drug: Antifungal

Uses: Used to treat fungal infections of the skin, vaginal thrush and infected nappy rash.

How it works: Alters the membranes of the fungal cells with the result that they can no longer multiply and the infection is halted.

Availability: POM

Possible adverse effects: Skin irritation, including a burning sensation, redness and itching, where the cream is applied.

Availability: Econazole is available as an ingredient in some over-the-counter preparations.

Other information: Wash hands well after application of drug. The cream should not be applied near the eyes, or allowed to come into contact with condoms or diaphragms. It is recommended that alternative contraceptive measures are taken if using this medicine for vaginal infection. It may be used in *pregnancy* and breastfeeding.

CAUTION

Children: This drug may be used to treat infections of childrens' skin.

ENALAPRIL

Brand name: Innovace
Type of drug: ACE inhibitor
Uses: To treat high blood pressure and heart failure.
How it works: It enables the blood vessels to relax, which allows them to increase in size. This reduces the pressure of the blood flowing through them.
Availability: POM
Possible adverse effects: Chest pain, dizziness, fatigue, indigestion, nausea, abdominal pains, headache, insomnia and blurred vision. Lying down after the medication may reduce symptoms. A dry cough may occur when first taking this medicine, but this side effect usually lessens with continued use. A cough that does not go away should be reported to the doctor or pharmacist.
Other information: This drug should be used with caution in patients with kidney problems. Blood tests are usually carried out to monitor the levels of potassium. Patients should avoid salt substitutes containing potassium, and should take care in hot weather, or if taking exercise, to avoid over-heating and dehydration.

CAUTION

Children: It is sometimes used in children to control high blood pressure.
Alcohol: Should only be consumed in strict moderation whilst taking this medicine because the combination may cause a large fall in blood pressure.
Driving and operating machinery: As this drug can cause dizziness and sedation, patients receiving this medication should not drive or perform such tasks until they are certain they are not experiencing any side effects.

ENOXAPARIN
Brand name: Clexane
Type of drug: Low molecular weight heparin
Uses: Used in prevention and treatment of the formation of blood clots in the veins of patients undergoing surgery who have been identified as being at high risk. It is also used in prevention and treatment of blood clots in the legs and lungs. It can also be used in the treatment of angina.
How it works: Alters the clotting mechanism of the blood to make the formation of clots less likely.
Availability: POM
Possible adverse effects: Rashes are common. Pain and reddening of the site of injection. Bleeding and bruising may occur which should be reported immediately. Occasionally it can cause reduced levels of platelets.
Other information: Avoid any products containing aspirin or other anti-inflammatory drugs, which can increase the risk of bleeding. Administered as an injection, usually in hospital. In certain situations, blood test monitoring is required.

EPHEDRINE
Brand name: Available only as a generic medicine
Type of drug: Decongestant
Uses: To relieve nasal congestion. Sometimes used in asthma and other lung diseases.
How it works: Ephedrine, when used as nose drops, causes narrowing of the blood vessels in the nose, which reduces swelling and eases congestion.
Availability: Ephedrine is available as an ingredient in some over-the-counter medicines.
Possible adverse effects: Nasal irritation, nausea, and headache.
Other information: Prolonged use is not recommended. When the medicine is withdrawn the congestion may return. This is known as 'rebound congestion'.

ENTACAPONE
Brand name: Comtess
Type of drug: Catechol-O-methyl transferase inhibitor

Uses: Treatment of Parkinson's disease.

How it works: This drug is used with levodopa. Levodopa increases the amount of a chemical messenger called dopamine in the brain, which is reduced in Parkinson's disease. Dopamine is broken down in the body by enzymes but Entacapone stops this enzyme breaking down dopamine, and so increases the effectiveness of the levodopa.

Availability: POM

Possible adverse effects: Difficulty sleeping, hallucinations, dizziness, drowsiness, confusion, nausea, dry mouth, vomiting, abdominal pain, diarrhoea, constipation and reddish brown urine. If urine is red in colour, this is no cause for concern. Involuntary and abnormal movements and facial flushing also occur.

Other information: Iron preparations should not be taken within three hours of taking entacapone.

CAUTION

Driving and operating machinery: Do not drive or perform skilled tasks until you are sure you are not experiencing side effects.

EPOETIN

(Formerly known as: erythropoietin)

Brand name: Eprex, NeoRecormon

Type of drug: Hormone

Uses: Treatment of anaemia due to kidney failure, cancer, or other causes.

How it works: For people who have suffered kidney failure, the drug stimulates the body to produce more red blood cells.

Possible adverse effects: Increased blood pressure, headache, and dizziness.

EPROSARTAN

Brand name: Teveten

Type of drug: Angiotensin 2 receptor antagonist

Uses: Used to treat high blood pressure.

How it works: Angiotensin 2 is a chemical naturally found in the body, which causes the blood vessels to constrict or become narrower, which increases blood pressure. Eprosartan prevents the actions of Angiotensin 2 allowing blood vessels to relax, and reducing blood pressure.

Availability: POM

Possible adverse effects: Flatulence, dizziness and joint pain.

Other information: This medicine should be taken with food.

CAUTION

Driving and operating machinery: As this drug can cause dizziness, patients receiving this medication should not drive or perform skilled tasks until they are certain they are not experiencing this or any other side effects.

EPOPROSTENOL

Brand name: Flolan

Type of drug: Prostaglandin

Uses: To stop blood clotting during dialysis, or to treat high blood pressure in the lungs.

How it works: It has many actions within the body. It can stop platelets, a constituent of the blood, from sticking together and forming blood clots; it is also a very powerful dilator of blood vessels which causes them to widen and reduces blood pressure.

Availability: POM

Possible adverse effects: Flushing of the face, headache, nausea, vomiting, colic and a drop in blood pressure.

Other information: This medicine is only administered via injection in hospital under the supervision of an experienced doctor.

ERGOCALCIFEROL

Brand name: Calciferol, Vitamin D2

Type of drug: Vitamin supplement

Uses: Prevention and treatment of certain types of vitamin D deficiency and osteoporosis.

How it works: Delivers vitamin D to those who are deficient. This may be due to inadequate diet, problems absorbing vitamin D from the gut, problems with the parathyroid gland or long-term liver disease.

Availability: Available in some over-the-counter products.

Possible adverse effects: Loss of appetite, nausea and vomiting, diarrhoea, weight loss, sweating, headache and thirst.

Other information: Blood tests may be undertaken to monitor the effectiveness of the drug. It can be used to treat children over 6 years who lack this vitamin.

ERGOMETRINE
Brand name: Syntometrine
Type of drug: Ergot alkaloid
Uses: Used to prevent bleeding from the uterus after childbirth.
How it works: Ergometrine causes narrowing of the blood vessels in the uterus, which reduces bleeding.
Availability: POM
Possible adverse effects: Nausea, vomiting, headache, abdominal pain, dizziness and palpitations.
Other information: Given as an injection or tablets, after childbirth.
CAUTION
Driving and operating machinery: It is recommended that you do not drive or perform other skilled tasks.

ERGOTAMINE
Brand name: Migril
Type of drug: Ergot alkaloid
Uses: To treat migraine in people for whom other treatment is not effective.
How it works: Ergotamine causes the narrowing of blood vessels in the brain, which stops the pain of the headache, and reduces the throbbing feeling.
Availability: POM
Possible adverse effects: Nausea, vomiting, headache, whiteness and coldness of the extremities due to reduced blood circulation and stomach pain. Ergotamine has also been shown to damage the heart and gut with prolonged use. If symptoms of a persistent cough, breathlessness, chest and severe abdominal pain occur, then consult a doctor.
Other information: Most effective when taken at the first signs of a migraine attack, when the 'aura' is perceived. In view of its potentially serious side effects, the drug should not be used for more than 24 hours;

this can be repeated 4 days later but no more than 2 courses should be taken in 1 month.

CAUTION

Alcohol: Should not be consumed whilst taking ergotamine, as this is something which often makes migraine worse.

Driving and operating machinery: Patients receiving this medication should not drive or perform skilled tasks until they are certain they are not experiencing side effects.

ERYTHROMYCIN

Brand name: Erythroped

Type of drug: Antibiotic

Uses: Treatment of a broad range of bacterial infections, including those of the throat, ear and lungs. Can also be helpful in treating acne.

How it works: Binds to enzymes within the bacterial cell which produce chemicals essential for the bacteria to survive. Without these chemicals the bacteria die.

Availability: POM

Possible adverse effects: Nausea and vomiting, abdominal discomfort and diarrhoea are commonly reported side effects.

Other information: Erythromycin is often used in patients allergic to penicillin. Should be taken an hour before food or on an empty stomach. Indigestion remedies should not be taken at the same time – but if required take 1 hour before or 2 hours after erythromycin. It is important to take as prescribed, and to complete the course. It may make the contraceptive pill less effective, and other means of contraception should be used throughout the treatment and for 7 days after completing it. It is used to treat infections in children.

ESOMEPRAZOLE

Brand name: Nexium

Type of drug: Ulcer healing drugs, proton pump inhibitor

Uses: Treatment and prevention of stomach and intestinal ulcers, and acid reflux causing heartburn.

How it works: Reduces the production of stomach acid which may cause or worsen gut irritation or ulceration.

Availability: POM

Possible adverse effects: Dry mouth, headache, nausea and diarrhoea. Occasionally it may affect blood cells. If allergic symptoms occur such as wheezing or an itchy rash, the patient should stop taking the medication and seek urgent medical advice.

Other information: The tablets should not be crushed or chewed, but swallowed whole. This medicine should be taken in the morning, half an hour before breakfast.

ESTRADIOL

(Formerly known as: oestradiol)

Brand name: Found in many hormone replacement therapy medicines

Type of drug: Female sex hormone

Uses: Treatment of the symptoms of the menopause and to prevent post-menopausal osteoporosis.

How it works: Replaces hormones lost during the menopause, with the result that symptoms such as hot flushes, night sweats and vaginal dryness are lessened.

Availability: POM

Possible adverse effects: Nausea, sore breasts, weight gain, dizziness, migraine, leg cramps, fluid retention, and high blood pressure. Also associated with an increased risk of clots in the legs and lungs, and raised lipids in the blood. Skin patches can sometimes cause a local rash.

Other information: There has been an increased risk of breast and endometrial cancer. For women who have not had a hysterectomy this medicine is usually prescribed with a progesterone substitute. Hormone replacement therapy does not provide contraception, and women are able to conceive a child for one to two years after their last period.

ESTRAMUSTINE

Brand name: Estracyt

Type of drug: Alkylating agent

Uses: To treat cancer of the prostate gland.

How it works: This drug is made up of a synthetic hormone and a nitrogen mustard. When the hormone binds to hormone receptors in the prostate gland and delivers the nitrogen mustard directly to its target, the mustard is then released and kills the cancer cells.

Availability: POM

Possible adverse effects: Nausea, vomiting, diarrhoea, breast tenderness, hair thinning and fluid retention. Anti-sickness medication will also be given.

Other information: This medicine is only given in hospital under the supervision of a doctor experienced in treating cancer, who will oversee and monitor treatment. Regular blood tests will be performed. Treatment with this drug may continue for up to three months. Milk and other calcium-rich diary foods can impair the absorption of the drug and should not be consumed within an hour of taking it. The capsules should be taken 1 hour before or 2 hours after meals. A barrier contraceptive should be used during treatment.

ETAMSYLATE

(Formerly known as: ethamsylate)

Brand name: Dicynene

Type of drug: Haemostatic

Uses: To stop heavy menstrual bleeding, and bleeding after surgery.

How it works: The precise way this drug works is unknown.

Possible adverse effects: Nausea, vomiting, diarrhoea, headache and fever.

Other information: Can be taken after food to help ease some of the side effects.

ETHAMBUTOL

Brand name: Only available as a generic medicine

Type of drug: Anti-tuberculosis

Uses: Treatment of tuberculosis (TB).

How it works: Used together with other drugs to destroy the organisms that cause TB. Ethambutol should be used if the bacteria is resistant to other drugs.

Availability: POM

Possible adverse effects: Generally uncommon, but it can occasionally cause eye problems such as temporary colour blindness, problems with focusing and a reduced visual field. Stopping the medication generally leads to improvement of these symptoms. However, this drug should not be discontinued unless advised by a doctor.

Other information: It is generally given for at least 2 months. Regular eye tests will be conducted. It is important to take the medicine regularly throughout the prescribed course and that the course is completed, as it will reduce the chances of the infection becoming resistant to treatment and reduces the chances of the infection coming back.

CAUTION

Children: Not recommended for children under 5 years old.

ETHOSUXIMIDE

Brand name: Emeside, Zarontin

Type of drug: Anti-convulsant

Uses: Treatment of certain types of epilepsy.

How it works: Reduces epileptic activity.

Availability: POM

Possible adverse effects: Relatively uncommon, however nausea, vomiting, diarrhoea, headache, dizziness, drowsiness and general apathy can occur in the early stages of treatment. These effects seem to diminish over time as long as the patient can tolerate them. Ethosuximide can also reduce the production of blood cells. Signs of infection, such as a sore throat, unexplained bleeding or bruising, generally feeling unwell or high temperature should be reported to the doctor immediately.

Other information: This medicine may be used in children of all ages.

CAUTION

Driving: The DVLA gives guidelines to epileptics wanting to drive. The most up-to-date should be consulted.

ETIDRONATE

Brand name: Didronel

Type of drug: Bisphosphonate

Uses: To treat Paget's disease. In combination with calcium tablets it is also used to prevent and treat osteoporosis.

How it works: Acts on the rate of bone growth and prevents bone cells from releasing calcium from the bones.

Availability: POM

Possible adverse effects: Diarrhoea, nausea, flatulence, indigestion, abdominal pain, constipation and vomiting.

Other information: Should be taken on an empty stomach. No food, milk or other dairy products, iron, antacids, or other minerals such as zinc, should be consumed 2 hours before, or 2 hours after, taking the etidronate tablet. When using this medicine for osteoporosis it will be taken in cycles of 14 days of etidronate tablets and 76 days of calcium supplements.

EZETIMIBE

Brand name: Ezetrol

Type of drug: Cholesterol absorption inhibitor

Uses: Ezetimibe is used in conjunction with other cholesterol lowering drugs to reduce the levels of cholesterol in the blood.

How it works: It stops the absorption of cholesterol in the intestine; the only cholesterol in the blood will be what the body makes.

Availability: POM

Possible adverse effects: Headache, abdominal pain, skin rash and diarrhoea.

Other information: This medicine should be used in conjunction with a low fat diet.

FAMCICLOVIR

Brand name: Famvir

Type of drug: Anti-viral

Uses: Treatment of herpes zoster, shingles, herpes simplex, and genital herpes.

How it works: Inactive in the form in which it is taken, when famciclovir enters the body it is converted into the active form penciclovir which stops the virus multiplying. This allows the immune system to deal with the infection more easily.

Possible adverse effects: Headache, vomiting and nausea.

Other information: Best used in the early stages of infection. For cold sores this means when the affected area starts to tingle. Take at regular intervals throughout the prescribed course, which should be completed.

CAUTION

Children: Not recommended.

FAMOTIDINE

Brand name: Pepcid

Type of drug: H$_2$ Receptor Antagonist

Uses: Treatment of ulcers of the stomach and gut and heartburn.

How it works: Reduces secretion of gastric acid and pepsin, an enzyme that helps in the digestion of protein in the stomach. This prevents irritation of the stomach or oesophagus from acid and promotes healing where the ulcers occur.

Availability: OTC

Possible adverse effects: Side effects are uncommon, but include headache, dizziness, constipation and diarrhoea.

Other information: Should be taken at night.

FELODIPINE

Brand name: Plendil, Cabren, Cardioplen, Felogen

Type of drug: Calcium channel blocker

Uses: Treating high blood pressure and preventing angina.

How it works: Relaxes blood vessels in the circulatory system, allowing blood to flow more easily, so reducing blood pressure. For angina it relaxes the blood vessels of the heart and allows more blood and oxygen to reach the heart muscle. This allows it to pump more effectively and relieves pain associated with angina.

Possible adverse effects: Headache, dizziness, flushing, rapid heart rate, fatigue and swelling of the ankles.

Other information: The tablets should be swallowed whole and not crushed or chewed. Should be taken in the morning with at least half a glass of water. Grapefruit juice should be avoided.

CAUTION

Alcohol: Should be consumed in moderation because may cause a greater than intended fall in blood pressure.

Driving and operating machinery: As this drug can cause dizziness and drowsiness, patients receiving this medication should not drive or perform skilled tasks until they are certain they are not experiencing these, or any other side effects.

FENBUFEN

Brand name: Lederfen

Type of drug: Anti-inflammatory

Uses: Treating mild to moderate pain in muscles and joints, as well as in rheumatoid arthritis, osteoarthritis and gout.

How it works: Not active in the form in which it is given but after being taken, is converted into active form by the liver. Reduces pain and inflammation by preventing the production of prostaglandins involved in the inflammatory process.

Possible adverse effects: Nausea, vomiting, indigestion, heartburn and rashes are reported. Gastrointestinal ulceration and/or bleeding may occur, so if you suffer severe stomach pain, or there is blood in your stools then seek urgent medical advice. If allergic symptoms occur such as wheezing or swelling of the face, the patient should stop taking the medication and seek urgent medical advice

Other information: Patients allergic to aspirin or indomethacin should not take it without advice from the doctor or pharmacist. It is important not to take more than the prescribed dose as this can cause kidney problems or bleeding. Do not take aspirin or other anti-inflammatory drugs except under the advice of a doctor as this will increase the risk of bleeding. Should be taken with or after meals to reduce stomach irritation.

FENOFIBRATE

Brand name: Lipantil, Suralip

Type of drug: Fibrate

Uses: Lowers the level of fats (lipids) in the blood which are thought to contribute to coronary heart disease, angina, heart attacks and stroke.

How it works: Inhibits an enzyme that produces lipids and promotes their breakdown.

Possible adverse effects: Nausea, vomiting, diarrhoea, flatulence, rashes, headache, fatigue and a sense of disorientation. Fenofibrate may also cause the skin to become more sensitive to sunlight, so take precautions such as covering the arms and legs, using a total sun block, wearing a wide-brimmed hat and sunglasses and avoiding the sun or sunlamps. Some patients may experience muscle pain, tenderness, or weakness. These side effects should be reported to the doctor or pharmacist.

Other information: Capsules should be taken with meals to maximise benefit. A special diet is usually used in conjunction with it to help keep cholesterol low.

FENTANYL

Brand name: Durogesic, Sublimaze

Type of drug: Opioid analgesic

Uses: Mainly to relieve pain during surgical operations, is also used to manage long-term and also severe pain.

How it works: Stops the transmission of pain messages through the spinal chord to the brain. This provides relief because pain is only felt once these signals reach the brain.

Availability: POM

Possible adverse effects: Nausea, vomiting, constipation, headache, confusion, hallucination, sweating, urine retention and skin rashes. Rashes are more common when a patch is used. In overdose may cause a decrease in the rate of breathing. If this effect is noticed a doctor or pharmacist should be consulted immediately.

Other information: By injection in hospital, by a patch applied to the skin or lozenges. The patch contains enough fentanyl to last for 72 hours, and the effect will last for 24 hours after removal. Soaps, oils and lotions should be avoided on the patch area, and the area used should be changed regularly. If the area the patch needs to be applied to needs cleaning use water only. Suitable parts of the body to place the patch include the upper arms and torso – hairy areas should be avoided. The patch should be pressed into place for approximately 30 seconds. The rate of release is increased when the temperature of the skin on which the patch is applied increases. Patients should not expose the patch to high temperatures.

Lozenges should be sucked for up to 15 minutes. No more than 4 doses should be taken in 24 hours.

Dependence may occur if the medication is taken for extended periods. This is different from 'tolerance' which may also occur, where higher doses are required to achieve the same level of pain relief. Tablets should be swallowed whole and not broken or crushed. The solution should be discarded 90 days after first opening the bottle by returning it to the pharmacy for safe disposal.

CAUTION

Children: Fentanyl lozenges look like lollipops and should be stored carefully away from children.

Alcohol: Should not be consumed since it may increase the severity of the side effects.

Driving and operating machinery: As this drug can cause dizziness and drowsiness, patients receiving this medication should not drive or perform skilled tasks until they are certain they are not experiencing these or any other side effects.

FERROUS SULPHATE/FERROUS GLUCONATE/FERROUS FUMARATE

Brand name: Only available as a generic medicine

Type of drug: Iron supplement

Uses: Replaces iron in conditions such as anaemia due to blood loss, or where it is deficient in the diet.

How it works: Iron is an essential component of red blood cells. If levels of iron are low then the number of produced red blood cells falls, resulting in anaemia. Taking an iron supplement replaces lost iron and allows the body to function normally.

Possible adverse effects: Nausea, vomiting, abdominal pain, blackening of stools, diarrhoea, or constipation.

Other information: Taking with meals often helps to relieve side effects, though it is best taken 1 hour before, or 2 hours after food. Treatment will continue for several months to replenish the body's stores of iron.

CAUTION

Children: Iron containing syrups are available for children.

Pregnancy: It is often given to pregnant women to prevent anaemia.

FEXOFENADINE

Brand name: Telfast

Type of drug: Antihistamine

Uses: Treatment of symptoms of hay fever and urticaria, or hives.

How it works: Blocks the action of histamine – a chemical released by the body in response to allergies. Histamine causes the majority of symptoms associated with allergies such as runny nose, itchy eyes and sneezing.

Possible adverse effects: Headache, nausea, drowsiness and dizziness.

Other information: Although marketed as a non-sedating antihistamine, it may still cause drowsiness.

CAUTION

Children: Can be used to treat children over 6 years of age but be aware that it is available in 2 strengths: 30mg and 120mg. 30mg twice daily can be given to children over 6 years, 120mg once daily can be given to children over 12 years of age.

Alcohol: Should only be consumed in moderation because the combination may increase the severity of drowsiness.

Driving and operating machinery: As this drug can cause dizziness and drowsiness, patients receiving this medication should not drive or perform skilled tasks until they are certain they are not experiencing these, or any other side effects.

FILGRASTIM

Brand name: Neupogen

Type of drug: Recombinant human granulocyte-colony stimulating factor.

Uses: Increases the levels of white blood cells in patients who have had chemotherapy, and other conditions where low white blood cell levels occur.

How it works: Stimulates the bone marrow to produce white blood cells, which boosts the body's ability to fight infection.

Possible adverse effects: Can cause muscle, joint and bone pain, fever, tiredness, nausea and diarrhoea. Mild painkillers may be required.

Other information: Treatment only given or started in hospital under supervision of a doctor experienced in treating cancer. Regular blood tests are required to assess the effects. Patients can be taught to give it to themselves. It can be used in the treatment of infection in children.

FINASTERIDE
Brand name: Proscar
Type of drug: Anti-androgens
Uses: Treatment of enlarged prostate, Benign Prostate Hyperplasia. (BPH) Also sometimes used to treat baldness.
How it works: Prevents the male hormone testosterone from being converted into the more active form dihydrotestosterone and results in shrinking of the prostate gland.
Possible adverse effects: Impotence, breast enlargement and tenderness, decreased sex drive, and rash.
Other information: Women of childbearing age must avoid handling broken or crushed tablets since they have a protective coating to prevent exposure. The use of condoms is recommended as the drug is excreted in semen. The effect of treatment may not become apparent for up to 6 months.

FLAVOXATE
Brand name: Urispas
Type of drug: Anti-cholinergic
Uses: To help urinary incontinence and other urinary problems.
How it works: Reduces involuntary contractions of the bladder muscle which cause an increased urge to urinate, passing small volumes of urine frequently. Allows the bladder to fill, and stops urine from leaking out.
Possible adverse effects: Drowsiness, headache, blurred vision, dry mouth, indigestion, nausea, vomiting, diarrhoea and fatigue.
CAUTION
Children: May be used in the treatment of children over 12 years of age.
Alcohol: Should be avoided or consumed in moderation as it increases the need to urinate frequently.
Driving and operating machinery: As this drug can cause dizziness and drowsiness, patients receiving this medication should not drive or perform

skilled tasks until they are certain they are not experiencing these or any other side effects.

FLECAINIDE
Brand name: Tambocor
Type of drug: Anti-arrhythmic
Uses: Prevention and treatment of a range of abnormal heart rhythms such as Wolff-Parkinson-White syndrome, atrial fibrillation and ventricular fibrillation.
How it works: Affects electrical impulses in the heart to establish a more regular and normal rhythm.
Avaialability: POM
Possible adverse effects: Dizziness and visual disturbances, hallucinations, tingling of the hands and feet, nausea and vomiting. Occasionally difficulty in breathing, fits and a reduction in blood cells also occur.
Other information: Treatment will usually be started in hospital, and regular appointments with the doctor are likely to be needed for monitoring.
CAUTION
Children: It may be used in children over the age of 12 years old.
Driving and operating machinery: As this drug can cause dizziness and drowsiness, patients receiving this medication should not drive or perform skilled tasks until they are certain they are not experiencing these or any other side effects.

FLUCLOXACILLIN
Brand name: Floxapen
Type of drug: Penicillin antibiotic
Uses: Treatment of infections of the ears, chest, skin, bone, and heart.
How it works: Damaging the outer, protective layer of bacteria, which leads to its destruction.
Availability: POM
Possible adverse effects: Nausea, and diarrhoea, which are usually mild. Can cause liver problems. If the skin becomes itchy and starts to turn yellow, inform your doctor. If allergic symptoms occur such as wheezing or swelling of the face, the patient should stop taking the medication and seek urgent

medical advice. Patients allergic to penicillin may also be allergic to flucloxacillin and should not take this without advice from the doctor.

Other information: Capsules should be swallowed whole and taken at regular intervals until the completion of the prescribed course. Should be taken 30 minues to 1 hour before meals and may reduce effectiveness of the contraceptive pill, so other methods of contraception should be used while taking it, and for at least 7 days after finishing. It may be used in children of any age.

FLUCONAZOLE

Brand name: Diflucan

Type of drug: Anti-fungal

Uses: Treatment of thrush (candidiasis) of the mouth and genital area and other fungal infections. Prevention of fungal infections in immunocompromised people such as patients undergoing bone marrow transplants and also used to treat some types of meningitis.

How it works: Damages the outer, protective layer of the fungus, which leads to its destruction.

Availability: POM

Possible adverse effects: Headache, dizziness, abdominal pain, diarrhoea, flatulence, nausea and skin rash. It can also cause liver problems.

Availability: As an ingredient in some over-the-counter preparations.

Other information: When prescribed for vaginal or penile thrush it is usually a single capsule. Where more than one capsule has been prescribed they should be taken at regular intervals throughout the prescribed course, and the course completed. For patients who may suffer a relapse of meningitis this drug may be administered indefinitely. May also be used to treat infection in children.

FLUDARABINE

Brand name: Fludara

Type of drug: Antimetabolite

Uses: Treatment of chronic leukaemia and some types of lymphoma in patients who have not responded to other treatments.

How it works: Stops multiplication of DNA in cancer cells, which stops the cells dividing and growing, ultimately leading to cell death.

Possible adverse effects: Infection is the most serious side effect of this medication due to its effects on the immune system. Any sign of infection, such as sore throat, unexplained bleeding or bruising, generally feeling unwell or high temperature should be reported to the doctor immediately. Antibiotics, antifungal and antiviral medicines may be prescribed to prevent infections. Fever, nausea, vomiting, diarrhoea, chills, problems with vision, fatigue, and fluid retention can occur. Low red blood cells can also occur.

Other information: Only given in hospital under the supervision of a doctor experienced in treating cancer. Regular blood tests are required to assess the effects. Immunity remains reduced for several months to years. Antibiotics, antifungal and antiviral medicines will usually be prescribed to try and stop any infection from developing. Regular blood tests will be carried out to monitor the effects of the medicine on the blood, and immune system.

CAUTION

Pregnancy: Effective contraceptive measures should be used throughout treatment and for 6 months afterwards, and the doctor informed if pregnancy is suspected.

FLUDROCORTISONE

Brand name: Florinef

Type of drug: Mineralocorticoid

Uses: Treatment of disorders of the adrenal glands, resulting in reduced quantities of essential hormones such as aldosterone.

How it works: Mimics aldosterone, which controls salt and water balance in the body. The main effect is to increase the amount of sodium and water reabsorbed from the urine by the kidney. This has the effect of increasing the volume of the blood, and hence blood pressure.

Possible adverse effects: Raised blood pressure, sodium and water retention, and low levels of potassium. Muscle weakness, numbness, appetite loss and nausea may be signs of low potassium and should be reported.

Other information: Only given in hospital under the supervision of a doctor experienced in treating endocrine problems. Regular blood tests are required to assess the effects. Patients are usually given a steroid card which explains what treatment they are receiving. This will allow appropriate treatment choices to be made. Should not be discontinued unless advised by a doctor, then it will be gradually withdrawn.

CAUTION

Children: When used in children the growth and development of the child will be carefully monitored because steroids can interfere with growth.

FLUOROURACIL

Brand name: Efudix

Type of drug: Antimetabolite

Uses: Treating a variety of cancers including skin cancer.

How it works: It is a modified version of one of the components used to make RNA. Due to the lack of RNA the cells cannot make other chemicals the body needs, and this causes a type of cellular suicide.

Possible adverse effects: Nausea, vomiting, diarrhoea, rashes and dermatitis can occur. The mouth and gut can also become very painful, and ulceration can occur leading to abdominal pain and blood in the vomit or faeces. Low blood counts occur so signs of infection, such as a sore throat, unexplained bleeding or bruising, generally feeling unwell or high temperature should be reported to the doctor immediately. When used as the cream the main adverse effect is a reddening of the skin. These reactions may be made worse by exposure to sunlight. Precautions include applying a total sun block, covering the arms and legs in long clothes, wearing a wide brimmed hat and sunglasses and not using sunlamps.

Other information: Only given in hospital under the supervision of a doctor experienced in treating cancer. Regular blood tests are required to assess the effects. After applying the cream the hands should be thoroughly washed. The cream should not be allowed to come into contact with the eyes, nose, or mouth.

CAUTION

Children: Not recommended for use in children. Infusions may be given.

Pregnancy: Should be avoided while taking this so appropriate contraception methods should be used.

Driving and operating machinery: Since it can cause dizziness and drowsiness, patients receiving this medication should not drive or perform skilled tasks until they are certain they are not experiencing these or any other side effects.

FLUOXETINE
Brand name: Prozac
Type of drug: Selective Serotonin Re-uptake Inhibitor
Uses: Treatment of depression, eating disorders such as bulimia nervosa, and obsessive-compulsive disorders.
How it works: Increases the amount of time that serotonin, a chemical messenger in brain, exists. This leads to an elevation of mood.
Possible adverse effects: Diarrhoea, nausea, vomiting, indigestion, dry mouth, headache, dizziness, insomnia, altered dreams, drowsiness, fatigue,weight loss, problems with sexual function, hair loss, problems with vision, sweating, flushing and pain of the muscles and joints. These side effects usually lessen with continued use. If allergic symptoms such as wheezing or swelling of the face occur, the patient should stop taking the medication and seek urgent medical advice
Other information: Treatment may last several months, and may take at least two to four weeks to have an effect. Although dependence is not a recognised complication of this drug, symptoms may appear on withdrawal of any drug of this class – including fluoxetine – such as nausea, weight loss, dizziness, drowsiness, headache and anxiety.
CAUTION
Alcohol: Consumption not recommended since it may make depression more severe.
Driving and operating machinery: As this drug can cause dizziness and drowsiness, patients receiving this medication should not drive or perform skilled tasks until they are certain they are not experiencing these or any other side effects.

FLUPENTIXOL
(Formerly known as: flupenthixol)
Brand name: Depixol
Type of drug: Antipsychotic

Uses: Treatment of schizophrenia and similar disorders.

How it works: Schizophrenia and similar disorders are believed to occur when too much dopamine, a chemical messenger, in the certain parts of the brain. This halts the action of dopamine and so reduces the symptoms associated with schizophrenia.

Possible adverse effects: Blurred vision, dizziness – especially when first standing up – nausea, weight gain, palpitations, tremors, feeling hot or cold, confusion, symptoms similar to those seen in patients with Parkinson's disease. Drowsiness may occur at the start of treatment. There may also be some effects on hormones in the body leading to breast enlargement and tenderness, problems with ejaculation in men, and an increased libido. Irregular and unintentional movements may occur and should be reported to the doctor immediately because they may be the start of a condition known as Tardive Dyskinesia. Any sign of feeling hot – especially when connected with problems urinating – fast heart beat, sweatiness, clamminess and muscular rigidity, should be reported to the doctor immediately because it may be the start of a condition called Neuroleptic Malignant Syndrome.

Other information: The control of severe symptoms may take up to 6 months. Tablets should be swallowed whole with a full glass of water. The tablets should not be taken with tea or coffee, or any medicines used for indigestion. It may cause an increased susceptibility to sunburn, and adequate precautions should be taken to prevent this such as covering exposed skin, using a total sun block, wearing a wide brimmed hat and sunglasses and staying out of the sun where possible.

CAUTION

Alcohol: Should not be consumed because it can worsen the effects of alcohol.

Driving and operating machinery: As this drug can cause dizziness and drowsiness – which may last into the next day – patients should not drive or perform skilled tasks until they are certain they are not experiencing these or any other side effects.

FLUPHENAZINE

Brand name: Moditen

Type of drug: Anti-psychotic

Uses: As a short-term treatment for anxiety, dangerous and impulsive behaviour, psychoses – where the patient's perception of the world is altered – and as an additional drug for treatment of schizophrenia.

How it works: Schizophrenia and other similar disorders are believed to occur when too much dopamine, a chemical messenger, is present in certain parts of the brain. Fluphenazine stops the action of dopamine, and so reduces the severity of the symptoms which are associated with schizophrenia.

Possible adverse effects: Symptoms of Parkinson's disease, abnormal – and sometimes unintentional – face and body movements, and restlessness. These should be reported immediately to a doctor. Drowsiness, dizziness (especially when first standing), dry mouth, constipation, incontinence and impaired mental skills. There may also be some effects on hormones in the body leading to breast enlargement and tenderness, problems with ejaculation in men and an increased libido. Feeling hot or cold has also been reported. Any sign of feeling hot – especially when connected with problems urinating – fast heart beat, sweatiness, clamminess and muscular rigidity, should be reported to the doctor immediately because it may be the start of a condition called Neuroleptic Malignant Syndrome. Patient must report any rashes that appear while on the medication.

Other information: Tablets should be swallowed whole with a full glass of water and should not be taken with tea or coffee or any medicines used for indigestion. It may cause an increased susceptibility to sunburn and adequate precautions should be taken to prevent this such as covering exposed skin, using a total sun block, wearing a wide brimmed hat and sunglasses, and staying out of the sun where possible.

CAUTION

Alcohol: Should not be consumed because it can worsen its effects.

Driving and operating machinery: As this drug can cause dizziness, drowsiness, and confusion – which may last into the next day – patients receiving this medication should not drive or perform skilled tasks until they are certain they are not experiencing these or any other side effects.

FLURBIPROFEN
Brand name: Froben
Type of drug: Non-steroidal anti-inflammatory
Uses: Mainly in the treatment and relief of pain in rheumatoid arthritis and osteoarthritis. Is also used for relief of inflammation after eye surgery and menstrual pain.
How it works: Inhibits the actions of an enzyme called cyclo-oxygenase. This enzyme produces chemical messengers that start, then continue the inflammatory process.
Possible adverse effects: Stomach and bowel pain or discomfort, breathlessness and allergic reactions. Gastrointestinal ulceration and/or bleeding may occur, so if you suffer severe stomach pain, or there is blood in your stools then seek urgent medical advice. If allergic symptoms occur such as wheezing or swelling of the face, the patient should stop taking the medication and seek urgent medical advice. In patients with asthma, aspirin can sometimes make these symptoms worse.
Availability: As an ingredient in some over-the-counter preparations.
Other information: Should be taken with or after food and milk to reduce stomach irritation.
CAUTION
Children: May be used in children over the age of 12 years old.

FUSIDIC ACID
Brand name: Fucidin
Type of drug: Antibiotic
Uses: A narrow spectrum antibiotic used in resistant infections and skin and bone infections.
How it works: Stops the production of chemicals essential to the survival of the bacteria. This allows the immune system a better chance to overcome the infection.
Possible adverse effects: When applied to the skin as a cream or ointment, or to the eyes as drops, the adverse effects are usually limited to a mild stinging or burning sensation. When taken by mouth the adverse effects include nausea, vomiting, stomach upsets, and jaundice, seen as yellowing of the skin and itching.

Other information: When prescribed by mouth the tablets or liquid should be taken regularly throughout the course which should be completed. The liquid should be taken with or after food.

FLUTAMIDE
Brand name: Drogenil
Type of drug: Anti-androgen
Uses: Treatment of advanced prostate cancer.
How it works: Prevents normal male hormones called androgens from working. Many types of prostate cancer require hormones to grow, so lack of the hormones prevents growth of the cancer.
Availability: POM
Possible adverse effects: Nausea, vomiting, breast enlargement, hot flushes, diarrhoea, weight gain, hair loss, reduced sex drive, muscle weakness, skin rash, dry skin, liver problems and itching may occur.
Other information: Patients may receive other medication with this drug as part of the chemotherapy regimen.
CAUTION
Alcohol: Can increase the likelihood of experiencing side effects and so should only be consumed in moderation.
Pregnancy: Should be avoided while taking this medicine so appropriate contraception methods should be used.

FLUTICASONE
Brand name: Flixonase, Flixotide
Type of drug: Corticosteroid
Uses: Control of the symptoms of asthma and hay fever.
How it works: By inhalation into the lungs it reduces inflammation of the airways, making breathing easier. With long term use it can reduce the number of asthma attacks. When inhaled into the nose it has the same effect on hay fever.
Possible adverse effects: Occasionally fungal infections can occur in the mouth, but gargling with water after each inhalation will prevent this in most cases. Nasal discomfort and a sore throat are also possible. With the inhaler for asthma an irritation may also be present in the throat. If

wheezing occurs after taking the dose then a doctor should be consulted as soon as possible.

Availability: As an ingredient in some over-the-counter preparations.

Other information: May be prescribed as an ointment, cream, nasal spray or inhaler. Creams and ointments should be applied sparingly. Keep away from eyes, around genital and rectal areas and any skin creases. Since it is used as a preventative measure in asthma, alternative medication is required during an asthma attack. It should be taken regularly as prescribed by the doctor and may take up to a week to work. Patients may sometimes refer to this inhaler as the preventer, or the 'red/orange' one. It is important that you follow the correct technique when using an inhaler. A 'spacer device' is available to make these inhalers easier to use. It may be prescribed to children of any age.

FLUVOXAMINE

Brand name: Faverin

Type of drug: Selective Serotonin Re-uptake Inhibitor

Uses: Treating depression and obsessive-compulsive disorders.

How it works: Increases the amount of time that serotonin, a specific chemical messenger in the brain, lasts. This leads to elevation of mood.

Possible adverse effects: Nausea, vomiting, weight loss, abdominal pain, diarrhoea, constipation, dry mouth indigestion, agitation, sweating, headache, dizziness and insomnia. These side effects usually lessen with use.

Other information: Treatment may last for several months and it may take at least 2 to 4 weeks to have an effect. Although dependence is not a recognised complication of this drug, symptoms such as nausea, weight loss, dizziness, drowsiness, headache, and anxiety may appear on withdrawal of any drug of this class – including fluoxetine.

CAUTION

Alcohol: This is not recommended because the alcohol itself may make depression more severe.

Driving and operating machinery: As this drug can cause dizziness and drowsiness, patients receiving this medication should not drive or perform skilled tasks until they are certain they are not experiencing these or any other side effects.

FOLIC ACID
Type of drug: Vitamin
Uses: Treatment of some types of anaemia and prevention of birth defects during pregnancy.
How it works: Replaces folic acid which is essential for the production of DNA in red blood cells, and other cells of the body
Possible adverse effects: Very uncommon. A rash may occur.
Availability: The 400mcg tablets used in pregnancy are available over-the-counter, but the 5mg tablets used for anaemia are only available on prescription.
Other information: Folic acid is found in all green vegetables such as spinach and broccoli. It may be used in children of all ages.
CAUTION
Pregnancy: It is used during the first 12 weeks of pregnancy to prevent neural tube defects such as spina bifida.

FORMOTEROL
(Formerly known as: eformoterol)
Brand name: Oxis
Type of drug: Beta$_2$ agonist
Uses: Treatment and prevention of moderate to severe asthma.
How it works: Relaxes the muscles that control the diameter of the lungs. This makes the airways larger and makes it easier for to breathe properly.
Possible adverse effects: A fine tremor, palpitations, flushing of the skin and headaches.
Other information: It is important to use the correct inhaler technique as taught and described in the leaflet supplied with the medicine. It needs to be taken regularly to be effective, not just during an asthma attack. It may be used to treat asthma in children.

FOSCARNET
Brand name: Foscavir
Type of drug: Anti-viral
Uses: Treating serious viral infections called by herpes viruses, such as cytomegalovirus infections of the eye.

How it works: Stops an enzyme called viral DNA polymerase from working. This enzyme is required for the virus to multiply.

Possible adverse effects: Anaemia, nausea, vomiting, diarrhoea, abdominal pain, headache, dizziness, chills, involuntary movement, weight loss, mood changes, fatigue and rashes. It can cause kidney damage so blood calcium level and kidney function tests need to be performed. It is important that lots of fluid is taken.

Other information: Usually only given in hospital under specialist supervision.

CAUTION

Driving and operating machinery: As this drug can cause dizziness and drowsiness, patients should not drive or perform skilled tasks until they are certain they are not experiencing these or any other side effects.

FOSINOPRIL

Brand name: Staril

Type of drug: ACE inhibitor

Uses: Treating high blood pressure and heart failure.

How it works: Allows the blood vessels to relax, which enables them to increase in size. This reduces the pressure of blood flow.

Possible adverse effects: Dizziness, cough, nausea, vomiting, diarrhoea, abdominal pain, chest, joint and muscle pain, fatigue and rashes. The cough is usually described as a dry cough, and will go away if patients keep taking the medicine.

Other information: Should be taken at least 2 hours before any antacids or indigestion remedies. Avoid salt substitutes containing potassium and take care in hot weather, or if exercising, to avoid over-heating and dehydration.

CAUTION

Children: It may be used in children above 12 years of age.

Alcohol: In moderation because of the risk of a greater the predicted drop in blood pressure.

FUROSEMIDE

(Formerly known as: frusemide)

Brand name: Lasix

Type of drug: Loop diuretic

Uses: Treatment of high blood pressure, heart failure and other conditions associated with fluid retention,

How it works: Acts on the kidneys to increase the amount of urine passed, which in turn, reduces excess fluid in the body. Fluid in the wrong places can cause high blood pressure, swollen ankles and breathlessness.

Possible adverse effects: Nausea, vomiting, problems with hearing and stomach problems. It may cause a large drop in levels of potassium in the blood, causing muscle cramps, and dizziness. Best taken in the morning so that it does not affect sleep. It may also be used in children of any age.

CAUTION

Alcohol: In moderation because the combination may cause a large drop in blood pressure.

Driving and operating machinery: As this drug can cause dizziness and drowsiness, patients should not drive or perform skilled tasks until they are certain they are not experiencing these or any other side effects.

GABAPENTIN

Brand name: Neurontin

Type of drug: Anti-epileptic

Uses: The treatment of epilepsy and nerveuropathic pain, such as trigeminal neuralgia.

How it works: An epileptic fit (or seizure) is thought to occur when the brain receives too many or abnormal signals. Gabapentin acts by reducing the number of signals that the brain receives. How it works to prevent nerve pain is less well understood.

Availability: POM

Possible adverse effects: When used for neuropathic pain the common adverse effects are drowsiness, dizziness, diarrhoea, dry mouth, fluid retention, weight gain, impaired mental function, problems with vision, memory loss and uncontrolled movement. When used as an anti-epileptic the common adverse effects are dizziness, drowsiness, problems with movement, fatigue, rapid eye movements, tremor, problems with vision, memory loss, joint pain, anxiety, indigestion, weight increase, and weakness of the muscles.

Other information: This medicine is only given in hospital under the supervision of a doctor experienced in treating epilepsy. First dose to be taken before bedtime to minimise drowsiness and dizziness. It is not advisable to stop taking this drug suddenly – the dosage should be reduced over at least a week. Gabapentin should be taken as instructed by the doctor, It should be taken at least 2 hours after any antacids or indigestion remedies because these interfere with the absorption of gabapentin into the body.

CAUTION

Children: This medicine can be used for children over 6 years of age.

Driving and operating machinery: As this drug can cause dizziness and drowsiness, patients receiving this medication should not drive or perform skilled tasks until they are certain they are not experiencing these, or any other side effects.

GANCICLOVIR

Brand name: Cymevene

Type of drug: Anti-viral

Uses: To treat and prevent infections with cytomegalovirus (CMV).

How it works: Ganciclovir prevents the virus multiplying inside cells by interfering with viral DNA.

Availability: POM

Possible adverse effects: Blood disorders, weight loss, decreased appetite, mood change, rashes, fever, nausea, vomiting, headache, confusion, dizziness, drowsiness, insomnia, funny tastes in the mouth, tingling in the hands and feet, fluid retention, eye pain, ear pain, cough, diarrhoea, flatulence, indigestion, constipation, abdominal pain, night sweats, joint and muscle pain, fatigue and a raised temperature.

Other information: This medicine is only given in hospital under the supervision of a doctor experienced in treating immunocompromised people, who will oversee and monitor treatment. Regular blood tests are required to assess the effects. Eye gel is available to treat CMV eye infections in addition to the intravenous form. Contraception should be used.

CAUTION

Children: This medicine may be used in children over 12 years of age.

Driving and operating machinery: As this drug can cause dizziness and drowsiness, patients should not drive or perform skilled tasks until they are certain they are not experiencing these, or any other side effects.

GEMFIBROZIL
Brand name: Lopid
Type of drug: Fibrate
Uses: To lower cholesterol and fat levels in the blood, which contribute to coronary heart disease, angina, heart attacks and stroke.
How it works: Gemfibrozil causes a lower level of lipids in the blood by preventing an enzyme that produces them, and promoting lipid breakdown.
Availability: POM
Possible adverse effects: Abdominal pain, diarrhoea, nausea, stomach pain, nausea, vomiting and flatulence.
Other information: These tablets should be taken with or after food. Must not be taken by people who are alcohol dependent, or who have gallstones or kidney problems. A fat-lowering diet and exercise regime should be maintained whilst on medication. Take with food to minimise the risk of gastric problems.
CAUTION
Alcohol: Should only be consumed in strict moderation whilst taking this medicine because the combination can cause an increase in the chances of muscle and joint pain or muscle cramps.

GENTAMICIN
Brand name: Genticin
Type of drug: Antibiotic
Uses: Treatment of serious infections affecting the lungs, kidneys, brain (meningitis) and heart. Also available as drops and ointment for the treatment of ear and eye infections.
How it works: Gentamicin stops bacteria from producing chemicals that are essential for their survival, leading to the death of the bacteria.
Availability: POM
Possible adverse effects: The two adverse effects that are potentially very serious; deafness or a persistent ringing in the ears, and kidney damage, which may require dialysis if severe. Use of the eye drops can be associated

with irritation, burning and stinging, itching, and a rash on application of the drops. If the drops cause an irritation or rash use of them should be stopped and the doctor consulted as soon as possible.

Other information: It is only given in hospital under the supervision of an experienced doctor, who will oversee and monitor treatment. It is often given with other antibiotic drugs. Regular blood tests are required to monitor the drug levels and kidneys. It is not generally given for longer than 7 days. The drops are unlikely to be absorbed into the body in sufficient quantity to cause any of the problems associated with injecting gentamicin. If the eye is being treated then contact lenses should be removed during the whole course of treatment. It can be used in children of all ages.

GLIBENCLAMIDE

Brand name: Daonil

Type of drug: Sulphonylurea

Uses: Used in the management of non-insulin dependent diabetes, for example in cases where the pancreas is still producing some insulin.

How it works: Glibenclamide increases the sensitivity of cells in the pancreas to glucose in the blood stream, the cells then increase their production of insulin which is required for glucose in the blood to enter cells. This leads to a decrease in the level of glucose in the blood.

Availability: POM

Possible adverse effects: Stomach upsets and headaches are the most common side effects experienced, although they are uncommon. If the levels of glucose in the blood fall too low (hypoglycaemia) the following symptoms may occur; feeling faint, weak, confused and sweaty.

Other information: Diabetics should have a normal, healthy diet and follow advice provided by the doctor, pharmacist or diabetic nurse. Blood and urine tests may be performed to monitor the effectiveness of the medication regime. The tablets should be taken with a full glass of water after the first main meal of the day.

CAUTION

Alcohol: Should only be consumed in strict moderation whilst taking this medication.

Driving and operating machinery: The DVLA has made recommendations about diabetics who wish to drive and the latest information should be consulted. Glibenclamide will impair the ability to drive if the levels of glucose in the blood are allowed to fall too low.

GLICLAZIDE
Brand name: Diamicron
Type of drug: Sulphonylurea
Uses: Used in the management of non-insulin dependent diabetes, for example in cases where the pancreas is still producing some insulin.
How it works: Gliclazide increases the sensitivity of cells in the pancreas to glucose in the blood stream. The cells increase their production of insulin which is required for glucose in the blood to enter cells. This leads to a decrease in the level of glucose in the blood.
Availability: POM
Possible adverse effects: Nausea, indigestion, diarrhoea and constipation have been reported with gliclazide. If the levels of glucose in the blood fall too low (hypoglycaemia) the following symptoms may occur; feeling faint, weak, confused and sweaty.
Other information: Diabetics should have a normal, healthy diet and follow advice provided by the doctor, pharmacist or diabetic nurse. Blood and urine tests may be performed to monitor the effectiveness of the medication regime. The tablets should be taken with a full glass of water after the first main meal of the day.
CAUTION
Alcohol: Should only be consumed in strict moderation.
Driving and operating machinery: The DVLA has made recommendations for diabetics who wish to drive, and the latest information should be consulted. Gliclazide will impair the ability to drive if the levels of glucose in the blood are allowed to fall too low.

GLUTARALDEHYDE
Brand name: Glutarol
Type of drug: Preparation for warts
Uses: Removal of warts on the hands and feet.
How it works: The precise way that gluteraldehyde works is not well

understood. It is thought that its antiviral properties kill the human papilloma virus responsible for warts.

Availability: POM

Possible adverse effects: Irritation of the skin surrounding the wart. This medicine may also stain the skin brown, but this disappears as soon as the medicine is stopped.

Availability: Glutaraldehyde is available as an ingredient in some over-the-counter preparations.

Other information: Avoid contact with mouth and eyes. Not to be used on facial or ano-genital warts. The skin should be soaked in warm water for 2 to 3 minutes and any hard skin removed with a pumice stone or emery board. The liquid should then be applied one drop at a time, trying not to get too much on the skin surrounding the wart. This medicine may be used by children of any age.

GLYCERYL TRINITRATE (GTN)

Brand name: Nitro-Dur, Nitrolingual

Type of drug: Nitrate

Uses: Relieves the symptoms of angina and to treat heart failure.

How it works: Dilates or widens the vessels of the heart allowing more blood to flow through them. This supplies more oxygen to the heart muscle and stops the pain associated with an angina attack. This also decreases the workload of the heart, making it more effective.

Availability: Glyceryl trinitrate tablets, patches and sprays are available over-the-counter.

Possible adverse effects: Flushing, throbbing headache, dizziness and a feeling of light-headedness after standing up are commonly reported with both the spray and tablets. Nausea, vomiting, low blood pressure, stomach pain and rapid heart rate may also occur after injection. With use of the patch there may be some local redness and irritation around the site it is put on.

Other information: The drug can be taken in tablet form, which is placed under the tongue, or as a skin patch, capsule, spray or ointment. At the first sign of chest pain or tightness the patient should sit down, and use the medication as directed by the doctor or pharmacist. The tablets should be allowed to dissolve under the tongue and the spray should be sprayed under the tongue. The patient should then remain seated for approximately 20 minutes until the pain goes away.

CAUTION

Driving and operating machinery: As this drug may reduce the blood pressure, causing dizziness, patients receiving this medication should not drive or perform skilled tasks until they are certain they are not experiencing these or any other side effects.

GONADOTROPHIN
See Human Menopausal Gonadotrophins and Chorionic Gonadotrophin

GOSERELIN
Brand name: Zoladex
Type of drug: Gonadorelin analogue
Uses: Treatment of hormone-related cancers such as those which occur in the prostate and breast. It is also used to treat endometriosis and also in fertility treatment.
How it works: Goserelin reduces hormone production of both androgens and oestrogens. Many types of prostate cancer require hormones to grow, so lack of the hormones prevents growth of the cancer. For endometriosis, it blocks the production of hormones by the ovaries, leading to a thinning of the endometrium, which stops endometriosis from becoming worse.
Availability: POM
Possible adverse effects: In both men and women adverse effects usually include hot flushes, sweating, headache and a decrease in sex drive. Osteoporosis may occur.
Other information: This medicine is only given in hospital under the supervision of a doctor experienced in treating cancer and gynaecological problems. Goserelin is administered as an implant which is inserted beneath the skin. For endometriosis the period of treatment does not usually exceed 6 months. Women who are receiving this medicine for endometriosis should use non-hormonal methods of contraception, such as a condom, until the first menstrual cycle after finishing treatment.

GRANISETRON
Brand name: Kytril
Type of drug: Anti-cancer
Uses: Prevents nausea and vomiting associated with anti-cancer drugs.
How it works: Blocks the messages to the brain that stimulate the feelings of nausea and instinct to vomit.
Availability: POM
Possible adverse effects: Headache and constipation. If allergic symptoms occur such as wheezing or swelling of the face, the patient should stop taking the medication and seek urgent medical advice.
Other information: It can be used in children of all ages.

GRISEOFULVIN
Brand name: Grisovin
Type of drug: Anti-fungal
Uses: Treatment of fungal infections of the nails, hair and skin where direct application to these areas is considered unsuitable, or has been tried and failed.
How it works: Disrupts the ability of the fungal cell to divide and therefore grow.
Availability: POM
Possible adverse effects: Headache, diarrhoea, nausea, vomiting, rashes, drowsiness and dizziness. This medicine may cause a rash in response to natural or artificial sunlight. If this occurs, patients should use a total sun block and stay out of the sun. Liver problems can occur with prolonged use and blood tests may be carried out to monitor the effects of this medicine on the liver.
Other information: Men must not father a child within 6 months of stopping the treatment. Should be taken around meal times to minimise stomach upset. The tablets should be taken regularly throughout the prescribed course, which should be completed. This medicine may be used in children of any age.
CAUTION
Pregnancy: Must be avoided during and for 1 month after stopping treatment.

Alcohol: Should only be consumed in strict moderation because the effects of alcohol can be made worse whilst taking griseofulvin.

Driving and operating machinery: As this drug can cause dizziness and drowsiness, patients should not drive or perform skilled tasks until they are certain they are not experiencing these, or any other side effects.

HALOPERIDOL

Brand name: Haldol

Type of drug: Antipsychotic

Uses: Treatment of schizophrenia, manias and violent and abnormal behaviour.

How it works: Haloperidol stops the action of a chemical messenger in the brain called dopamine. Schizophrenia and related disorders are thought to be due to an increase in the amount of dopamine available in the brain. Blocking the action of dopamine helps to control the symptoms of the disease.

Availability: POM

Possible adverse effects: Dizziness, drowsiness, dry mouth, constipation, inability to pass urine, anxiety, a rash that develops when skin is exposed to sunlight, stomach upsets, and weight gain may occur. Unwanted effects include abnormal, involuntary movements, stiffness, restlessness and a condition that is like Parkinson's disease with shakiness, difficulty in movement and stiffness. Any sign of feeling hot, especially when connected with problems urinating, fast heart beat, sweatiness or clamminess and muscular rigidity should be reported to the doctor immediately because it may be the start of a rare but serious condition called Neuroleptic Malignant Syndrome.

Other information: Should not be discontinued unless advised by a doctor but any side effects should be reported and should not be used at the same time as other anti-depressants. It can cause a rash in response to sunlight which should be avoided, especially between the hours of 11:00 and 14:00 when the sun is strongest. Sensible precautions to prevent this include applying a total sun block, covering the arms and legs in long clothes, wearing a wide brimmed hat and sunglasses, and not using sunlamps. This drug can be given to children of all ages.

CAUTION

Alcohol: Should be avoided whilst taking this medication because it may cause an increase in the severity of dizziness and drowsiness experienced. *Driving and operating machinery:* As this drug can cause dizziness and drowsiness, patients should not drive or perform skilled tasks until they are certain they are not experiencing these, or any other side effects.

HEPARIN

Brand name: Calciparine

Type of drug: Anti-coagulant

Uses: Prevents formation of blood clots and assists in their breakdown in both medical conditions such as heart attack, or deep vein thrombosis, and to stop clots forming whilst patients are having dialysis, surgery or other procedures.

How it works: Alters the clotting mechanism of the blood to make the formation of clots less likely.

Availability: POM

Possible adverse effects: Excessive bleeding is a risk, so the dosage may be monitored by blood tests. In some patients, reduced numbers of platelets in the blood occurs after receiving heparin therapy so this will also be monitored. Bruising may appear around the site of the injection.

Other information: Heparin is usually given in hospital, by injection. Patients must avoid aspirin and aspirin-like medications unless told to use them by the doctor or pharmacist, as these will increase their risk of bleeding. This drug may be used in pregnancy and breastfeeding.

CAUTION

Children: This medicine may be used in children who need to be anticoagulated.

HOMATROPINE

Brand name: Minims homatropine

Uses: Preparation of the eye for surgery, and inflammation of the eye

How it works: Homatropine stops the muscles controlling the iris from working. This results in the pupil becoming larger.

Availability: POM

Possible adverse effects: Irritation and stinging pains in the eye and possibly conjunctivitis. A rash may appear on the eyelids and skin surrounding the eye.

Other information: Darkly pigmented eyes usually require larger amounts of the drug to work.

CAUTION

Driving and operating machinery: As this drug can cause visual problems, patients receiving this medication should not drive or perform skilled tasks until they are certain they are not experiencing this or any other side effects.

HUMAN MENOPAUSAL GONADOTROPHINS

Brand name: Menogon, Menopur, Merional

Type of drug: Gonadotrophin

Uses: To treat infertility due to an abnormalities of the pituitary gland (an area of the brain that produces hormones required for normal sexual function), and other causes of infertility as long as the ovaries, uterus and Fallopian tubes are normal.

How it works: Stimulates the production of oestrogen and progesterone in women, and testosterone in men. This may lead to normal menstruation in women and sperm production in men.

Availability: POM

Possible adverse effects: There may be itching, redness and swelling at the site of injection, nausea and vomiting. It can cause ovaries to become overactive, producing swelling which will be noticed as abdominal pain, and an increased frequency of urination.

Other information: This medicine is only given in hospital under the supervision of a doctor experienced in treating infertility, who will oversee and monitor treatment. Regular tests are required to assess the effects.

CAUTION

Pregnancy: Patients should be informed about possibility of multiple pregnancies occurring.

HYDRALAZINE

Brand name: Apresoline

Type of drug: Peripheral vasodilator

Uses: Treatment of moderate-to-severe high blood pressure in combination with other medicines and heart failure

How it works: Enables the blood vessels to relax, which allows them to increase in size. This reduces the pressure of the blood flowing through them, which causes the blood pressure to fall and reduces the work of the heart

Availability: POM

Possible adverse effects: Increase in heart rate, flushing of the skin, chest pain, headache, muscle and joint pain, diarrhoea, nausea, vomiting. It can also cause dizziness due to low blood pressure. In treatment that lasts over 6 months, and at higher doses a combination of joint pain, associated with a fever and a rash may occur. If this happens consult a doctor as soon as possible.

Other information: Take medication with meals to enhance drug absorption and minimise gastric irritation.

CAUTION

Pregnancy: It can be used to control pregnancy-induced hypertension.

Alcohol: Hydralazine may worsen the effects of alcohol on the body.

Driving and operating machinery: As this drug can cause dizziness and drowsiness, patients receiving this medication should not drive or perform skilled tasks until they are certain they are not experiencing these, or any other side effects.

HYDROCORTISONE

Brand name: Corlan, Hydrocortone, Solu-Cortef

Type of drug: Corticosteroid

Uses: Used to suppress allergic reactions and inflammation. It is also used to replace the hormone cortisol in diseases associated with the adrenal glands. It is also used to treat skin conditions such as eczema.

How it works: Replaces the natural hormone cortisol, when the adrenal glands are not producing sufficient quantities. Suppresses the production of cells and chemicals that can cause and continue inflammation.

Availability: Hydrocortisone is available over-the-counter as an ingredient in some preparations.

Possible adverse effects: When used as a supplement to replace cortisol the following may occur: fluid retention, raised blood pressure, changes in the levels of sodium, potassium and calcium in the blood, muscle pain and weakness. Osteoporosis has been reported, especially when used by women who have passed the menopause, as well as indigestion, oral thrush, headache, mood changes, acne, increased sweating. It may take longer for wounds to heal, the skin may become thinner and bruise more easily, and on long-term therapy may cause blood glucose leading to diabetes.

When used as a cream or ointment, the adverse effects tend to be mild irritation. With creams rubbed into the skin, the least amount necessary should be used. Creams and ointments can cause thinning of the skin and increased or decreased colouration of the skin, and can make infections worse – this is usually only with long-term treatment. If the condition does not improve, or appears to worsen, a doctor should be consulted.

Other information: This medicine is only given in hospital under the supervision of a doctor experienced in treating endocrine diseases. Regular blood and other tests are required to assess the effects. Patients will usually be given a steroid card if they are to be on long-term treatment, which they should show to anybody who may treat them. This allows correct treatments to be chosen. In children growth and development will be monitored because hydrocortisone can stunt the growth.

CAUTION

Children: It may be used in children of all ages for replacement of cortsiol. When used for mouth ulcers, hydrocortisone should not be used by children under 12 years of age.

Driving and operating machinery: As this drug can cause dizziness and drowsiness, visual problems and muscle wasting, patients receiving this medication should not drive or perform skilled tasks until they are certain they are not experiencing these or any other side effects.

HYDROXYCHLOROQUINE

Brand name: Plaquenil

Type of drug: Antimalarial

Uses: Treatment of juvenile and rheumatoid arthritis, and skin conditions aggravated by sunlight.

How it works: Believed to act on the immune system to reduce inflammation in the affected joints.

Possible adverse effects: Changes in eye colour, visual problems, nausea, diarrhoea, weight loss, abdominal pain and skin rashes may occur.

Other information: Only given in hospital under the supervision of a doctor experienced in treating rheumatic diseases who will oversee and monitor treatment. Regular blood tests and eye examinations are required. It may take between several weeks to see the beneficial effects of this medication. If antacids or indigestion remedies are to be taken, at least 4 hours must be left between these and taking the hydroxychloroquine tablet. It should be taken with a meal or small glass of milk.

CAUTION

Children: This medicine can be used in children to treat arthritis.

Driving and operating machinery: As this drug can cause visual problems, patients receiving this medication should not drive or perform skilled tasks until they are certain they are not experiencing this or any other side effects.

HYDROXOCOBALAMIN

Brand name: Cobalin-H, Neo-Cytamen

Type of drug: Vitamin

Uses: Used to treat pernicious anaemia and other causes of vitamin B_{12} deficiency.

How it works: Replaces the vitamin B_{12}, which is deficient in people suffering with these types of anaemia.

Availability: POM

Possible adverse effects: Itching, hot flushes, fever, chills, nausea, dizziness, and pain at the site of injection. Rarely, allergic reactions may occur in which case the doctor should be consulted.

Other information: Administered on alternate days initially and then every 3 months thereafter. Treatment will usually be for life.

HYOSCINE

Brand name: Buscopan, Scopoderm TTS

Type of drug: Anti-cholinergic

Uses: To treat irritable bowel spasms and motion sickness. Also an ingredient in eye drops.

How it works: Reduces nerve impulses reaching the gut wall and so reduces painful gut contractions. It blocks many other nerves in the body leading to reduced production of saliva and widening of the pupil of the eye.

Availability: Some preparations containing hyoscine are available over-the-counter.

Possible adverse effects: Drowsiness, dry mouth, visual problems, difficulty in passing urine and constipation.

Other information: Can cause constipation, so the intake of fluid should be kept high whilst taking this medication.

CAUTION

Children: Children over 3 years of age may use the tablet form of this medicine for travel sickness, and children over 10 years of age may use the patch. Children over 6 years of age may use this for bowel problems.

Alcohol: Should only be consumed in moderation whilst taking hyoscine because it may increase the severity of drowsiness associated with the medicine.

Driving and operating machinery: As this drug can cause drowsiness, dizziness, visual problems and muscle wasting, patients receiving this medication should not drive or perform skilled tasks until they are certain they are not experiencing these, or any other side effects.

IBUPROFEN

Brand name: Brufen, Ibugel, Nurofen

Type of drug: Non-steroidal anti-inflammatory

Uses: Treatment of symptoms of conditions such as rheumatoid and osteoarthritis, back pain and gout. Also effective for headaches, menstrual pain, soft tissue injuries, and backache.

How it works: Inhibits the actions of an enzyme called cyclo-oxygenase, which produces chemical messengers that initiate and continue the inflammatory process.

Possible adverse effects: Heartburn and indigestion which can be minimised by taking the medicine with food or milk. Gastrointestinal ulceration and/or bleeding may occur, so if you suffer severe stomach pain, or there is blood in your stools then seek urgent medical advice. Nausea, vomiting, diarrhoea, abdominal pain, and fluid retention have also been reported.

Availability: As an ingredient in many over-the-counter preparations.

Other information: Asthmatics should not take this medication unless discussed with a doctor or pharmacist. If wheezing or difficulty breathing does occur patients should stop taking the medication and see their doctor. Those allergic to aspirin may also be allergic to ibuprofen and should not take it without advice from the doctor or pharmacist. This medicine can be used to treat children.

IDARUBICIN

Brand name: Zavedos

Type of drug: Anthracycline

Uses: Treatment of some types of leukaemia and breast cancer.

How it works: Inserts itself into the strands of DNA of the cancer, and then permanently damages the DNA, preventing the cancer cell from multiplying. This eventually causes the death of the cancer cells.

Possible adverse effects: Nausea, vomiting, diarrhoea, abdominal pain, a burning sensation of the hands and feet (which usually allays within 4 weeks), hair loss and loss of appetite are common side effects. Idarubicin can also cause damage to the heart and reduces the production of blood cells and suppresses the immune system increasing the risk of infection. Any sign of infection, such as a sore throat, unexplained bleeding or bruising, high temperature or generally feeling unwell should be reported to the doctor immediately. The urine may be stained red.

Other information: This medicine is only given in hospital under the supervision of a doctor experienced in treating cancer. Regular blood tests are required to assess the effects. Additional medicines to combat side effects may be prescribed. Children may be treated using this medicine.

CAUTION

Pregnancy: A barrier method of contraception is recommended during treatment to prevent pregnancy although fertility is often reduced by chemotherapy.

Alcohol: Should be avoided or consumed in moderation.

Driving and operating machinery: Patients receiving this medication should not drive or perform skilled tasks until they are certain they are not experiencing any side effects.

IDOXURIDINE

Brand name: Herpid, Iduridin

Type of drug: Antiviral

Uses: Treatment of herpes infections of the skin, such as cold sores.

How it works: Stops the virus from multiplying, allowing the immune system to deal with the infection more easily.

Availability: POM

Possible adverse effects: Irritation and a stinging sensation when applied to the skin. This will usually lessen of its own accord.

Other information: Do not mix with any other solutions or medication. Avoid sharing towels and flannels with others. Always wash hands before and after application. If the solution gets into the eye, it should be washed out thoroughly with cold tap water.

CAUTION

Children: It may be used in children over the age of 12 years old.

IMIPRAMINE

Brand name: Tofranil

Type of drug: Tricyclic anti-depressant

Uses: Treatment of depression and of children who have a bed-wetting problem.

How it works: Inhibits the re-uptake of brain chemicals, which results in a heightening of mood. It also encourages appetite and enables users to lead a more normal daily life. Sedative effect is also useful for people who find difficulty in sleeping at nights.

Availability: POM

Possible adverse effects: Sweating, dry mouth, headache, tremor, hot flushes, blurred vision, anxiety, insomnia, confusion, drowsiness and nausea, vomiting, anorexia, or weight gain and constipation. These usually lessen with continued use. Take with milk or food if it upsets the stomach.

Other information: The full effects may not be experienced for up to 4 weeks after starting treatment. Should not be discontinued unless advised by a doctor, and then it will gradually be reduced. Should be taken with milk or food if it appears to upset the stomach. It can have a 'hangover' effect – a feeling of tiredness, disorientation and sedation when waking in the morning, so it is advisable to take this drug prior to going to sleep at night in order to avoid daytime sleepiness.

CAUTION

Children: This medicine can be used in children over 6 years of age.

Alcohol: Should not be consumed since it may stop imipramine from working as effectively and worsen side effects.

Driving and operating machinery: As this drug can cause dizziness, drowsiness and blurred vision, patients receiving this medication should not drive or perform skilled tasks until they are certain they are not experiencing these or any other side effects.

INDAPAMIDE

Brand name: Natrilix

Type of drug: Thiazide diuretic

Uses: Treatment of high blood pressure.

How it works: Acts on the kidneys to increase the amount of urine passed, which in turn reduces excess fluid in the body. Fluid in the wrong places can cause high blood pressure, swollen ankles and breathlessness. In addition to water, salts are also lost from the body into the urine.

Availability: POM

Possible adverse effects: Headache, dizziness, fatigue, cramps, weight loss, indigestion, constipation and vertigo, particularly on standing up. Occasionally skin rashes may appear – these should be reported to your doctor.

Other information: Best taken in the morning. The modified release tablets should not be crushed or chewed but swallowed whole.

CAUTION

Alcohol: Should only be consumed in moderation since it may cause a greater than anticipated drop in blood pressure.

INDOMETACIN

(Formerly known as: indomethacin)

Brand name: Indocid

Type of drug: Non-steroidal anti-inflammatory

Uses: Treatment of conditions such as rheumatoid arthritis, osteoarthritis, ankylosing spondylitis and gout. It can also be used to close the hole in the heart, called the ductus ateriosus, sometimes found in premature babies.

How it works: Inhibits the actions of an enzyme called cyclo-oxygenase which produces chemical messengers that start and continue the inflammatory process.

Availability: POM

Possible adverse effects: When taken by mouth, headache, dizziness, and indigestion abdominal pain, confusion, tinnitus, ulcers and diarrhoea may be experienced. Gastrointestinal ulceration and/or bleeding may also occur. If you suffer severe stomach pain or there is blood in your stools then seek urgent medical advice.

Other information: Do not take aspirin or similar medication without consulting a doctor first. Do not take more than the recommended dose as this may cause kidney damage and increase the risk of bleeding. This medicine should be taken with or after meals to minimise problems associated with the stomach. Patients with asthma should consult a doctor or pharmacist before usage because it may precipitate an asthma attack. Patients who are allergic to aspirin may also be allergic to indometacin and should not take it without consulting the doctor or pharmacist.

CAUTION

Driving and operating machinery: As this drug can cause dizziness, drowsiness, and confusion, patients receiving this medication should not drive or perform skilled tasks until they are certain they are not experiencing these or any other side effects.

INSULIN

Brand name: Humalog, Human Actrapid, Human Insulatard, Human Mixtard, Human Monotard, Human Ultratard, Humulin, Pork Insulatard, Pork Mixtard, among others.

Type of drug: Anti-diabetic

Uses: Treatment of insulin-dependent diabetes mellitus.

How it works: Provides the body with the hormone insulin, which is made by the pancreas and lacking in diabetics. Insulin is crucial for the body to be able to use the available sugars to create energy.

Availability: POM

Possible adverse effects: Most of the adverse effects are associated with a low blood sugar level (hypoglycaemia), and include light-headedness, confusion, sweating and dizziness. These can usually be prevented by a correction to the dose. Serious allergic reactions are rare. As insulin needs to be injected into the body, local irritation at the site of injection can occur. This is will usually lessen with time, and rotation of the sites where insulin is injected.

Other information: Should be stored in the fridge. An overdose should be reported to a doctor immediately. People prescribed insulin should carry a warning card or bracelet. Other medication should not be taken without consulting a doctor or pharmacist. There are three main sources of insulin: pigs – porcine; cows – bovine; and human insulin. The latter is the main type used as it less likely to cause allergic reactions. Insulins can be short-, intermediate- and long-acting, and there are also mixtures.

Short-acting insulin works over the course of a few hours and is usually used to control the surge in glucose levels in the blood that occurs after meals. Long-acting insulins are used to provide cover throughout the day, with the requirement that meals are eaten regularly.

Blood or urine tests are carried out to assess the blood sugar control. For more information about insulin therapy or diabetes in general a doctor, pharmacist or diabetic nurse should be consulted. This medicine is used in children.

CAUTION

Pregnancy: Insulin can be used to control diabetes during pregnancy and to control diabetes brought on by pregnancy.

Alcohol: Only be used in strict moderation as it will increase the risk of having hypoglycaemic attacks.

Driving and operating machinery: The DVLA has strict requirements for diabetics about driving, and the latest information should be consulted.

INTERFERON

Brand name: Betaferon, Immukin, Intron-A, Roferon-A, Viraferon, Wellferon

Type of drug: Anti-viral and anticancer

Uses: There are three types of Interferon. Interferon Alpha is used to treat leukaemia, some cancers and active hepatitis. Interferon Beta is used for multiple sclerosis. Interferon Gamma is used with antibiotics for people with granulomatous disease.

How it works: Interferons are a natural part of the body's armoury in fighting infectious diseases, and can activate or repress the body's immune system; they have antiviral properties and can cause regression of some cancers.

Availability: POM

Possible adverse effects: Headaches, nausea, vomiting, rashes, joint and muscle pain, high temperature, depression, hair loss, chills, pain where injection takes place and fatigue. Taking at night and with paracetamol may lessen these effects.

Other information: The initial treatment is at a hospital under the supervision of an experienced doctor. Regular blood tests are required initially to assess the effects. Patients can be taught to administer to themselves.

CAUTION

Pregnancy: Should be avoided while taking this medicine so appropriate contraception methods should be used.

Driving and operating machinery: As this drug can cause dizziness and drowsiness, patients receiving this medication should not drive or perform skilled tasks until they are certain they are not experiencing these, or any other side effects.

IPRATROPIUM BROMIDE

Brand name: Atrovent, Rinatec

Type of drug: Antimuscarinic bronchodilator

Uses: Treatment of lung diseases such as asthma and chronic bronchitis.

How it works: Acts on the nerves in the airways of the lungs and makes them widen, thus easing breathing.

Availability: POM

Possible adverse effects: Headache, nausea, and a dry mouth. May cause a cough after it has been used, but if wheezing or breathlessness worsens, a doctor should be consulted and the medicine not used.

Other information: Patients are taught the correct procedure to use the inhaler, which may be used with a 'spacer' device.

CAUTION

Children: Children over 6 years old may be treated with inhalers.

ISOCARBOXAZID

Brand name: Only available as a generic medicine

Type of drug: Monoamine-oxidase inhibitor

Uses: Treatment of depression.

How it works: Stops the body breaking down chemicals in the brain which lift mood, while its more general stimulant effect is also useful.

Availability: POM

Possible adverse effects: Can react with certain types of food such as alcohol, cheese and dairy products, pickled herring, broad beans, Bovril, Oxo and Marmite to cause dangerously high blood pressure. These foods should therefore be avoided. If frequent headaches occur patients should stop taking and seek medical advice. Hypotension (low blood pressure) leading to feelings of dizziness, dry mouth, fluid retention, nausea, vomiting, blurred vision, insomnia, drowsiness and fatigue.

Other information: Do not eat any food that you do not believe to be fresh while on this medication. Any foodstuff which has been hung, cured, smoked or otherwise preserved should be avoided. A pharmacist should be consulted before taking any over-the-counter remedies, especially for coughs and colds.

CAUTION

Alcohol: Must not be consumed.

Driving and operating machinery: As this drug can cause drowsiness, dizziness, and blurred vision, patients receiving this medication should not drive or perform skilled tasks until they are certain they are not experiencing these side effects.

ISONIAZID

Brand name: Only available as a generic medicine

Type of drug: Antibiotic

Uses: Treatment and prevention of tuberculosis.

How it works: Stops production of chemicals essential to the survival of the organism, resulting in its death. Combined with other drugs it also destroys the organisms that cause TB.

Availability: POM

Possible adverse effects: Problems are uncommon. Fever, nausea, vomiting, and stomach upset can occur. A tingling in the hands and feet, constipation, dry mouth, difficulty starting to urinate, and vertigo may occur due to irritation of the nerves. Pyridoxine, a form of vitamin B, is commonly given to prevent this side effect.

Other information: Therapy is often necessary for 4 to 6 months and can continue for 2 years. Patients should keep taking the medicine as prescribed until told they can stop by a doctor. It should be taken 30 minutes to 1 hour before food. Isoniazid is also suitable for the treatment of children.

CAUTION

Alcohol: Should be consumed in strict moderation.

ISOSORBIDE DINITRATE/MONONITRATE

Brand name: Isoket, Imdur, Ismo

Type of drug: Nitrate

Uses: Treatment of angina and heart failure.

How it works: Dilates the vessels of the heart allowing more blood to flow through. This supplies more oxygen to the heart muscle and stops pain associated with an angina attack. These drugs also dilate the main veins leading back to the heart, reducing the pressure of the blood entering the heart, and allows it to work more efficiently.

Availability: Some preparations containing nitrates are available without prescription.

Possible adverse effects: Throbbing headache (which usually goes away after a couple of days), dizziness and flushing are relatively common. Occasionally a sudden drop in blood pressure occurs. At the start of treatment nausea and vomiting may occur but this usually eases with continued therapy.

Other information: The effectiveness of this medicine can lessen with time due to tolerance. Blood pressure should also be monitored. The tablets should be swallowed whole and not chewed. This medicine should be taken until advised otherwise by a doctor.

CAUTION

Alcohol: Should be consumed in moderation because the combination may increase the severity of any falls in blood pressure caused by the medicine.

Driving and operating machinery: As this drug can cause dizziness, patients receiving this medication should not drive or perform skilled tasks until they are certain they are not experiencing this or any other side effects.

ISOTRETINOIN

Brand name: Isotrex, Roaccutane

Type of drug: Retinoid

Uses: Treatment of severe acne that has not responded to other therapy.

How it works: Slows down the reproduction of skin cells.

Availability: POM

Possible adverse effects: When applied as a gel it can cause stinging, burning, irritation, and redness or peeling of the skin but this often settles with time. When taken orally it can cause dryness of the eyes, lips, skin, and nose, redness of the skin, skin rash, sweating, thinning of the hair, joint pain and mood changes.

If diarrhoea develops while on treatment the doctor should be informed immediately. May cause visual problems at night so extra care is required when driving or working in low lighting. The skin may also become more sensitive to sunlight, and the use of sunlamps should be avoided. If exposed to the sun, legs and arms should be covered, a total sun block should be worn, as well as a wide brimmed hat and sunglasses.

Other information: A specialist dermatologist in a hospital will start the oral form of this medicine. A course of treatment usually lasts several months when applied to the skin. If taking this medication orally the course will last at least sixteen weeks. It should be taken with or after meals to minimise stomach upsets. Avoid foods rich in vitamin A such as liver.

CAUTION

Pregnancy and breastfeeding: This drug must not be taken while pregnant, planning to become pregnant or breastfeeding because of the adverse effects it may have on the child. Women will have a pregnancy test prior to starting treatment to ensure that they are not pregnant, and must use effective means of contraception while using this medicine, and for at least one month afterwards.

Alcohol: Consumed in strict moderation.

Driving and operating machinery: As this drug can cause visual problems, patients receiving this medication should not drive or perform skilled tasks until they are certain they are not experiencing these, or any other side effects.

ISPAGHULA HUSK

Brand name: Fybogel

Type of drug: Laxative

Uses: Treatment of constipation particularly in patients with colostomy, haemorrhoids, ileostomy, diverticular disease and irritable bowel syndrome.

How it works: Absorbs water, which causes the drug to swell in size and in turn increases the bulk of the stool. For diarrhoea this is the excess fluid that causes the stools to be runny. In constipation this makes the stool larger and softer and easier to pass. In diarrhoea, some of the excess fluid is absorbed making the stool more firm.

Availability: OTC

Possible adverse effects: Flatulence and abdominal swelling.

Other information: Plenty of fluid should be taken. Do not take just before bedtime. This medicine is safe to use in pregnancy and breast-feeding.

CAUTION

Children: It may be used by children of 6 years of age and above.

ISRADIPINE
Brand name: Prescal
Type of drug: Calcium channel blocker
Uses: Treatment of high blood pressure.
How it works: Causes widening of the veins and arteries, which makes it easier for the heart to push blood around the body. This has the effect of reducing the blood pressure and enables the heart to work more efficiently.
Availability: POM
Possible adverse effects: Dizziness, flushing and headache.
Other information: Any episodes of palpitations or irregular heartbeat should be reported. Should be taken as directed unless told to stop by the doctor and must not be taken with grapefruit juice.

ITRACONAZOLE
Brand name: Sporanox
Type of drug: Antifungal
Uses: Treatment and prevention of severe fungal infections.
How it works: Damages the outer, protective layer of the fungus, which leads to its death.
Availability: POM
Possible adverse effects: Indigestion, nausea, constipation and abdominal pain are the most commonly reported side effects. Headache, menstrual irregularities in women and dizziness may also occur. Liver problems can sometimes arise, so any sign of jaundice, unusually dark urine or nausea should be reported.
Other information: The capsules should be taken with food to maximise absorption and therefore effectiveness. The liquid should be taken half an hour before meals or on an empty stomach. Any antacids or indigestion remedies should be taken two hours after, because it needs stomach acid to be effective. The capsules should be swallowed whole, not chewed or crushed. This medicine should be taken regularly until told to stop by a doctor.
CAUTION
Children: This medicine is only licensed for children over 12 years of age. However in certain circumstances under the supervision of a hospital specialist, it may be used for younger children.

KETOCONAZOLE

Brand name: Nizoral

Type of drug: Antifungal

Uses: Treatment of fungal infection of the skin and scalp irritation. It is also used to treat infections inside the body.

How it works: Treats infections caused by a fungus by damaging the outer protective layer of the fungus.

Availability: Preparations containing ketoconazole for use on the scalp, and for fungal infection of the skin are available over-the-counter.

Possible adverse effects: When applied to the skin or scalp, irritation, redness, and inflammation may occur. Patients with grey or dyed hair may notice a change in hair colour. When taken by mouth, indigestion, nausea, vomiting, diarrhoea, abdominal pain, changes in the menstrual cycle, dizziness, and a preference for darkened rooms are the most commonly reported adverse effects. Taking the medicine with meals should reduce the severity of stomach upsets. The tablets may also cause damage to the liver over a period of time and pale stools, darkened urine, fever, or jaundice – a yellowing of the skin and whites of the eye – and itching of the skin should be reported to the doctor immediately as they may indicate liver problems.

Other information: Antacids or indigestion remedies should not be taken for at least two hours after taking ketoconazole tablets. If the cream of shampoo gets into the eyes they should be thoroughly washed out with cold tap water.

CAUTION

Children: Children over 1 year of age may be given this medicine.

Pregnancy and breastfeeding: Treatments for the scalp, and skin may be used during pregnancy, but not the oral medication.

Alcohol: Should not be consumed whilst taking ketoconazole because there is a risk of an unpleasant reaction occurring, with flushing, fluid retention and swelling of the ankles, nausea, vomiting and headache.

KETOPROFEN

Brand name: Oruvail

Type of drug: Analgesic, non-steroidal anti-inflammatory

Uses: To relieve the symptoms of rheumatoid arthritis, osteoarthritis, gout and ankylosing spondylitis. This medication is also used to relieve period pain.

How it works: Ketoprofen works by inhibiting the actions of an enzyme called cyclo-oxygenase. This enzyme produces chemical messengers that start and continue the inflammatory process.

Availability: Preparations for application to the skin are available over-the- counter.

Possible adverse effects: Nausea, vomiting, indigestion, abdominal pain, diarrhoea, constipation, dizziness, drowsiness, confusion, mood changes, and insomnia may occur whilst using this medicine. Gastrointestinal ulceration and/or bleeding may occur, so if you suffer severe stomach pain or there is blood in your stools then seek urgent medical advice.

Other information: Patients who have asthma should not take this medication unless prescribed by a doctor as it can make their condition worse. If wheezing or difficulty breathing does occur patients should stop taking the medication and see their doctor. Patients allergic to aspirin may also be allergic to ketoprofen and should not take it without advice from the doctor or pharmacist.

CAUTION

Pregnancy: This drug may be taken during pregnancy but should be stopped at least one week before the expected delivery date

KETOROLAC TROMETAMOL
Brand name: Acular
Type of drug: Non-steroidal anti-inflammatory
Uses: To prevent and reduce pain and inflammation following surgery, including eye surgery.
How it works: Ketorolac works by inhibiting the actions of an enzyme called cyclo-oxygenase. This enzyme produces chemical messengers that start and continue the inflammatory process.
Availability: POM
Possible adverse effects: Stinging, and burning sensations when eye drops are used, although this diminishes with time. Occasionally blurring of vision may occur. When taken orally, there may be dry mouth,

flushing, rapid heart rate and muscle pains. Gastrointestinal ulceration and/or bleeding may also occur, so if you suffer severe stomach pain, or there is blood in your stools, then seek urgent medical advice.

Other information: Patients allergic to aspirin may also be allergic to ketorolac and should not take it without advice from the doctor or pharmacist. Patients should not wear soft contact lenses.

CAUTION

Driving and operating machinery: It can cause stinging of the eye and blurred vision, patients should not drive or perform skilled tasks until they are certain they are not experiencing these side effects.

KETOTIFEN

Brand name: Zaditen

Type of drug: Antihistamine

Uses: The prevention of asthma and symptoms of hay fever.

How it works: Blocks the action of histamine – a chemical released by the body in response allergies. Histamine causes the majority of symptoms associated with allergies such as runny nose, itchy eyes and sneezing.

Availability: POM

Possible adverse effects: When taken orally, drowsiness, dry mouth, weight gain and dizziness have been reported within the first few days of treatment but tend to lessen with time. The eye drops may cause a stinging or burning sensation in the eye, which wears off after a short time.

Other information: Tablets should be taken with food. Should not be discontinued unless advised by a doctor but any side effects should be reported.

CAUTION

Children: Children over 2 years of age can take this medicine.

Alcohol: Should only be consumed in moderation because of the increased drowsiness that the combination of alcohol and the drug may give rise to.

Driving and operating machinery: As this drug can cause drowsiness, blurred vision and dizziness, patients should not drive or perform skilled tasks until they are certain they are not experiencing these side effects.

LABETALOL

Brand name: Trandate

Type of drug: Beta-blocker

Uses: The treatment of high blood pressure.

How it works: Reduces blood pressure by allowing the blood vessels of the body and heart muscle to relax. This increases the diameter and therefore decreases the blood pressure. This drug also slows the heart.

Availability: POM

Possible adverse effects: Dizziness (particularly on standing up), headache, tiredness, mood changes, lethargy, nasal congestion and sweating. Scalp tingling may be experienced during the early days of therapy. If there is coldness of the hands and feet, pale stools, darkened urine, fever, yellowing of the skin and whites of the eye and itching of the skin seek medical advice.

Other information: Asthmatics may notice an increase in the severity of asthma or wheezing and breathlessness whilst taking this medicine. If this occurs consult a doctor as soon as possible.

CAUTION

Pregnancy and breastfeeding: Should not be used while breastfeeding but is safe in pregnancy and used to treat pregnancy-induced hypertension

Alcohol: Should only be consumed in moderation because the combination may cause a greater than expected drop in blood pressure.

Driving and operating machinery: As this drug can cause dizziness and drowsiness, patients receiving this medication should not drive or perform skilled tasks until they are certain they are not experiencing these or any other side effects.

LACIDIPINE

Brand name: Motens

Type of drug: Calcium channel blocker

Uses: Treatment of high blood pressure

How it works: Relaxes the blood vessels in the circulatory system allowing blood to flow more easily, and thereby reducing blood pressure.

Availability: POM

Possible adverse effects: Headache, flushing, fluid retention and dizziness. Report any chest pain or difficulty breathing to the doctor immediately.

Other information: It may take at least four weeks for the required effect to become noticeable. Grapefruit juice should be avoided.

CAUTION

Driving and operating machinery: As this drug can cause dizziness, patients receiving this medication should not drive or perform skilled tasks until they are certain they are not experiencing this or any other side effects.

LACTULOSE

Brand name: Duphalac

Type of drug: Laxative

Uses: The treatment of constipation.

How it works: Softens the faeces by increasing the amount of water in the bowel and stool making stools softer. This allows the gut to resume normal motions.

Availability: OTC

Possible adverse effects: Stomach cramps and wind may occur during the early days of treatment but usually diminish with time. If diarrhoea occurs, reduce or stop medicine.

Other information: Available as a liquid, the medicine may be taken for a few days before the effect becomes noticeable.

LAMIVUDINE

Brand name: Epivir, Zeffix

Type of drug: Antiviral

Uses: Treatment of HIV and Hepatitis B infection.

How it works: To the virus, lamivudine appears as a chemical it needs to manufacture its DNA, though it has been modified so that once it is incorporated, the virus is unable to multiply.

Availability: POM

Possible adverse effects: Headache, tiredness, dizziness, sleeplessness, fever, chills, bone and muscle pain, throat and tonsil discomfort, nausea, diarrhoea and vomiting. When being used for treatment of HIV, rashes and hair loss are also reported. Occasionally it can cause liver problems.

Other information: This medicine is only administered in hospital under the supervision of a doctor experienced in treating infectious diseases. Regular blood tests are required to check the progress of the diseases being treated, and the function of the liver. It is important to take this drug as prescribed.

CAUTION

Children: May be used in children over 3 months old for treatment of HIV.

Driving and operating machinery: As this drug can cause dizziness and drowsiness, patients should not drive or perform skilled tasks until they are certain they are not experiencing these or any other side effects.

LAMOTRIGINE

Brand name: Lamictal

Type of drug: Antiepileptic

Uses: Treatment of epilepsy.

How it works: An epileptic fit (or seizure) occurs when the nerves in the brain become overactive. Lamotrigine acts to stop this overactivity and so reduces the chances of a seizure.

Availability: POM

Possible adverse effects: Rashes are the most commonly reported, especially within the first 8 weeks of treatment. This may be associated with a fever and facial swelling. If any of these symptoms appear, seek medical advice as soon as possible. Headache, tiredness, nausea, dizziness, irritability, confusion, tremor, blurred vision, drowsiness and liver problems may also occur. Lamotrigine may be used alone or with other drugs to control epilepsy. Blood tests are taken to assess the effect of the drug on the liver.

CAUTION

Children: This medicine may be used in children over 2 years of age.

Driving and operating machinery: As this drug can cause dizziness and drowsiness, patients receiving this medication should not drive or perform skilled tasks until they are certain they are not experiencing these side effects. The DVLA has specific requirements for patients suffering from epilepsy who wish to drive. The latest information from the DVLA should be consulted before attempting to drive.

LANSOPRAZOLE

Brand name: Zoton

Type of drug: Proton pump inhibitor

Uses: Treating ulcers of the stomach and gut, and for acid reflux which causes heartburn.

How it works: Reduces the production of stomach acid, allowing the stomach and intestines to recover and heal. When used for reflux disease it stops production of excess acid that can travel back up the oesophagus or gullet, which becomes irritated and inflamed because it has no protection against the stomach acid.

Availability: POM

Possible adverse effects: Headache, dizziness, fatigue, diarrhoea, constipation, abdominal pain, nausea, vomiting, flatulence, abdominal pain and dry mouth or throat.

Other information: Should be taken before meals. Other indigestion remedies and antacids must be taken at least one hour after lansoprazole to maximise effectiveness.

CAUTION

Driving and operating machinery: As this drug can cause dizziness, patients receiving this medication should not drive or perform skilled tasks until they are certain they are not experiencing these, or any other side effects.

LATANOPROST

Brand name: Xalatan

Type of drug: Prostglandin analogue

Uses: Treatment of glaucoma.

How it works: Mimics natural chemicals produced by the body called prostglandins. They increase the loss of the fluid from within the eye and thus reduce the pressure inside the eyeball.

Availability: POM

Possible adverse effects: Changes in colour of the iris of the eye, changes to the eye lashes such as length and thickness, irritation, inflammation of the eyelids and eye pain.

Other information: Should be stored in the fridge when not in use. If more than one type of eye drop is being used, at least five minutes should pass between putting each type of drop in. Patients who wear soft contact lenses should leave at least 15 minutes before putting the lenses in.

Driving and operating machinery: As this drug can cause blurring in vision, patients receiving this medication should not drive or perform skilled tasks until they are certain they are not experiencing these or any other side effects.

LERCANIDIPINE
Brand name: Zanidip
Type of drug: Calcium channel blocker
Uses: Treatment of mild to moderately high blood pressure.
How it works: Relaxes the blood vessels in the circulatory system allowing blood to flow more easily, and therefore reducing blood pressure.
Availability: POM
Possible adverse effects: Headache, dizziness, ankle swelling, facial flushing and headache.
Other information: May take at least two weeks before the required effect is noticed. Avoid grapefruit juice with this medicine, as this will reduce the absorption and therefore its effectiveness.
CAUTION
Alcohol: Should not be consumed whilst taking this medicine because the combination of alcohol and the drug may cause a greater than intended fall in blood pressure.
Driving and operating machinery: As this drug can cause dizziness, patients receiving this medication should not drive or perform skilled tasks until they are certain they are not experiencing these or any other side effects.

LEUPRORELIN
Brand name: Prostap
Type of drug: Gonadorelin analogue
Uses: Treating prostate cancer and endometriosis.
How it works: Goserelin suppresses the release of hormones which stimulate the release of testosterone and oestrogen. In women this leads to a thinning of the endometrium, which stops endometriosis from worsening. In men it leads to a suppression of testosterone production and subsequent decrease in size of the prostate. It also prevents growth of prostate cancers that are dependent on hormones for survival.

Availability: POM

Possible adverse effects: Fluid retention, fatigue, muscle weakness, diarrhoea, nausea, vomiting, weight change, fevers and chills, hot flushes, joint and muscle pain, dizziness, insomnia, dizziness and irritation where the medicine was injected. Men may also expect impotence and a loss of sex drive. Women may experience changes in their menstrual cycle, mood changes, vaginal dryness, changes in breast size, and breast tenderness. This treatment can lead to osteoporosis in both sexes. It is administered by a 'depot injection', which means one injection contains enough drug to last either one or three months. Specialist doctors will supervise treatment with this drug in cancer patients.

CAUTION

Pregnancy: Effective non-hormonal contraceptive measures, such as a condom, should be used.

Driving and operating machinery: As this drug can cause dizziness and drowsiness, patients receiving this medication should not drive or perform skilled tasks until they are certain they are not experiencing these, or any other side effects.

LEVETIRACETAM

Brand name: Keppra

Type of drug: Antiepileptic

Uses: Treatment of partial epileptic seizures.

How it works: An epileptic fit (or seizure) occurs when the nerves in the brain become overactive. Levetiracetam acts to stop this overactivity, and so reduces the chances of seizure.

Availability: POM

Possible adverse effects: Drowsiness, general weakness, lethargy and dizziness are the most common. Mood changes, headache, tremors, muscle rigidity, weight loss, double vision and rash may also occur.

Other information: Should not be discontinued unless advised by a doctor, and then it will gradually be reduced.

CAUTION

Children: May not be prescribed for children.

Alcohol: Avoid because the effects of the combination are as yet unknown.

Driving and operating machinery: As this drug can cause dizziness and drowsiness, patients receiving this medication should not drive or perform skilled tasks until they are certain they are not experiencing these or any other side effects.

LEVOBUNOLOL
Brand name: Betagan
Type of drug: Beta-blocker
Uses: Treatment of glaucoma.
How it works: Stops the production of the aqueous humor, a fluid in the eye. This reduces the pressure inside the eye, leading to improvement of glaucoma.
Availability: POM
Possible adverse effects: Burning and stinging when applied to the eye, impaired vision and inflammation of the eyelids and conjunctivitis.
Other information: Patients should not wear soft contact lenses for at least 15 minutes after putting in the drops. Asthmatic patients should report any chest pain or breathlessness to the doctor immediately.
CAUTION
Driving and operating machinery: As this drug can cause impaired vision, patients should not drive or perform skilled tasks until they are certain they are not experiencing these or any other side effects.

LEVOCABASTINE
Brand name: Livostin
Type of drug: Antihistamine
Uses: To reduce the symptoms which occur with hay fever.
How it works: Blocks the action of histamine – a chemical released by the body in response to allergies. Histamine causes the majority of symptoms associated with allergies such as runny nose, itchy eyes and sneezing.
Availability: Over-the-counter as eye drops and a nasal spray.
Possible adverse effects: Headache, local irritation and stinging, blurred vision and breathlessness.
Other information: Patients are advised not to wear soft contact lenses whilst using levocabastine because the preservative can discolour them.

CAUTION

Children: Those over the age of 9 years old may be treated with this medicine when prescribed by a doctor. However if buying this medication over-the-counter it may not be sold for use by children who are under 12 years old.

Alcohol: Should be avoided because of an increased risk of drowsiness associated with the combination.

Driving and operating machinery: As this drug can cause drowsiness and blurred vision, patients receiving this medication should not drive or perform any skilled tasks until they are certain that they are not experiencing these or any other side effects.

LEVOFLOXACIN

Brand name: Tavanic

Type of drug: Quinolone antibiotic

Uses: Treating chest and urinary tract infections.

How it works: Acts on the DNA of the bacteria to stop them multiplying, resulting in their death.

Availability: POM

Possible adverse effects: Nausea and diarrhoea are the most common. May also increase the chances of seizure in epileptic patients.

Other information: Levofloxacin hould not be taken at the same time as indigestion remedies, milk and medicines containing iron or zinc. Should be taken at regular intervals until the prescribed course is completed.

CAUTION

Driving and operating machinery: Patients receiving this medication should not drive or perform skilled tasks until they are certain they are not experiencing any side effects.

LEVOTHYROXINE

(Formerly known as: thyroxine)

Brand name: Eltroxin

Type of drug: Thyroid hormone

Uses: Treatment of thyroid hormone deficiency.

How it works: Replaces thyroxine, a vital hormone which is usually produced by the thyroid gland.

Availability: POM

Possible adverse effects: Insomnia, diarrhoea, nervousness, restlessness, flushing, sweating, dislike of hot weather, excessive weight loss, muscular weakness, tremor and heart rhythm disturbances. Report signs of a headache or diarrhoea to the doctor.

Other information: This medicine is prescribed for children of all ages.

CAUTION

Driving and operating machinery: Patients receiving this medication should not drive or perform skilled tasks until they are certain they are not experiencing any side effects.

LIOTHYRONINE

Brand name: Tertroxin

Type of drug: Thyroid hormone

Uses: Treatment of thyroid hormone deficiency.

How it works: Replaces the hormone produced by the thyroid gland, which allows the body to function normally.

Availability: POM

Possible adverse effects: Insomnia, diarrhoea, nervousness, restlessness, flushing, sweating, dislike of raised temperatures, excessive weight loss, muscular weakness, tremor and heart rhythm disturbances. Report any sign of a headache or diarrhoea to the doctor.

CAUTION

Driving and operating machinery: Patients receiving this medication should not drive or perform skilled tasks until they are certain they are not experiencing any side effects.

LISINOPRIL

Brand name: Zestril

Type of drug: ACE inhibitor

Uses: Treating high blood pressure, heart failure and kidney problems due to diabetes.

How it works: It allows the blood vessels to relax, which enables them to increase in size. This reduces the pressure of the blood flowing through them and decreases blood pressure.

Availability: POM

Possible adverse effects: Dizziness, headache, fatigue, diarrhoea, vomiting and a dry cough. Report any signs of light-headedness or infection to the doctor.

Other information: Do not take any over-the-counter products – especially to treat a cold – without checking with your pharmacist first. Do not use salt substitutes that contain potassium. Blood tests may be carried out to monitor the kidneys and to check the level of potassium in the blood.

CAUTION

Alcohol: Should only be consumed in moderation whilst taking this medicine because the combination may cause a greater than expected drop in blood pressure.

Driving and operating machinery: As this drug can cause dizziness and drowsiness, patients receiving this medication should not drive or perform skilled tasks until they are certain they are not experiencing these side effects.

LITHIUM

Brand name: Camcolit, Liskonum, Priadel

Type of drug: Antipsychotic

Uses: Treatment and prevention of mania associated with manic depression. It is also occasionally used for the treatment of severe depression.

How it works: Lithium is believed to increase the production – and decrease the breakdown – of serotonin, a chemical messenger in the brain. This has the effect of lifting mood and halting depression.

Possible adverse effects: Nausea, disorientation, feeling dazed and muscle weakness may occur initially but diminish given time. Weight gain, fluid retention and a need to urinate more frequently are reported. However if weight loss, nausea, vomiting, muscle weakness, lack of co-ordination, drowsiness, blurred vision, inability to move and muscle twitching occur, the patient should not take any more tablets and seek medical advice immediately.

Other information: It may take two to three weeks for this drug to take effect. An overdose should be treated as an emergency. Long-term treatment (more than five years) can lead to kidney problems, and blood tests will be carried out to monitor blood lithium levels and the kidneys. It will only be started under the supervision of a specialist. It is important to drink lots of fluid. Patients are often given a warning card for them to give to anybody who treats them. This enables appropriate treatments to be selected so as not to interfere with the lithium. Patients should keep this card on them at all times.

CAUTION

Alcohol: Avoid because it may cause dehydration and lead to levels of lithium in the blood rising too high.

LODOXAMINE

Brand name: Alomide

Type of drug: Anti-inflammatory eye drops

Uses: Treating allergic reactions involving the eye.

How it works: Lowers the production of histamine – a chemical released by the body in response to allergies. Histamine causes the majority of symptoms such as runny nose, itchy eyes and sneezing.

Availability: POM

Possible adverse effects: A burning or stinging sensation once the drops are put into the eye, blurred vision, itchy eyes, crusting around the eye, and tear formation.

Other information: Patients should not wear soft contact lenses whilst receiving treatment with lodoxamine the preservatives in the eye drops can damage and discolour the lenses.

CAUTIONS

Children: May be prescribed for children over 4 years of age

Driving and operating machinery: Patients receiving this medication should not drive or perform skilled tasks until they are certain they are not experiencing any side effects.

LOFEPRAMINE

Brand name: Gamanil

Type of drug: Tricyclic anti-depressant

Uses: The long-term treatment of depression.

How it works: Inhibits the re-uptake of brain chemicals, which results in a heightening of mood. It also encourages appetite and enables patients to lead a more balanced daily life.

Availability: POM

Possible adverse effects: Dizziness, sleep disturbances, agitation, confusion, headache, dry mouth, constipation, problems with vision, nausea, vomiting, sweating and flushing.

Other information: This drug should not be discontinued unless advised by a doctor, and then it will gradually be reduced. Smoking while taking this drug may reduce its beneficial effects.

CAUTION

Alcohol: Should not be consumed whilst taking this medicine

Driving and operating machinery: As this drug can cause dizziness and drowsiness, patients should not drive or perform skilled tasks until they are certain they are not experiencing these or any other side effects.

LOFEXIDINE

Brand name: BritLofex

Type of drug: Drug used for opioid dependence

Uses: Management of symptoms drug-dependent people experience when withdrawing from heroin or other opium-based drugs.

How it works: Acts on the central nervous system to produce a relaxant effect without the corresponding fall in blood pressure. This relieves some of the symptoms of withdrawing from opiates.

Possible adverse effects: Drowsiness, dry mouth, throat and nose and a slow pulse.

Other information: Should not be discontinued unless advised by a doctor, and then it will gradually be reduced.

CAUTION

Alcohol: Should be avoided because of an increased risk of drowsiness which is associated with the combination.

Driving and operating machinery: As this drug can cause drowsiness, patients should not drive or perform skilled tasks until they are certain they are not experiencing this or any other side effects.

LOPERAMIDE

Brand name: Imodium

Type of drug: Antimotility drug

Uses: Treating diarrhoea.

How it works: Acts on the muscles of the intestinal wall, slowing down the movement of the gut.

Availability: OTC

Possible adverse effects: Constipation and dizziness.

Other information: If diarrhoea continues for more than 48 hours despite taking this medication, seek medical advice. Should not be used by people who have existing bowel problems such as ulcerative colitis.

CAUTION

Children: Those over 4 years of age may be treated with this medicine when prescribed by a doctor.

Driving and operating machinery: As this drug can cause dizziness, patients should not drive or perform skilled tasks until they are certain they are not experiencing this or any other side effects.

LORATADINE

Brand name: Clarityn

Type of drug: Antihistamine

Uses: Treatment of hay fever and other allergic conditions such as recurrent urticaria (itching).

How it works: Blocks the action of histamine – a chemical released by the body in response to allergies. Histamine causes the majority of symptoms associated with allergies such runny nose, itchy eyes and sneezing.

Availability: As an ingredient in over-the-counter preparations.

Possible adverse effects: Headache, nausea, tiredness.

CAUTION

Children: Those over 2 years of age may be treated with this medicine if prescribed by a doctor.

Driving and operating machinery: Although described as 'non-drowsy' this medicine may still cause drowsiness in a minority of patients. Do not drive or perform skilled tasks until you are certain that you are not experiencing this or any other side effects.

LORAZEPAM

Brand name: Ativan

Type of drug: Benzodiazepine

Uses: Treatment of long-term anxiety and as a pre-medication for general surgical and dental procedures. It is also used to treat epilepsy.

How it works: Anxiety is believed to be caused by an increase in the transmission of signals through nerves in particular parts of the brain. Lorazepam acts on these nerves to stop the signals going any farther. This has the effect of relieving anxiety and encouraging sleep. It works the same way for epilepsy, because an epileptic fit occurs when signals are sent through the brain in bursts.

Availability: POM

Possible adverse effects: Drowsiness, dizziness, muscle weakness and problems with movement. Mood changes, changes in appetite, confusion, reduced alertness, nausea, problems sleeping, visual problems, stomach upset, and a change in sex drive have also been reported.

Other information: Treatment generally lasts for a maximum of about 4 weeks. The effectiveness of the medicine seems to diminish after a treatment period of several weeks. Both tolerance and dependence can occur, especially with prolonged treatment. In people who have used this drug for several months or years, it should be gradually reduced before stopping.

CAUTION

Children: Those over 5 years of age can be prescribed this medicine as part of the pre-medication before an operation.

Alcohol: Should be avoided because of the increased risk of drowsiness associated with the combination.

Driving and operating machinery: As this drug can cause dizziness and drowsiness and muscle weakness, patients receiving this medication should not drive or perform skilled tasks until they are certain they are not experiencing these, or any other side effects.

LOSARTAN POTASSIUM

Brand name: Cozaar

Type of drug: Angiotensin 2 receptor antagonist.

Uses: Treatment of high blood pressure and kidney protection for diabetics.
How it works: Stops the action of a chemical called angiotensin II. This chemical is produced by an enzyme called ACE, and causes the blood vessels to constrict. Usage halts these effects and allows blood vessels to widen, thus reducing blood pressure.
Availability: POM
Possible adverse effects: Dizziness caused by a fall in blood pressure, especially on standing up, diarrhoea, abnormal taste in the mouth and headache.
Other information: Patient should avoid salt alternatives that use potassium, because losartan can increase the level of potassium in the blood. This medicine is sometimes used instead of ACE inhibitors for patients who cannot tolerate the cough that those drugs can produce.
CAUTION
Alcohol: Can cause a much greater drop in blood pressure than the doctor would expect and so should only be consumed in moderation.
Driving and operating machinery: As this drug can cause dizziness, patients receiving this medication should not drive or perform skilled tasks until they are certain they are not experiencing this or any other side effects.

MAPROTILINE
Brand name: Ludiomil
Type of drug: Antidepressant
Uses: Treatment of depression when there is also a need for a sedative effect.
How it works: It inhibits the re-uptake of chemical messengers in the brain, which results in a heightening of mood. It also encourages appetite and enables users to lead a more normal daily life. Its sedative effect is also useful for people who have difficulty sleeping at nights.
Availability: POM
Possible adverse effects: Dry mouth, blurred vision, drowsiness, changes in appetite, impaired memory, light-headedness – especially on standing up, muscle weakness, interrupted sleep and insomnia, weight gain, rapid beating of the heart, constipation, skin rash, and a loss of libido. These side effects usually lessen with continued use. Convulsions can also occur with this medication.

Other information: It may take between 2 and 4 weeks to feel beneficial effects of this medication.

CAUTION

Alcohol: Should be avoided because the combination may worsen the side effects, and possibly reduce the effectiveness of this medicine.

Driving and operating machinery: Patients should not drive or perform skilled tasks until they are certain they are not experiencing any side effects.

MEBEVERINE

Brand name: Colofac

Type of drug: Antispasmodic

Uses: The alleviation of episodes of painful spasms in the bowel, which often occur with conditions such as irritable bowel syndrome.

How it works: Relaxes the muscles in the bowel wall.

Availability: Preparations containing mebeverine are available OCM.

Possible adverse effects: Side effects are rare, but rashes and other allergic reactions can occur.

Other information: Take medication with plenty of water. This medicine should be taken at least 20 minutes before meals. Once the desired effect has been established, which may take a number of weeks, the amount taken may be slowly reduced. A sachet is available which is combined with ispaghula husk, and this should not be taken before bedtime.

CAUTION

Children: It may be prescribed for children over 10 years of age.

MEDROXYPROGESTERONE

Brand name: Provera, Depo-Provera

Type of drug: Sex hormone, Progestogen, contraceptive

Uses: Treatment of a range of disorders related to the menstrual cycle, including endometriosis. It is available as an injection for long-acting contraception. It is also used in conjunction with other drugs to treat some cancers affecting the breast and uterus.

How it works: This medicine mimics the action of the female sex hormone, progesterone, the lack of which is thought to be a factor in some menstrual disorders.

Availability: POM

Possible adverse effects: Side effects include mood changes, depression, dizziness, headache, growth of facial hair, hair loss, nausea, indigestion, fluid retention, weight changes, changes in breast size, and breast tenderness. Use of this drug may increase the risk of blood clots in the leg veins or lungs. If chest pain or leg pain and swelling occur that cannot be explained then seek urgent medical advice.

CAUTION

Pregnancy: A pregnancy test is usually carried out before starting this medicine to ensure the patient is not pregnant. If the patient becomes, or suspects she is pregnant, a doctor should be informed.

MEFENAMIC ACID

Brand name: Ponstan

Type of drug: Painkiller, non-steroidal anti-inflammatory

Uses: To treat period pains, rheumatoid arthritis and osteoarthritis, and joint and muscle pain.

How it works: Mefenamic acid works by stopping the action of an enzyme called cyclo-oxygenase that is involved in the inflammatory process.

Availability: POM

Possible adverse effects: The most common side effect is diarrhoea. Patients should stop taking the medicine if this occurs. Gastrointestinal ulceration and/or bleeding may occur, so if you suffer severe stomach pain, or there is blood in your stools then seek urgent medical advice. Other side effects include rash, drowsiness, nausea, vomiting, and abdominal pain. If allergic symptoms occur such as wheezing or swelling of the face patients should stop taking the medication and seek urgent medical advice.

Other information: Patients allergic to aspirin may also be allergic to mefanamic acid and should not take this medicine without advice from the doctor or pharmacist.

MEFLOQUINE

Brand name: Lariam

Type of drug: Antimalarial

Uses: To prevent or treat malaria.

How it works: The drug kills the malaria parasite before it can reproduce.

Availability: POM

Possible adverse effects: Side effects can be serious and include dizziness, headache, confusion, loss of balance, hallucinations, nausea, vomiting, diarrhoea and disturbed sleep. Any signs of depression or confusion may indicate a toxic effect. The drug should be discontinued, and medical advice sought. Side effects may last for several weeks after the final dose has been taken because mefloquine persists in the body for a long time.

Other information: Mefloquine is effective against different types of malaria, including choloroquine-resistant and other persistent strains. However malarial strains that are resistant to mefloquine are increasingly being reported, so it is important to discuss the most effective prevention of malaria before travelling abroad. This medicine is usually started 2 to 3 weeks before entering the malaria zone to allow the drug to reach effective levels in the blood before the person is exposed to the malaria parasite; also side effects may become apparent during this time. It needs to be continued for 4 weeks after returning from a malarial area and it is not generally taken for longer than 12 months in total. Because it is long-acting, it is taken once weekly, on the same day of the week. It should be taken after a meal and always taken with a large glass of water. The tablets should not be chewed or crushed, but swallowed whole.

In addition to medication, it is important to take precautions against being bitten by mosquitoes, as this is how malaria is transmitted. Other recommendations include using mosquito repellents, wearing long sleeves and trousers after dusk, avoiding swamps and marshy areas where possible and using mosquito nets around the bed.

Patients with epilepsy, depression, or other psychiatric disorders should not take mefloquine as it may worsen these conditions.

CAUTION

Children: It may be prescribed for children over 3 months of age.

Driving and operating machinery: As this drug can cause dizziness and drowsiness, patients should not drive or perform skilled tasks until they are certain they are not experiencing these or any other side effects.

MEGESTROL
Brand name: Megace
Type of drug: Sex hormone, progestogen
Uses: Treatment of some types of breast and uterine cancer.
How it works: Mimics the action of the female sex hormone, progesterone. Its main function when administered for cancers is to suppress the production of oestrogen, which the cancer needs to survive and grow; this leads to a reduction in the size of the tumour.
Availability: POM
Possible adverse effects: Weight gain, fluid retention, nausea and vomiting. Irregular bleeding form the uterus due to incomplete suppression of the menstrual cycle may also occur. Use of this drug may increase the risk of blood clots in the leg veins or lungs. If chest pain, or leg pain and swelling occur that cannot be explained then seek urgent medical advice.
Other information: This medicine needs to be taken for at least 2 months to achieve the desired effect.

MERCAPTOPURINE
Brand name: Puri-Nethol
Type of drug: Chemotherapy
Uses: The treatment of some types of leukaemia and in inflammatory bowel disease.
How it works: Mercaptopurine stops the production of chemicals that make up DNA. DNA production is required for cells to multiply, and failure to do this leads to the eventual death of the cell.
Availability: POM
Possible adverse effects: The main adverse effect of this medicine is the reduced production of blood cells. Nausea, vomiting and liver problems can also occur.
Other information: This medicine is only used in hospital under the supervision of a doctor experienced in treating leukaemia, who will

oversee and monitor treatment. Regular blood tests are required to assess the effects. Any sign of infection, such as a sore throat, unexplained bleeding or bruising, generally feeling unwell or high temperature should be reported to the doctor immediately.

CAUTION

Children: Strict guidelines are to be followed when prescribed for children.

Pregnancy: Effective contraceptive measures should be used whilst receiving treatment. If you do become pregnant report to your doctor immediately.

MESALAZINE

Brand name: Asacol, Asacol MR, Ipocol, Mesren, Pentasa

Type of drug: Aminosalicylate

Uses: Both to treat and prevent flare-ups in ulcerative colitis and Crohn's disease.

How it works: Related to aspirin, this medicine is believed to work by stopping the production of chemicals that cause inflammation in the bowel.

Availability: POM

Possible adverse effects: The main side effects are generally due to stomach upsets such as nausea, abdominal pain and diarrhoea. Allergic reactions may occur. Any rash should be reported to a doctor. Regular blood tests are usually carried out because it may cause some blood disorders. Any sign of sore throat, unexplained bleeding or bruising, a high temperature, or feeling unwell should be reported to the doctor immediately.

Other information: If in the form of tablets, patients are advised to swallow them whole, not chew or crush them. If given as a suppository or enema, it should be retained for as long as possible. Patients who are allergic to aspirin or similar medicines should inform the doctor before taking mesalazine.

METFORMIN

Brand name: Glucophage

Type of drug: Anti-diabetic

Uses: Management of non-insulin dependent diabetes, for example, in cases where the pancreas is still producing some insulin.

How it works: Acts to reduce blood sugar levels by increasing the uptake of sugars into the muscles and other tissues and decreasing the breakdown of sugar stores in the body.

Availability: POM

Possible adverse effects: Appetite loss, nausea, vomiting, diarrhoea and abdominal discomfort are not uncommon side effects when the medicine is first taken but tend to decrease with time. Another commonly reported side effect is a metallic taste in the mouth. Lactic acidosis is a rare, but serious, complication of this medicine, so any unexplained shortness of breath, difficulty in breathing or feeling very cold should be reported to the doctor immediately.

Other information: Diabetic patients are advised to follow the normal requirements for a healthy lifestyle, as well as specific recommendations given to them by their doctor, diabetic nurse or pharmacist.

CAUTION

Alcohol: Can make the patient more susceptible to lactic acidosis.

METHADONE

Brand name: Methadose

Type of drug: Painkiller, opioid analgesic

Uses: Treatment of severe pain and for treating opiate dependence such as heroin addiction.

How it works: Chemically similar to morphine. It stops the transmission of pain messages through the spinal cord to the brain. It is also used as a substitute for heroin during the detoxification and maintenance of people who were dependent on it.

Availability: POM

Possible adverse effects: Constipation, drowsiness, nausea and vomiting may all occur during the initial stages of treatment, although they usually subside as treatment progresses. Decreased blood pressure and slower breathing are more serious side effects of this drug.

Other information: The medicine should be taken in accordance with the directions of the doctor or pharmacist.

CAUTION

Alcohol: This should be avoided while taking methadone, as it will increase the likelihood of experiencing side effects, which may have serious consequences.

Driving and operating machinery: This drug can cause drowsiness, patients should not drive or perform any skilled tasks until they are certain that they are not experiencing this side effect.

METHENAMINE HIPPURATE

(Formerly known as: hexamine hippurate)

Brand name: Hiprex

Type of drug: Antibiotic

Uses: To prevent and treat recurrent infections of the urinary system.

How it works: Forms formaldehyde in the urine, that kills bacteria and other organisms that may try to live and grow in the bladder.

Availability: POM

Possible adverse effects: These occur rarely, but stomach and bowel upsets, bladder irritation and rashes have all been reported.

Other information: This drug is mainly used for patients with a catheter permanently inserted into the bladder, because they are at more risk of infection. Take at regular intervals until directed otherwise by a doctor.

CAUTION

Children: This medicine may be used in children over 6 years of age.

METHOCARBAMOL

Brand name: Robaxin, Robaxisal forte

Type of drug: Muscle relaxant

Uses: To treat muscular pain and spasms.

How it works: The way this drug works is not well understood, but it is thought to act on the spinal cord by stopping the messages that tell muscles to contract.

Availability: POM

Possible adverse effects: Drowsiness, dizziness, confusion, indigestion, and nausea.

Other information: This medicine is usually given in combination with other drugs for treatment of the condition, and is only usually used for short periods of time to provide temporary relief.

CAUTION

Alcohol: Should be avoided because of an increased risk of drowsiness which is associated with the combination.

Driving and operating machinery: As this can cause drowsiness, patients should not drive or perform skilled tasks until they are certain they are not experiencing this, or any other side effects.

METHYLCELLULOSE

Brand name: Celevac

Type of drug: Laxative

Uses: Treatment of chronic constipation, particularly that associated with diverticular disease and irritable bowel syndrome (diarrhoea may also be a feature of these conditions). Used as an additional treatment for obesity.

How it works: Absorbs water, which causes the drug to swell in size and in turn increases the bulk of the stool. In constipation this makes the stool larger and softer and easier to pass. In diarrhoea, some of the excess fluid is absorbed making the stool more firm. Its use for appetite control is also related to the swelling of the drug as it then occupies more space in the stomach, reducing the desire to eat.

Availability: This medicine is available over-the-counter.

Possible adverse effects: Side effects are only rarely reported. Of those that are abdominal discomfort and flatulence are common.

Other information: Do not take just before bedtime. In constipation, the patient is generally encouraged to drink plenty of fluids, and where possible to increase fibre and bran in the diet. The tablets should be taken with plenty of water. However, when used for diarrhoea the tablets should be taken with as little fluid as is necessary to swallow the tablets, and fluids should not be consumed for half an hour before or after taking it.

METHYLDOPA

Brand name: Aldomet

Type of drug: Antihypertensive

Uses: To treat high blood pressure.

How it works: Acts by stopping the brain sending signals that narrow the blood vessels. This reduces the force needed to push blood through the vessels and so reduces blood pressure.

Availability: POM

Possible adverse effects: Drowsiness may occur at the start of treatment. Other adverse effects include: dry mouth, mood changes, nightmares, skin rashes, weakness of the muscles, headaches, diarrhoea, liver disturbances and fluid retention can occur. This medicine may affect the production of blood cells. Any occurrence of a high temperature, unexplained bleeding and bruising, rashes, yellowing of the eyes and skin or generally feeling unwell should be reported to the doctor immediately.

Other information: This medicine is used to treat high blood pressure associated with pregnancy. It may be prescribed for children.

CAUTION

Alcohol: Should be avoided. It may lead to a greater than expected drop in blood pressure, and increased drowsiness.

Driving and operating machinery: As this drug can cause drowsiness, patients should not drive or perform skilled tasks until they are certain they are not experiencing this or any other side effects.

METHYLPHENIDATE

Brand name: Ritalin, Equasym, Concerta

Type of drug: Stimulant

Uses: This medicine is used to treat children with severe attention deficit hyperactivity disorder (ADHD).

How it works: This medicine has different effects depending upon the age of the patient. In adults methylphenidate acts as a stimulant, though in children it calms them down, and increases attention spans.

Availability: POM

Possible adverse effects: Stomach and bowel upsets, nervousness and insomnia are common at the start of treatment. Skin rashes and occasionally liver disturbances may occur.

Other information: Treatment should only be initiated by a specialist. It is used as part of a programme which includes psychological, educational and social support. Growth and development will also be monitored. Caffeine found in some fizzy drinks, tea, coffee, and other stimulants should be avoided.

CAUTION

Children: This medicine may be prescribed for children over 6 years old.

METHYSERGIDE

Brand name: Deseril

Type of drug: Antimigraine

Uses: Prevention of recurrent severe migraine, cluster and other headaches.

How it works: This medicine acts on the blood vessels in the brain, preventing their narrowing and expansion that gives rise to headaches.

Availability: POM

Possible adverse effects: Nausea, drowsiness and dizziness, vomiting, abdominal discomfort, indigestion, tingling or numbness in the hands and/or feet and weight gain. Unexplained chest pain should be reported to the doctor immediately. Retroperitoneal fibrosis is a rare but serious complication of this medicine, so unexplained back or abdominal pain or difficulty in passing urine should be reported to the doctor immediately.

Other information: Hospital specialists administer this medicine and supervise its use. In addition to medication, other measures to prevent migraine attacks, such as avoiding caffeine, alcohol and overtiredness should be taken where possible.

CAUTION

Alcohol: This should be avoided whilst taking this medicine because the combination may make some of the side effects, such as drowsiness, worse.

Driving and operating machinery: As this drug can cause drowsiness and dizziness, patients should not drive or perform skilled tasks until they are certain they are not experiencing these, or any other side effects.

METOCLOPRAMIDE

Brand name: Maxolon

Type of drug: Anti-sickness

Uses: Relief of nausea and vomiting.

How it works: Acts directly on the gut to increase the speed at which food is propelled from the stomach into the intestine.

Availability: POM

Possible adverse effects: Drowsiness, headache, dizziness, restlessness and diarrhoea are reported. In young people and the elderly involuntary or unintentional movements or spasms of the face and other muscles can occur. This requires urgent medical attention.

Other information: It should be taken 30 minutes before eating.

CAUTION

Driving and operating machinery: As this drug can cause dizziness and drowsiness, patients receiving this medication should not drive or perform skilled tasks until they are certain they are not experiencing these or any other side effects.

METRONIDAZOLE

Brand name: Anabact, Flagyl, Metrogel, Metrotop, Rozex

Type of drug: Antibiotic

Uses: Treatment of a variety of infections, particularly those affecting the abdomen, gut, pelvis and mouth, pressure sores and leg ulcers.

How it works: This antibiotic is effective against bacteria and other organisms that do not require oxygen to survive.

Availability: POM

Possible adverse effects: Side effects include nausea, loss of appetite, upset stomach, an unpleasant taste and furred tongue.

Other information: This medicine should be taken after meals with plenty of water.

Other information: Children may be prescribed this medicine.

CAUTION

Alcohol: Should not be consumed whilst taking this medicine, as it leads to facial flushing, throbbing headache, increased heart rate, nausea and vomiting, which can be severe.

MICONAZOLE

Brand name: Daktarin, Gyno-Daktarin

Type of drug: Antifungal

Uses: Treatment of fungal infections affecting the skin or nails and thrush affecting the mouth or genitals.

How it works: Miconazole stops production of important chemicals used in the cell membrane of the fungus. Disruption of the membrane leads to the death of the fungal cell.

Availability: Miconazole is available in some preparations for sale over-the-counter, and may be combined with steroids

Possible adverse effects: When applied to the skin or used as a vaginal preparation it can occasionally cause irritation. When used for infection in the mouth or gut, this medicine can cause nausea, vomiting and diarrhoea.

Other information: The medicine should be used regularly in accordance with the instructions from the doctor or pharmacist and the course completed. It may be used to treat children of all ages.

MIFEPRISTONE

Brand name: Mifegyne

Type of drug: Hormone antagonist

Uses: To induce or aid in termination of pregnancy.

How it works: It stops the actions of progesterone necessary for pregnancy to continue.

Availability: Specialist centres authorised by the government to carry out terminations of pregnancy in the UK.

Possible adverse effects: Nausea, headache, vomiting, cramping pains and vaginal bleeding which is sometimes severe.

Other information: Women with bleeding disorders or on medication which increases the risk of bleeding must inform their doctor before taking this medicine Aspirin or similar medication should not be taken for at least 8-12 days after taking this drug, as it may increase the risk of bleeding. It is usually combined with another drug called gemeprost to complete the termination. A follow up visit to the centre is usually required to ensure that successful, complete termination has occurred.

MINOCYCLINE

Brand name: Minocin

Type of drug: Tetracycline antibiotic

Uses: Commonly used to treat acne. However it is also used to treat a variety of infections including pneumonia and some sexually transmitted diseases. It may be used in people with chronic bronchitis to prevent infection.

How it works: Minocycline stops the production of chemicals essential for the successful multiplication of the bacteria. As the bacteria cannot reproduce it allows the body's immune system a better chance to clear the infection.

Availability: POM

Possible adverse effects: Nausea, vomiting, weight loss and dizziness. It can cause a change of colour in bodily fluids such as tears and sweat. An unusual side effect on prolonged use is discolouration of the teeth, which can turn them yellow, grey or brown and there may be a reduction in the amount of enamel on the teeth. For this reason it is not usually given to children under 12 years. It can also cause a rash to develop on exposure to sunlight. Any rashes should be reported to the doctor

Other information: The tablets should be taken with a full glass of water. The whole course should be completed, and the medicine taken regularly throughout. Antacids, indigestion remedies, vitamins or other supplements, iron tablets, or medicines containing zinc, iron, calcium, magnesium, or aluminium should be taken at least 3 hours before this medicine. Milk may still be consumed whilst taking this medicine.

CAUTION

Pregnancy: Women of a childbearing age should ensure that they use suitable, effective measures of contraception whilst using this medicine. If patients suspect that they have become pregnant they should seek medical advice.

Driving and operating machinery: As this drug can cause dizziness, patients should not drive or perform skilled tasks until they are certain they are not experiencing these or any other side effects.

MINOXIDIL

Brand name: Loniten, Regaine

Type of drug: Anti-hypertensive

Uses: Treatment of high blood pressure and a treatment for hair loss.

How it works: Increases the size of the blood vessels, which reduces the force needed to pump blood through them, and so reduces blood pressure. The way minoxidil prevents hair loss is not fully understood but is probably due to increased blood flow to the scalp.

Availability: POM except for scalp lotions.

Possible adverse effects: Fluid retention leading to weight gain, ankle swelling and breast tenderness. An increased heart rate may occur. Additional medication may be prescribed to combat these effects. Nausea, increased hair growth and skin rashes are other recognised side effects. If persistent itching, or irritation of the scalp occurs when using the solution for hair growth, the medication should be stopped.

Other information: When used for high blood pressure, it is often in combination with other medicines. The solution for hair growth is available over-the-counter and is only effective in some patients.

MISOPROSTOL

Brand name: Cytotec

Type of drug: Prostaglandin analogue

Uses: Treatment and prevention of gastric and duodenal ulcers.

How it works: Reduces the amount of acid produced in the stomach with the result that the ulcerated areas have a chance to heal. Misoprostol also acts to increase the production of a protective layer of cells that stop the released acid from irritating the stomach.

Availability: POM

Possible adverse effects: Diarrhoea can sometimes be severe, requiring the medicine to be stopped. Indigestion, abdominal pain and abnormal vaginal bleeding may occur whilst taking this medicine

Other information: This medication is sometimes prescribed to protect the stomach from the irritant effects of aspirin and aspirin type drugs. Side effects may be reduced if each dose is taken with food. Ulcers will generally heal after about 4 to 8 weeks of treatment.

CAUTION

Pregnancy: Women of a childbearing age should ensure that they use suitable, effective measures of contraception whilst using this medicine. If patients suspect that they have become pregnant they should seek medical advice.

MITOMYCIN

Brand name: Mitomycin C Kyowa

Type of drug: Chemotherapy, cytotoxic antibiotic

Uses: Treatment of a variety of cancers both on its own and in combination with other medicines. This may be given as an injection or as infusion into the veins or directly to the area for treatment such as into the bladder.

How it works: Binds to the DNA in cancer cells and stops them multiplying. This causes the cells to die and the tumour to reduce in size.

Availability: POM

Possible adverse effects: Headache, drowsiness, fatigue, nausea, vomiting and a reduction in blood cells.

Other information: This medicine is only given in hospital under the supervision of a doctor experienced in treating cancer, who will oversee and monitor treatment. Regular blood tests are required to assess the effects. Any sign of infection, such as a sore throat, unexplained bleeding or bruising, generally feeling unwell or high temperature should be reported to the doctor immediately.

CAUTION

Driving and operating machinery. As this drug can cause drowsiness and dizziness, patients should not drive or perform skilled tasks until they are certain they are not experiencing these, or any other side effects.

MOCLOBEMIDE

Brand name: Manerix

Type of drug: Antidepressant

Uses: Treatment of depression.

How it works: This drug stops the body breaking down chemicals in the brain that are known to lift mood. This leads to a progressive improvement in mood.

Availability: POM

Possible adverse effects: Dry mouth, blurred vision, confusion, dizziness, headache and interrupted sleep are some of the recognised side effects, but these usually lessen with continued use. Serious adverse effects, such as a marked rise in blood pressure, can occur if certain types of food and medicines are consumed. Foods to be avoided include yeast extract, pickled herring, mature cheese, Bovril, Oxo and Marmite. If a throbbing headache occurs, urgent medical advice should be sought.

Other information: It may take between 2 and 4 weeks to feel the beneficial effects of this medication.

CAUTION

Alcohol: Should not be consumed whilst taking this medicine.

Driving and operating machinery: As this drug can cause dizziness and confusion, patients receiving this medication should not drive or perform such tasks until they are certain they are not experiencing any side effects.

MORPHINE

Brand name: MST Continus, Oramorph, Sevredol

Type of drug: Painkiller, opioid analgesic

Uses: Relief of severe pain such as that caused by cancer, heart attack or injury.

How it works: This drug stops the transmission of pain messages through the spinal cord to the brain.

Availability: POM

Possible adverse effects: Nausea, vomiting, itching and constipation are common and often require additional medication to combat these effects. Drowsiness, difficulty in passing urine, changes in mood, lower blood pressure and slower heart rate may also occur. Allergic reactions include rash, swelling of the face and/or tongue and difficulty breathing – if any allergic symptoms occur, the patient should stop taking the medication and seek urgent medical advice

Other information: Dependence may occur if the medication is taken for extended periods. Tolerance to the medicine, which is where the body becomes used to the effects of morphine may also occur, and higher doses are required to achieve the same level of pain relief. Tablets should be swallowed whole not broken or crushed. Solution should be discarded 90 days after first opening the bottle by returning it to the pharmacy for safe disposal. Patients are often advised to record usage and painful events that require extra pain relief to allow the doctor to calculate the best dose for the patient.

CAUTION

Children: Children over 1 year of age may be prescribed this medicine.

Alcohol: This should be avoided whilst taking this medicine, because drowsiness and other side effects of morphine may be enhanced.

Driving and operating machinery: As this drug can cause dizziness and drowsiness, patients receiving this medication should not drive or perform such tasks until they are certain they are not experiencing any side effects.

MOXONIDINE

Brand name: Physiotens

Type of drug: Antihypertensive

Uses: To treat mild to moderately raised blood pressure.

How it works: Stops the brain sending signals that narrow the blood vessels. This reduces the force needed to push blood through the vessels, and so reduces blood pressure.

Availability: POM

Possible adverse effects: Headache, dry mouth, dizziness, nausea, and drowsiness.

Other information: Do not stop taking this drug suddenly without consulting a doctor first.

CAUTION

Alcohol: Should only be consumed in moderation whilst taking this medicine because the combination may cause a larger than expected drop in blood pressure.

Driving and operating machinery: As this drug can cause drowsiness and dizziness, patients receiving this medication should not drive or perform skilled tasks until they are certain they are not experiencing any side effects.

MYCOPHENOLATE MOFETIL

Brand name: CellCept

Type of drug: Immunosuppressant

Uses: Given with other medicines to prevent rejection of the kidney, heart and liver following a transplant operation.

How it works: Stops the production of cells within the immune system, which means that they cannot attack the transplanted organ.

Availability: POM

Possible adverse effects: Vomiting, diarrhoea, headache, dizziness, headache, decreased weight and abdominal pain. As this medication increases the patient's risk of infections through its effect on the immune system, other medicines are often administered to prevent infections. It can also cause changes in the blood cells.

Other information: This medicine is only given in hospital under the supervision of a doctor experienced in looking after patients who have undergone transplants. Regular blood tests are required to assess the effects. Any sign of infection, such as a sore throat, unexplained bleeding or bruising, generally feeling unwell or high temperature should be reported to the doctor immediately.

CAUTION

Children: May be used in kidney transplants for children over 2 years of age.
Pregnancy: Patients should avoid pregnancy while taking this medicine, and effective contraceptive measures should be used before, during, and for 6 weeks after using this medicine.

NABILONE

Brand name: Only available as a generic medicine
Type of drug: Cannabinoid anti-emetic
Uses: Treatment of nausea and vomiting in patients undergoing cancer treatment where other medicines have not worked.
How it works: Chemically very closely related to a constituent of cannabis, its precise actions are unknown, but it is thought to act in the brain to stop nausea and vomiting.
Availability: POM
Possible adverse effects: Drowsiness, vertigo, dry mouth, depression and euphoria.
Other information: This drug can cause mood and behavioural changes. It is only used in hospitals and is usually taken on the night before chemotherapy is administered and again approximately three hours before chemotherapy.

CAUTION

Alcohol: Should be avoided because the combination may increase the severity of any drowsiness experienced.
Driving and operating machinery: Patients should not drive while taking

this medicine because it will affect the ability to drive and perform skilled tasks. These effects may last for several days after taking the medicine.

NADOLOL
Brand Name: Corgard
Type of drug: Cardiac, beta-blocker
Uses: Treatment of high blood pressure, angina, prevention of migraine headaches and some types of fast heartbeat.
How it works: Slows the rate at which the heart beats, reducing its workload and making it more efficient. The drug also acts on blood vessels leading to lower blood pressure. In migraine it is thought to stop the narrowing of blood vessels in the brain.
Availability: POM
Possible adverse effects: Side effects are rare but those that have been reported include stomach upsets, nightmares, light-headedness when standing up, cold hands and feet, tiredness and trouble sleeping.
Other information: This medicine should not be stopped suddenly unless advised by the doctor. Nadolol should only be prescribed with caution for people with asthma or other lung disorders because it can make the conditions worse. Any sign of wheezing, breathlessness or chest pain should be reported to the doctor or pharmacist.

NAFARELIN
Brand name: Synarel
Type of drug: Gonadorelin analogues
Uses: Treatment of endometriosis.
How it works: Nafarelin suppresses the release of hormones which stimulate the release of testosterone and oestrogen. In women this leads to a thinning of the endometrium, which stops endometriosis from becoming worse.
Availability: POM
Possible adverse effects: Irregular bleeding, hot flushes, change in sex drive, nausea, vomiting, breast enlargement and tenderness, constipation.
Other information: Only available as an inhaler for the nose. Avoid use of nasal decongestants for at least 30 minutes after treatment.

CAUTION
Pregnancy: Barrier contraception should be used. If patients suspect they may have become pregnant, they should inform their doctor.

NAPROXEN
Brand name: Naprosyn
Type of drug: Non-steroidal anti-inflammatory
Uses: To treat symptoms of rheumatoid arthritis, ankylosing spondylitis and osteoarthritis. Also used in the treatment of gout, migraine and pain following surgery.
How it works: Inhibits the actions of an enzyme called cyclo-oxygenase. This enzyme produces chemical messengers that start and continue the inflammatory process.
Availability: POM
Possible adverse effects: Gastrointestinal problems such as indigestion and nausea, headache, problems with concentration and a ringing in the ears. Gastrointestinal ulceration and/or bleeding may occur, so if you suffer severe stomach pain, or there is blood in your stools then seek urgent medical advice. If allergic symptoms such as wheezing or swelling of the face occur, the patient should stop taking the medication and seek urgent medical advice.
Other information: Patients allergic to aspirin may also be allergic to naprosyn and should not take this medicine without advice from the doctor or pharmacist.
CAUTION
Children: It may be used in children over 5 years of age to treat arthritis.
Driving and operating machinery: Patients receiving this medication should not drive or perform skilled tasks until they are certain they are not experiencing any side effects.

NARATRIPTAN
Brand name: Naramig
Type of drug: Antimigraine
Uses: To stop a migraine attack that has already started.
How it works: Increases the levels of a chemical messenger, serotonin, in

the brain. When increased levels of serotonin are available the blood vessels in the brain constrict which stops the headache.

Availability: POM

Possbile adverse effects: Tingling sensations, drowsiness, dizziness, nausea, vomiting, rapid or slow heart beat and feeling hot.

Other information: The tablets should be swallowed whole with water.

CAUTION

Children: It may be prescribed for children over 12 years of age.

Driving and operating machinery: As this drug can cause dizziness and drowsiness, patients should not drive or perform skilled tasks until they are certain they are not experiencing these, or any other side effects.

NEDOCROMIL SODIUM

Brand name: Rapitil, Nilade

Type of drug: Anti-inflammatory

Uses: To treat symptoms of eye allergies. It is also used for asthma.

How it works: Stops certain types of cell from producing chemicals that cause inflammation, so reduces any irritation in the eye and lungs.

Availability: POM

Possible adverse effects: Stinging and burning sensations in the eye after putting in the drops, these usually subside with time. Unpleasant taste with both the inhaler and eye drops.

Other information: Patients should not wear soft contact lenses whilst using this medicine. Those wearing hard lenses should take them out before using the drops and put back in 10 minutes after using them. The inhaler is used regularly to prevent the occurrence of asthma attacks, rather than just during an attack.

CAUTION

Children: Those over 6 years of age may use this medicine.

Driving and operating machinery: As this drug may cause visual problems, patients should not drive or perform skilled tasks until they are certain they are not experiencing this or any other side effects.

NEFOPAM

Brand name: Acupan

Type of drug: Non-opioid analgesic
Uses: Relieves moderate pain associated with surgery, injury or cancer.
How it works: Stops the transmission of pain messages through the spinal cord to the brain.
Availability: POM
Possible adverse effects: Nausea, dry mouth, dizziness, light-headedness, drowsiness, stomach pain and diarrhoea. Some of these effects might be lessened by lying down after taking this medicine.
Other information: A harmless pink discolouration of the urine may occur.
CAUTION
Children: It may be prescribed for children over 12 years of age.
Alcohol: Should be avoided because of the increased risk of drowsiness associated with the combination.
Driving and operating machinery: As this drug can cause dizziness and drowsiness, patients should not drive or perform skilled tasks until they are certain they are not experiencing these or any other side effects.

NEOMYCIN
Brand name: Only available as a generic medicine
Type of drug: Antibiotic
Uses: Reduces the amount of bacteria in the bowels before surgery. It is also used to treat infections of the eyes, ears and skin.
How it works: Stops bacteria from producing chemicals that are essential for their survival.
Availability: POM
Possible adverse effects: Tablets may cause nausea, vomiting and also diarrhoea. A potentially serious side effect is deafness or a persistent ringing in the ears. Use of the drops, cream or ointment can also be associated with irritation, burning, stinging, itching, and a rash on application.
Other information: If the eye is being treated then contact lenses should be removed during the whole course of treatment.
CAUTION
Children: This medicine may be given to children over 6 years of age.

NEOSTIGMINE

Brand name: Only available as a generic medicine

Type of drug: Muscle stimulant

Uses: Treatment of myasthenia gravis, a rare autoimmune condition, and urinary retention.

How it works: Stops the breakdown of a chemical messenger in the brain and nerves called acetylcholine, which allows better control over the muscles in myasthenia.

Availability: POM

Possible adverse effects: Abdominal cramps, excessive saliva, dizziness, drowsiness, nausea, headache, vomiting, blurred vision and diarrhoea. In patients with asthma, neostigmine can make their symptoms worse.

Other information: This medicine should be taken when maximum strength in the muscles is needed. It lasts for about 4 hours. It is recommended that it is taken when the patient gets up and before meals. This medicine may be used in children of all ages.

CAUTION

Driving and operating machinery: Patients should not drive or perform skilled tasks until they are certain they are not experiencing any side effects.

NICARDIPINE

Brand name: Cardene

Type of drug: Calcium channel blocker

Uses: Treatment of angina and raised blood pressure.

How it works: Relaxes the blood vessels in the circulatory system allowing blood to flow more easily therefore reducing blood pressure. For angina it relaxes the blood vessels of the heart and allows more blood and oxygen to reach the heart muscle. This allows it to pump effectively and relieves the pain of angina.

Availability: POM

Possible adverse effects: Dizziness, headache, palpitations, nausea, abdominal discomfort, and swelling of the ankles and feet.

Other information: Avoid grapefruit juice. If chest pain occurs whilst taking this medicine consult a doctor immediately.

CAUTION

Alcohol: Should only be consumed in moderation because this combination can cause a greater than expected drop in blood pressure.

NICORANDIL

Brand name: Ikorel

Type of drug: Potassium channel activator, and nitrate

Uses: Treatment and prevention of the symptoms of angina.

How it works: Widens both veins and arteries so that more blood can reach the heart muscle and the workload of the heart is reduced.

Availability: POM

Possible adverse effects: Headache, nausea, flushing and generally feeling weak. Patients can develop painful mouth ulcers that may stop them from continuing with this medicine.

CAUTION

Alcohol: Should only be consumed in moderation whilst taking this medicine because the combination may cause a drop in blood pressure.

Driving and operating machinery: Patients receiving this medication should not drive or perform skilled tasks until they are certain they are not experiencing any side effects.

NIFEDIPINE

Brand name: Adalat, Coracten

Type of drug: Calcium channel blocker

Uses: Treatment of angina and high blood pressure.

How it works: Relaxes the blood vessels in the circulatory system allowing blood to flow more easily, therefore reducing blood pressure. For angina it relaxes the blood vessels of the heart and allows more blood and oxygen to reach the heart muscle. This allows the heart to pump more effectively and relieves the pain associated with angina.

Availability: POM

Possible adverse effects: Headache, dizziness, feeling tired, constipation, dizziness and ankle swelling.

Other information: Patient should swallow the medication whole, and not chew or crush the capsules or tablets. When using the long acting tablet they must be taken at roughly the same time each day, preferably with breakfast. These tablets must not be taken with grapefruit juice. The coating of the tablet may appear in the stools because it is not broken down in the gut; this does not mean the medicine has not been effective.

CAUTION

Alcohol: Should only be consumed in moderation whilst taking this medicine because the combination may cause a drop in blood pressure.

Driving and operating machinery: Patients receiving this medication should not drive or perform skilled tasks until they are certain they are not experiencing any side effects.

NITROFURANTOIN

Brand name: Macrobid, Macrodantin

Type of drug: Anti-bacterial

Uses: Treatment of urinary-tract infections.

How it works: Nitrofurantoin passes into the urine where the drug becomes active against bacteria causing the infection.

Availability: POM

Possible adverse effects: Side effects are common and include stomach irritation and upset, nausea and vomiting, anorexia, diarrhoea. Urine may be coloured yellow or brown. If symptoms such as cough, fever, chills and difficulty breathing develop, seek the advice of a doctor as it can cause liver and lung problems.

Other information: Should not be taken by people with G6PD deficiency, an inherited blood disorder, as it can cause jaundice and low red blood cells. Take with milk or food to minimise side effects. It should be taken at regular intervals and the prescribed course completed.

CAUTION

Children: This medicine may be used in children over 3 months of age.

NIZATIDINE

Brand name: Axid

Type of drug: H_2-receptor antagonist

Uses: Treatment of gastric and duodenal ulcers and heartburn.

How it works: Reduces the secretion of gastric acid, and pepsin, an enzyme that helps in the digestion of protein. This promotes healing of the stomach lining where the ulcers occur.

Availability: As an ingredient in some over-the-counter preparations.

Possible adverse effects: Diarrhoea and upset stomach, headaches, sweating, dizziness and skin rashes.

Other information: Smoking increases the production of gastric acid so will lessen the effectiveness of the treatment.

NORETHISTERONE

Brand name: Micronor, Noriday, Primolut N, Utovlan

Type of drug: Progestogen

Uses: To treat a range of menstrual disorders, including endometriosis. Is also in some contraceptive pills. It is sometimes used to treat endometrial cancer.

How it works: Acts in a similar way to the female hormone progesterone. This hormone has many actions and suppresses ovulation, as well as the menstrual cycle.

Availability: POM

Possible adverse effects: Breakthrough bleeding between periods, weight gain, change in mood, nausea, and rashes have been reported. Liver problems can also occur.

Other information: When used as a contraceptive on its own, it must be taken at the same time each day.

NORFLOXACIN

Brand name: Utinor

Type of drug: Antibiotic

Uses: Treatment of urinary tract infections.

How it works: It acts on the DNA of the bacteria to stop them multiplying, which results in their death.

Availability: POM

Possible adverse effects: Nausea, heartburn, abdominal cramps, diarrhoea, headache, dizziness, anxiety. It can lead to fits in epileptic patients.

Other information: The patient is advised to take this medication 1 hour before or 2 hours after meals, antacids, indigestion remedies, supplements or vitamins. The tablets should be taken regularly and the prescribed course completed. A rash may develop when skin is exposed to sunlight or sunlamps. Patients should avoid the sun or use total sun blocks when going outside.

CAUTION

Driving and operating machinery: Patients receiving this medication should not drive or perform skilled tasks until they are certain they are not experiencing any side effects.

NORTRIPTYLINE

Brand name: Allegron

Type of drug: Tricyclic antidepressant

Uses: Treatment of depression. It is also used for bed-wetting in children.

How it works: It inhibits the re-uptake of brain chemicals, which results in a heightening of mood. It also encourages appetite and enables users to lead a more normal daily life. Its sedative effect is also useful for people who have difficulty sleeping at nights.

Availability: POM

Possible adverse effects: Confusion, disorientation, numbness and tingling in the hands and feet, which must be reported to the doctor. Other side effects include dry mouth, blurred vision, constipation, rashes, nausea, vomiting and weight changes.

Other information: This medicine may take up to 4 weeks before it has an effect.

CAUTION

Children: It may be prescribed for children over 7 years

Alcohol: Should be avoided because the combination can worsen any confusion and disorientation.

Driving and operating machinery: As this drug can cause dizziness and drowsiness, patients receiving this medication should not drive or perform skilled tasks until they are certain they are not experiencing these or any other side effects.

NYSTATIN
Brand name: Nystan
Type of drug: Anti-fungal
Uses: Treatment of yeast infections such as thrush and other infections of the skin, mouth, throat, gut and vagina.
How it works: Stops the cell wall of the fungus from acting as a barrier, and the contents of the fungal cell leak out causing the death of the cell.
Availability: POM
Possible adverse effects: Adverse effects are uncommon but with tablets and suspension they can cause irritation of the mouth and nausea.
Other information: Good hygiene is essential to prevent re-infection. Always finish the course prescribed in order to minimise the risk of re-infection. Should be used regularly as prescribed. This medicine may be prescribed for children of all ages.

OCTREOTIDE
Brand name: Sandostatin
Type of drug: Hormone
Uses: Treating acromegaly – the abnormal growth of the body due to excessive pituitary gland activity. It may also be used to treat nausea, vomiting and certain tumours.
How it works: Mimics the action of a naturally occurring messenger in the brain called somatostatin, which reduces the production of growth hormones from the pituitary gland.
Availability: POM
Possible adverse effects: Stomach upsets, abdominal pain, loss of appetite, nausea, vomiting, and diarrhoea.
Other information: This drug can cause gallstones, so patient is advised to report serious abdominal discomfort promptly. When used for cancer this medicine does not actually kill the cancer, but relieves the symptoms it causes.
CAUTION
Driving and operating machinery: Patients receiving this medication should not drive or perform skilled tasks until they are certain they are not experiencing any side effects.

OESTROGEN
See Conjugated Estrogen

OFLOXACIN
Brand name: Tarivid
Type of drug: Quinolone antibiotic
Uses: Treatment of infections of the urinary tract, chest, genital tract and eyes.
How it works: Acts on the DNA of the bacteria to stop them multiplying, resulting in their death.
Availability: POM
Possible adverse effects: Nausea, vomiting, stomach upset, dizziness, sleep disorders, headache, nervousness, visual disturbances. Stinging and irritation of the eye may occur when using the eye drops. May increase the tendency to have fits in epileptics.
Other information: Patients are advised to drink plenty of fluids. Prolonged exposure to the sun should be avoided. If being treated for eye infection, do not wear soft contact lenses. This medicine should be taken regularly, and the prescribed course completed. This medicine must be taken two hours before any antacids or indigestion remedies.
CAUTION
Alcohol: Can increase the likelihood of experiencing side effects and so should only be consumed in moderation.
Driving and operating machinery: As this drug can cause dizziness and drowsiness, patients should not drive or perform skilled tasks until they are certain they are not experiencing any other side effects.

OLANZAPINE
Brand name: Zyprexa
Type of drug: Antipsychotic
Uses: Treatment of schizophrenia.
How it works: Schizophrenia and related disorders are thought to be due to an excessive amount of one of the brain's chemical messengers, dopamine. Olanzapine reduces dopamine levels and affects other messengers in the brain.

Availability: POM

Possible adverse effects: Dizziness, drowsiness, increased appetite, weight gain, dry mouth and blurred vision. Dry mouth and constipation tend to lessen with time.

Other information: Do not take any over-the-counter preparations unless advised by a pharmacist. This medicine must not be stopped suddenly, unless on the advice of a doctor. It may take between 2 and 4 weeks to feel the beneficial effects of this medication.

CAUTION

Alcohol: Should not be consumed whilst taking this medicine

Driving and operating machinery: As this drug can cause dizziness and drowsiness, patients should not drive or perform skilled tasks until they are certain they are not experiencing these or any other side effects.

OLMESARTAN

Brand name: Olmetec

Type of drug: Angiotensin 2 receptor antagonist.

Uses: Treatment of high blood pressure.

How it works: This medicine stops the action of a chemical called angiotensin II. which is produced by an enzyme called ACE, and causes the blood vessels to narrow. Olmesartan stops these effects and allows the blood vessels to become wider, which reduces the blood pressure.

Availability: POM

Possible adverse effects: Dizziness, cough, abdominal pain, upset stomach, constipation, diarrhoea, joint, muscle and chest pain.

Other information: May affect levels of potassium in the blood, so blood tests may be performed. It should be taken at approximately the same time each day.

CAUTION

Alcohol: Should be consumed in moderation because the combination may cause a greater than required drop in blood pressure.

Driving and operating machinery: As this drug can cause dizziness and drowsiness, patients receiving this medication should not drive or perform skilled tasks until they are certain they are not experiencing these side effects.

OLSALAZINE

Brand name: Dipentum

Type of drug: Aminosalicylate

Uses: Treatment and prevention of flare-ups of ulcerative colitis;

How it works: The way this medicine works is not yet entirely understood. Related to aspirin, this medicine is believed to work by stopping the production of chemicals which that cause inflammation in the bowel.

Availability: POM

Possible adverse effects: Diarrhoea, headaches and dizziness, stomach upset and cramps, joint pains and rashes. Allergic reactions may occur. Any rash should be reported to a doctor. Regular blood tests are usually carried out because this medicine may cause low numbers of blood cells. Any sign of sore throat, unexplained bleeding or bruising, a high temperature or feeling unwell should be reported to the doctor.

Other information: Patients with an allergy to aspirin should not take this medicine without consulting a doctor or pharmacist. It should be taken after a meal as this will relieve some of the stomach upsets associated with this medicine.

OMEPRAZOLE

Brand name: Losec, Zanprol

Type of drug: Proton pump inhibitor

Uses: Treatment of stomach and gut ulcers, acid reflux causing heartburn and, in conjunction with other drugs, the treatment of *Helicobacter Pylori* infection.

How it works: Reduces the production of stomach acid, allowing the stomach and intestines to recover and heal. When used for reflux disease, it stops production of excess acid that can travel back up the oesophagus or gullet – which becomes irritated and inflamed because it has no protection against the acid of the stomach.

Availability: OTC

Possible adverse effects: Headache, dizziness, dry mouth, nausea, flatulence, constipation, diarrhoea and other stomach upsets.

Other information: If patients find it hard to swallow capsules then tablets are available which may be dispersed in water. If capsules are prescribed they may be opened and mixed with yoghurt or fruit juice, though the contents of the capsule should not be crushed or chewed.

CAUTION

Children: Can be used in children over 2 years of age. Treatment will usually be started by a specialist in hospital for this age group.

Driving and operating machinery: As this drug can cause dizziness, patients receiving this medication should not drive or perform skilled tasks until they are certain they are not experiencing this side effect.

ONDANSETRON

Brand name: Zofran

Type of drug: $5HT_3$ antagonist

Uses: Treating nausea and vomiting resulting from surgery or chemotherapy treatment.

How it works: Blocks the messages to the brain which stimulate the feelings of nausea and instinct to vomit.

Availability: POM

Possible adverse effects: Headache, fatigue, constipation, flushing.

Other information: The Zofran Melt form of this medicine should be allowed to dissolve on the tongue and then swallowed.

CAUTION

Children: This medicine may be used for children over 2 years of age.

ORLISTAT

Brand name: Xenical

Type of drug: Lipase inhibitor

Uses: Used in the treatment of severe obesity where dietary measures have failed.

How it works: Stops the absorption of fats from the gut. This means that a reduced amount of extra weight is put on, but does not reduce weight unless combined with other measures, such as exercise and a balanced low calorie diet.

Availability: POM

Possible adverse effects: Oils and fats in the stools. Flatulence has also been reported.

Other information: Should be taken up to one hour before meals. If a meal contains little fat or is missed then the corresponding dose of medicine should be missed as well. As the fats are not being absorbed, then fat-soluble vitamins A,D,E and K may become deficient and so supplements may be required, to be taken at bedtime.

ORPHENADRINE

Brand name: Disipal

Type of drug: Anticholinergic

Uses: Treatment of Parkinson's disease, and Parkinson's-like conditions.

How it works: Acts on the part of the brain which controls muscle tone, with the result that muscle stiffness and spasm – which are characteristic of Parkinsonism – are relieved.

Availability: POM

Possible adverse effects: Dry mouth, blurred vision, insomnia, confusion, headache, difficulty in passing water, and constipation.

Other information: This medicine must not be discontinued unless advised by a doctor. Then it will be gradually reduced.

CAUTION

Alcohol: Can increase the severity of drowsiness and so should only be consumed in moderation.

Driving and operating machinery: As this drug can cause dizziness and drowsiness, patients receiving this medication should not drive or perform skilled tasks until they are certain they are not experiencing these or any other side effects.

OXPRENOLOL

Brand name: Trasicor

Type of drug: Beta-blocker

Uses: Prevention of angina, treatment of high blood pressure, and to treat some abnormal heart rhythms.

How it works: Slows the rate at which the heart beats, reducing its workload and making it more efficient, which means oxygen can be more easily carried around the heart and relieve the symptoms of angina. A reduced heart rate is also thought to help lower the blood pressure.

Availability: POM

Possible adverse effects: Fatigue, headache and dizziness, cold hands and feet, constipation, stomach upsets and reduced sex drive. In patients with asthma, oxprenolol can make the symptoms worse, so if any signs of chest pain, tightness, or wheezing occur then seek urgent medical advice.

Other information: This medicine must not be stopped suddenly unless on the advice of a doctor.

CAUTION

Alcohol: Can increase the likelihood of side effects such as dizziness and so should only be consumed in moderation.

Driving and operating machinery: As this drug can cause dizziness and drowsiness, patients receiving this medication should not drive or perform skilled tasks until they are certain they are not experiencing these, or any other side effects.

OXYBUTYNIN

Brand name: Cystrin, Ditropan

Type of drug: Antimuscarinic

Uses: Treatment of urinary incontinence and other urinary problems.

How it works: Involuntary contractions of the bladder muscle cause an increased urge to urinate, passing small volumes of urine frequently. Oxybutynin reduces these contractions, which allows the bladder to fill, and stops urine from leaking out.

Possible adverse effects: Dizziness, blurred vision, abdominal discomfort, dry mouth, and stomach upsets.

Other information: The medicine may be discontinued periodically to see if the patient still requires it.

CAUTION

Children: May be prescribed for those over 5 years of age.

Alcohol: Can increase the need to urinate more frequently so should only be consumed in moderation.

Driving and operating machinery: As this drug can cause dizziness and drowsiness, patients should not drive or perform skilled tasks until they are certain they are not experiencing these or any other side effects.

OXYCODONE

Brand name: Oxycontin, Oxynorm

Type of drug: Opioid analgesic

Uses: Relief from severe pain.

How it works: This drug stops the transmission of pain messages through the spinal cord to the brain. Pain is relieved because it is only felt once these signals reach the brain.

Availability: POM

Possible adverse effects: Nausea, vomiting, constipation, stomach upsets, headache and dizziness, confusion, drowsiness, sweating, mood changes and chills. If allergic symptoms such as wheezing or swelling of the face occur, the patient should stop taking the medication and seek urgent medical advice

Other information: Tolerance may develop as, over time, more of the drug is required to obtain the same effect. The tablets and capsules should be swallowed whole and not chewed. Dependence can also occur.

CAUTION

Alcohol: Should not be consumed whilst taking this medicine.

Driving and operating machinery: As this drug can cause dizziness and drowsiness, patients receiving this medication should not drive or perform skilled tasks until they are certain they are not experiencing these or any other side effects.

OXYTETRACYCLINE

Brand name: Terramycin

Type of drug: Tetracycline antibiotic

Uses: Treatment of infection of the chest, urine and skin.

How it works: Stops the production of chemicals essential for the successful multiplication of the bacteria. As the bacteria cannot reproduce it allows the body's immune system a better chance to clear cope with infection.

Availability: POM

Possible adverse effects: Nausea, vomiting, diarrhoea, upset stomach and rashes. It cause a change of colour of bodily fluids such as tears and sweat. An unusual, peculiar side-effect with prolonged use is the discolouration of teeth, which turns them yellow, grey, or brown. There may also be a reduction in the amount of enamel on the teeth. It can also cause a rash to develops on exposure to sunlight, If a rash develops, consult a doctor.

Other information: The medicine should be taken at regular intervals, and the prescribed course completed. Milk and other dairy products, as well as antacids or indigestion remedies, can reduce the amount of medicine absorbed, so it should be taken 1 hour before or 2 hours after meals or dairy produce – including milk in coffee and tea. It may reduce the effectiveness of the contraceptive pill, and so extra precautions should be taken whilst, and for 2 weeks after, taking this medicine.

CAUTION

Children: It may be used in those over 12 years of age.

Pregnancy: If women suspect that they have become pregnant while taking this medicine they should seek medical advice as soon as possible.

PANTOPRAZOLE

Brand name: Protium

Type of drug: Proton pump inhibitor

Uses: Treatment of stomach and gut ulcers, and indigestion.

How it works: Reduces the production of stomach acid, which allows the stomach and intestines to recover and heal. When used for reflux diseases, it stops the production of excess acid which can travel back up the gullet or oesophagus, irritating and inflaming the oesophagus and causing pain.

Availability: POM

Possible adverse effects: Headache, abdominal pain, diarrhoea, dizziness and rash.

CAUTION

Driving and operating machinery: As this drug can cause dizziness and drowsiness, patients receiving this medication should not drive or perform skilled tasks until they are certain they are not experiencing these, or any other side effects.

PARACETAMOL

Brand name: A generic medicine and as many over-the-counter brands

Type of drug: Analgesic

Uses: Mild to moderate pain.

How it works: Makes the nerves less responsive to painful signals.

Availability: OTC

Possible adverse effects: Although rare, can include rashes and itching. If too much is taken, sometimes fatal liver damage can result.

Other information: As a maximum dose in adult patients who are otherwise healthy, 2 tablets may be taken 4 times a day. Patients should be aware that many over-the-counter products contain paracetamol, and to check with a pharmacist before using any of these. This medicine can be used in children of all ages. It may be taken during pregnancy and while breastfeeding.

PAROXETINE

Brand name: Seroxat

Type of drug: Selective serotonin re-uptake inhibitor

Uses: Treatment of mild to moderate depression, panic disorders and obsessive-compulsive disorders.

How it works: It increases the amount of time that serotonin, a specific chemical messenger in brain exists. This leads to elevation in mood.

Availability: POM

Possible adverse effects: Nausea, sweating, blurred vision, dry mouth, dizziness, weight changes, weakness, inability to sleep and tremor. These side effects usually lessen with continued use.

Other information: Some symptoms of withdrawal may be experienced if the drug is stopped suddenly. Best taken in the morning with meals. It will take approximately 4 weeks to have an effect.

CAUTION

Alcohol: Should be avoided because it may lower effectiveness .

Driving and operating machinery: As this drug can cause dizziness and drowsiness, patients receiving this medication should not drive or perform skilled tasks until they are certain they are not experiencing these or any other side effects.

PENICILLAMINE

Brand name: Distamine, Pendramine

Type of drug: Disease modifying anti-rheumatic drug

Uses: Treating rheumatic disease and used for copper and lead poisoning.

How it works: The exact way in which it helps with the treatment of rheumatoid arthritis is unknown; it appears to have anti-inflammatory properties. When used in the treatment of copper and lead poisoning, it binds the metals in the blood in a form that the body can excrete in urine.

Availability: POM

Possible adverse effects: Nausea, weight loss, vomiting and mouth ulcers. It can also cause skin rashes which should be reported to your doctor, as well as low blood cells. Any sign of infection, such as a sore throat, unexplained bleeding or bruising, generally feeling unwell or high temperature should be reported to the doctor immediately.

Other information: This medicine is only given in hospital under the supervision of a doctor experienced in treating rheumatic diseases. Regular blood tests are required to assess the effects. Penicillamine should be taken on an empty stomach or at least 30 minutes before meals. Vitamin supplements or iron tablets should not be taken within 2 hours of taking this medicine. It may be a few months before the benefits are felt.

PENTAZOCINE

Brand name: Only available as a generic medicine

Type of drug: Opioid analgesic

Uses: Treating moderate to severe pain.

How it works: Stops transmission of pain messages through the spinal cord to the brain.

Availability: POM

Possible adverse effects: Sedation, dizziness, nausea, vomiting, dry mouth, blurred vision, low blood pressure.

CAUTION

Alcohol: Should be avoided because of it may increase the severity of the sedative effects.

Children: May be prescribed for children over 6 years of age.

Driving and operating machinery: As this drug can cause dizziness and drowsiness, patients receiving this medication should not drive or perform skilled tasks until they are certain they are not experiencing these or any other side effects.

PERGOLIDE

Brand name: Celance

Type of drug: Dopaminergic drug

Uses: Treating the symptoms of Parkinson's disease.

How it works: This drug may be used with levodopa, which increases the amount of chemical messenger dopamine in the brain, which is reduced in Parkinson's disease. Dopamine is broken down in the body by enzymes but pergolide stops this, and so increases dopamine levels and the effectiveness of levodopa.

Availability: POM

Possbile adverse effects: Nausea, abdominal pain, indigestion, headache, sleepiness, hallucinations, constipation, confusion and a drop in blood pressure. Report difficulty breathing, chest pain or breathlessness to the doctor as soon as possible as occasionally lung damage can occur.

CAUTION

Driving and operating machinery: Patients receiving this medication should not drive or perform skilled tasks until they are certain they are not experiencing side effects.

PERICYAZINE

Brand name: Neulactil

Type of drug: Antipsychotic

Uses: Management of schizophrenia and other psychiatric disorders

How it works: Schizophrenia and other similar disorders are believed to occur when too much of the brain's chemical messenger dopamine is present. Pericyazine acts by stopping the action of dopamine, and so reduces the symptoms associated with schizophrenia.

Availability: POM

Possible adverse effects: Dizziness, light-headedness when standing up, symptoms similar to those seen in patients with Parkinson's disease. Drowsiness may occur at the start of treatment with this medicine.

There may also be some effects on hormones in the body leading to breast enlargement and tenderness, problems with ejaculation in men, and an increased sex drive. Irregular and unintentional movements may occur and should be reported to the doctor immediately because they may be the start of a condition known as Tardive Dyskinesia.

Other information: Care must be taken when handling the tablets or liquid because it can cause an adverse skin reaction. Also this medicine may cause an increased susceptibility to sunburn, and adequate precautions should be taken to prevent this. such as covering exposed skin, using a total sun block, wearing a wide-brimmed hat and sunglasses and staying out of the sun where possible.

CAUTION

Alcohol: Should be avoided because of an increased risk of drowsiness associated with the combination.

Driving and operating machinery: As this drug can cause dizziness and drowsiness, patients should not drive or perform skilled tasks until they are certain they are not experiencing these or any other side effects.

PERINDOPRIL

Brand name: Coversyl

Type of drug: ACE inhibitor

Uses: Treating raised blood pressure and congestive heart failure.

How it works: Enables the blood vessels to relax, which allows them to increase in size. This reduces the pressure of the blood flowing through them.

Availability: POM

Possible adverse effects: Low blood pressure, leading to light-headedness and dizziness, nausea, flushing, disorientation, problems with vision and hearing, upset stomach, rash, cramps and cough. Some of these effects are caused by a rise in potassium levels in the blood. The cough usually lessens with continued use.

Other information: Tablets should be taken in the morning before breakfast. Patients should not use potassium-rich salt substitutes and should take care in hot weather or if taking exercise, to avoid over-heating and dehydration.

CAUTION

Alcohol: Should be avoided because of the risk of a greater-than-expected fall in blood pressure.

Driving and operating machinery: As this drug can cause dizziness and drowsiness, patients receiving this medication should not drive or perform skilled tasks until they are certain they are not experiencing these or any other side effects.

PERMETHRIN

Brand name: Lyclear
Type of drug: Insecticide
Uses: Treating head lice and scabies.
How it works: Paralyses the parasites that cause the infestation.
Availability: OTC
Possible adverse effects: Burning and stinging. Any itching, redness or swelling of the scalp should be reported to your doctor or pharmacist as this may indicate an allergic reaction.
Other information: Avoid contact with the eyes, and do not apply to broken or infected skin

CAUTION

Children: May be used for those aged over 2 months.

PETHIDINE

Brand name: Pethidine
Type of drug: Opioid analgesic
Uses: For moderate to severe pain relief, such as during labour or after an operation.
How it works: Pethidine stops the transmission of pain messages through the spinal cord to the brain.
Availability: POM
Possible adverse effects: Dizziness, drowsiness, sweating, dry mouth, nausea, confusion, vomiting.
Other information: Relatively short-acting compared to other opioid analgesics. However, with repeated use the risk of side effects increase and with repeated high doses fits may occur. Tolerance may also occur which

means increasing the dosage to obtain the same effectiveness. Dependency can also develop.

CAUTION

Alcohol: Should not be consumed while taking this medicine.

Driving and operating machinery: As this drug can cause dizziness and drowsiness, patients receiving this medication should not drive or perform skilled tasks until they are certain they are not experiencing these, or any other side effects.

PHENOBARBITAL

(Formerly known as: phenobarbitone)

Brand name: Phenobarbitol Sodium, Gardenal Sodium

Type of drug: Anticonvulsant

Uses: Treatment of epilepsy.

How it works: An epileptic fit (or seizure) occurs when the brain receives too many signals via the nervous system. Phenobarbital stops some of those signals getting through, and so reduces the chances of a seizure occurring.

Availability: POM

Possible adverse effects: Drowsiness, light-headedness, fatigue, visual problems, problems with movement, skin rashes and rapid eye movement.

Other information: Patient must not stop taking the drug suddenly, as some symptoms of withdrawal may be experienced.

CAUTION

Children: It may be prescribed for epilepsy in children. While in adults sedation is common, it can also cause hyperactivity in children.

Alcohol: Should be avoided because the combination will reduce the reaction time of patients, and cause excessive drowsiness.

Driving and operating machinery: The DVLA has specific requirements for patients suffering from epilepsy who wish to drive. The latest information of the DVLA should be consulted before attempting to drive. It may also affect the ability to drive by slowing reaction time.

PHENOTHRIN

Brand name: Full Marks

Type of drug: Insecticide
Uses: Treatment of head and pubic lice.
How it works: Kills lice.
Availability: OTC
Possible adverse effects: The lotion contains alcohol which may aggravate the skin, especially if eczema is present. This drug can also worsen asthma so any breathlessness or wheezing should be reported to a doctor or pharmacist.
Other information: The mousse may discolour bleached hair. If using the lotion, it must not come into contact with naked flames or other heat sources such as hair dryers.

PHENOXYMETHYLPENICILLIN
(Also called penicillin, or penicillin V)
Brand name: Only available as a generic medicine
Type of drug: Penicillin antibiotic
Uses: Treating a wide variety of infections and to prevent infection in people without a spleen.
How it works: Phenoxymethylpenicillin stops an enzyme in the bacterial cell wall, called transpeptidase, working, leading to the death of the bacteria.
Availability: POM
Possible adverse effects: Nausea, diarrhoea, itching and rashes are relatively common with this medicine. A potentially fatal allergic reaction can occur in some individuals. This will be seen as a rash around the midriff, high fever, and swelling of the neck, mouth, and tongue, itching and breathlessness. If this occurs see the doctor immediately.
Other information: Penicillin may impair the effectiveness of the contraceptive pill and other effective measures should be taken while, and for 7 days after taking this medicine.

PHENYLEPHRINE
Brand name: Minims phenylephrine
Type of drug: Sympathomimetic
Uses: Phenylephrine is commonly used as a decongestant, to dilate the pupil of the eye, and less commonly used for treating low blood pressure.

How it works: By causing the blood vessels in the nose to narrow, phenylephrine relieves the sensation of a blocked nose. When injected this effect occurs on all blood vessels and raises blood pressure. When used as eye drops, it makes the pupil larger.

Availability: In some over-the-counter preparations.

Possbile adverse effects: Raised blood pressure, nausea, vomiting and headache. Stinging of the eye when used as eye drops.

Other information: Prolonged use of the nasal drops as a decongestant may result in congestion recurring once the drops are stopped. For this reason they should not be used for longer than seven days.

CAUTION

Driving and operating machinery: As this drug can cause blurred vision, patients should not drive or perform skilled tasks until they are certain they are not experiencing these or any other side effects.

PHENYTOIN

Brand name: Epanutin

Type of drug: Antiepileptic

Uses: Treatment of epilepsy.

How it works: An epileptic fit (or seizure) occurs when the brain receives too many signals via the nervous system. Phenytoin stops some of those signals getting through, and so it reduces the chances of a seizure occurring.

Availability: POM

Possible adverse effects: Dizziness, drowsiness, a feeling of disorientation, confusion, nausea and vomiting and difficulty in sleeping. With continued use it may cause the face to change appearance, with bigger gums and an increase of facial hair. It can lower the number of blood cells so patients should seek immediate medical advice if fever, sore throat, bleeding and bruising occurs. Blood tests may be performed to monitor phenytoin levels.

Other information: May impair the effectiveness of the contraceptive pill, and patients may be asked to take a higher than normal dose to compensate for this. This medicine can be used in the treatment of epilepsy in children.

CAUTION

Alcohol: Should not be consumed while taking this medicine

Driving and machinery: The DVLA has special rules for epileptics who wish to drive, and these should be consulted. However this medicine is not reported as affecting the ability to drive.

PILOCARPINE

Brand name: Available as a generic eye drop and Salagen

Type of drug: Parasympathomimetic

Uses: Treatment of acute and chronic glaucoma and dry mouth.

How it works: When used in the eye it causes a narrowing of the pupil. When taken by mouth it increases saliva production.

Availability: POM

Possible adverse effects: Changes to vision, including blurring and poor sight at night. Headaches and irritation of the eye are also possible. When taken by mouth this medicine may also cause dizziness, chills, flushing, stomach upsets, diarrhoea, constipation, runny nose and sweating.

Other information: May be prescribed as eye drops or inserts placed under the eye-lid.

CAUTION

Driving and operating machinery: As this drug can cause dizziness and patients receiving this medication should not drive or perform skilled tasks until they are certain they are not experiencing these or any other side effects.

PINDOLOL

Brand name: Visken

Type of drug: Beta-blocker

Uses: Treatment of high blood pressure, and to prevent angina.

How it works: Pindolol slows the heart rate, reducing its workload and making it more efficient. A reduced heart rate is also thought to lower blood pressure.

Availability: POM

Possible adverse effects: Tiredness, cold hand and feet, headache, dizziness and light-headedness especially when standing up, upset stomach and problems with vision. This drug can make asthma worse.

Other information: Asthmatics should consult the doctor or pharmacist before taking this medicine.

CAUTION

Alcohol: Can cause large falls in blood pressure so should only be consumed in moderation.

Driving and operating machinery: As this drug can cause blurred vision, dizziness and drowsiness, patients receiving this medication should not drive or perform skilled tasks until they are certain they are not experiencing these or any other side effects.

PIOGLITAZONE

Brand name: Actos

Type of drug: Antidiabetic

Uses: Treatment of non-insulin dependent diabetes

How it works: Increases the amount of insulin secreted by the pancreas to which in turn reduces the levels of sugar in the blood.

Availability: POM

Possible adverse effects: Although rare, side effects that have occured include: abdominal pain, diarrhoea and vomiting. If blood sugar levels become too low, they will require urgent correction.

Other information: Should be taken before main meals. A healthy diet, exercise and weight loss where appropriate are important, as well as any recommendations from the doctor, diabetic nurse or pharmacist. Regular intermittent glucose testing will be required while taking this medicine.

CAUTION

Alcohol: Can affect blood sugar levels so should only be consumed in moderation.

PIPERAZINE

Brand name: Pripsen

Type of drug: Anthelmintic

Uses: Treating threadworm and roundworm infestations.

How it works: Paralyses the worms and enables the body to eliminate them.

Availability: Available in some over-the-counter preparations.

Possible adverse effects: Nausea, drowsiness, diarrhoea and allergic reactions can occur when taken by mouth.

Other information: Adults should take this medicine at night, while children should take it in the morning. A second dose may be required in some patients to kill worms hatched after the first dose.

CAUTION

Children: This medicine may be prescribed for children over 3 months of age.

PIROXICAM

Brand name: Feldene

Type of drug: Non-steroidal anti-inflammatory

Uses: Relieves the symptoms of gout, osteoarthritis, rheumatoid arthritis and ankylosing spondylitis.

How it works: Inhibits the enzyme cyclo-oxygenase. This enzyme produces chemical messengers which trigger the inflammatory process.

Availability: Some over-the-counter preparations for application to the skin.

Possible adverse effects: Stomach pain, diarrhoea, constipation, vomiting and nausea. Gastrointestinal ulceration and/or bleeding may occur, so if you suffer severe stomach pain, or there is blood in your stools, seek urgent medical advice.

Other information: Patients allergic to aspirin, may also be allergic to piroxicam and should not take this medicine without advice from the doctor or pharmacist.

PIZOTIFEN

Brand name: Sanomigran

Type of drug: Anti-migraine

Uses: Prevention of migraine.

How it works: Migraine appears to result from spasms within the blood vessels of the brain. Pizotifen enhances the actions of chemical messenger serotonin, which acts on the blood vessels.

Availability: POM

Possible adverse effects: Drowsiness, increased appetite.

Other information: Can cause weight gain during long periods of use. In addition to this medicine, patients are encouraged to identify triggers for their migraine such as tiredness, coffee, the contraceptive pill – and where to avoid them. This medicine may be used in children.

CAUTION

Alcohol: Should be avoided because of an increased risk of drowsiness associated with the combination.

Driving and operating machinery: As this drug can cause drowsiness, patients receiving this medication should not drive or perform skilled tasks until they are certain they are not experiencing this or any other side effects.

PRAMIPEXOLE

Brand name: Mirapexin

Type of drug: Dopaminergic

Uses: Treatment of Parkinson's disease

How it works: Parkinson's disease is caused by a reduction of dopamine, a chemical messenger, in the brain. Pramipexole mimics dopamine, so relieving symptoms of the disease.

Availability: POM

Possible adverse effects: Uncontrolled movement, nausea, dizziness, light-headedness when standing up and constipation commonly occur at the start of treatment but will go away if patients continue taking the medicine. Insomnia and daytime sleepiness have also occurred, as have visual problems and fluid retention. Pramipexole may be given with other medicines for the disease.

CAUTION

Alcohol: Avoided as it will increase the severity of some adverse effects.

Driving and operating machinery: Because of the known risk of daytime sleepiness, which may be quick to appear, patients receiving this medication should not drive or perform skilled tasks until they are certain they are not experiencing this or any other side effects.

PRAVASTATIN

Brand name: Lipostat

Type of drug: HMG-CoA reductase inhibitor

Uses: Treating raised blood cholesterol levels.

How it works: Stops an enzyme in the liver called HMG-CoA reductase from producing cholesterol, so reducing the cholesterol levels in the blood.

Availability: POM

Possible adverse effects: Nausea, constipation, flatulence, insomnia, dizziness, chest pain, fatigue. Aches, pains or muscle cramps can occur due to inflammation of the muscles – these will generally improve on stopping the medicine. Liver damage is possible, so if yellowing of the skin or itching occurs, stop the medication and inform your doctor or pharmacist.

Other information: Pravastatin is best taken at bedtime, as this is when the body produces the most cholesterol.

CAUTION

Alcohol: Should only be consumed in moderation, and in accordance with instructions from the doctor.

Driving and operating machinery: As this drug can cause dizziness, patients receiving this medication should not drive or perform skilled tasks until they are certain they are not experiencing these side effects.

PRAZOSIN

Brand name: Hypovase

Type of drug: Alpha- blocker

Uses: Treating high blood pressure and conditions caused by poor circulation, such as Raynaud's disease. Also relieves symptoms associated with an enlarged prostate gland.

How it works: Prazosin causes the blood vessels to dilate, or become wider, which reduces the force needed to get blood through them. This leads to a reduction in blood pressure.

Availability: POM

Possible adverse effects: Dizziness and fainting when first standing up, nausea, headache, faintness and drowsiness. The first dose may cause a very large drop in blood pressure and will be given when the patient is lying down.

Other information: Patients must not stop taking this medicine suddenly.

CAUTION

Alcohol: Should be avoided while taking this medicine as the combination may cause a greater than predicted drop in blood pressure.

Driving and operating machinery: As this drug can cause dizziness and drowsiness, patients receiving this medication should not drive or perform skilled tasks until they are certain they are not experiencing these or any other side effects.

PREDNISOLONE

Brand name: Deltacortril, Minims prednisolone, Precortisyl, Predenema, Predfoam, Pred Forte, Predsol

Type of drug: Corticosteroid

Uses: Treating a range of inflammatory diseases and allergies. It may also be given in treatment of leukaemias and lymphoma, together with other drugs.

How it works: Steroids work by suppressing the production of cells, chemicals and enzymes that cause inflammation.

Availability: POM

Possible adverse effects: Indigestion is the most common, though more serious side effects are possible when it is taken for long periods, which include slowed growth in children, changes in the menstrual cycle, changes in face shape, hair growth, increased susceptibility to infection, osteoporosis and bone weakness, weight gain, disturbed sleep, depression, anxiety, fluid retention, thinning of the skin, increased bruising and bleeding, glaucoma, raised blood pressure, raised blood sugar, and stomach upsets. Gastrointestinal ulceration and/or bleeding may occur, so if you suffer severe stomach pain, or there is blood in your stools then seek urgent medical advice. Due to its effects on the immune system, there is an increased risk of infection, so signs of infection, such as sore throat, generally feeling unwell or high temperature should be reported to the doctor immediately. When used as eye drops for inflammation of the eye, the commonly reported side effect is an increase in pressure inside the eyeball.

Other information: This medication is best taken after meals in the morning. Evening doses should be taken before 6pm. Patients using the eye drops should not wear soft contact lenses while using the medicine. Those who are on this medicine for a long time, or who take high doses, will need to have the dose reduced gradually over a period of weeks.

Patients will be issued with a steroid card that contains the details of the medicine and how it should be taken. This should be handed to anybody who treats the patient while, and for at least a year after taking the medicine, to allow appropriate choice to be made about treatment. Patients may be given immunisations before receiving treatment for prolonged periods because some diseases such as chickenpox and measles may be more severe in patients taking this medicine. Patients should also avoid contact with anybody who has these diseases.

PRIMIDONE

Brand name: Mysoline

Type of drug: Anticonvulsant

Uses: Treating epilepsy.

How it works: Inactive in the form that it is taken, it is converted into phenobarbital, which prolongs the anticonvulsant effect. An epileptic fit (or seizure) occurs when the brain receives too many signals via the nervous system. Primidone and phenobarbital stop some of those signals getting through, and so reduce the chances of a seizure.

Availability: POM

Possible adverse effects: Drowsiness, light-headedness, fatigue, visual problems, problems with movement and rapid eye movement.

Other information: This medicine can reduce the effectiveness of oral contraceptives, so patients should use alternative measures.

CAUTION

Children: While in adults sedation is common, it can cause hyperactivity in children.

Alcohol: Should be avoided because the combination will slow the reaction time of the patient.

Driving and machinery: The DVLA has specific requirements for patients suffering from epilepsy who wish to drive. The latest information should be consulted before attempting to drive. This medicine may also affect the ability to drive by slowing the reaction time of the patient.

PROCHLORPERAZINE

Brand name: Buccastem, Stemetil

Type of drug: Anti-emetic and anti-psychotic

Uses: Treatment of nausea and vomiting. This medicine can also be used to treat psychiatric disorders at higher doses.

How it works: Acts on the part of the brain responsible for the sensation of nausea and vomiting by stopping the action of the chemical messenger dopamine. Increased levels of dopamine are thought to be responsible for some psychiatric complaints, hence the use of prochlorperazine as an antispychotic.

Availability: Prochlorperazine is available as an ingredient in some over-the-counter medicines.

Possible adverse effects: Drowsiness, dry mouth, dizziness and involuntary movements similar to those seen in people with Parkinson's disease. If patients experience muscular rigidity, or a sensation of feeling hot (that cannot otherwise be explained) they should stop taking the medicine and seek medical advice. Otherwise this drug should not be stopped abruptly when treating psychiatric disorders.

Other information: Patients should avoid exposure to sun, sunlamps and extremes of temperature.

CAUTION

Children: May be used in those over 1 year of age if necessary.

Alcohol: Should be avoided because of an increased risk of drowsiness associated with the combination.

Driving and operating machinery: As this drug can cause dizziness and drowsiness, patients should not drive or perform skilled tasks until they are certain they are not experiencing these, or any other side effects.

PROCYCLIDINE

Brand name: Kemadrin

Type of drug: Antimuscarinic

Uses: Treating the symptoms of Parkinson's disease.

How it works: Relieves muscle rigidity and excess salivation by acting in a part of the brain that controls movement. It is particularly effective in the early stages of the disease.

Availability: POM

Possible adverse effects: Dizziness, dry mouth, constipation and blurred vision.

CAUTION

Driving and operating machinery: As this drug can cause dizziness and blurred vision, patients receiving this medication should not drive or perform skilled tasks until they are certain they are not experiencing these or any other side effects.

PROGESTERONE

Brand name: Cyclogest, Gestone

Type of drug: Female sex hormone

Uses: Treating a variety menstrual problems and in hormone replacement therapy (HRT) in women with an intact uterus.

How it works: The same as the natural hormone progesterone, and acts to relieve symptoms such as irritability and tension.

Availability: POM

Possible adverse effects: Changes in the menstrual cycle are common; when used as suppositories, diarrhoea and flatulence are also reported.

Other information: Consult a doctor if there is excessive bleeding.

PROGUANIL

Brand name: Paludrine

Type of drug: Anti-malarial

Uses: Prevention of infection with malaria.

How it works: Proguanil prevents the malaria parasite producing folic acid, which it needs to live. This stops the infection before it can spread throughout the body.

Availability: OTC

Possible adverse effects: Stomach irritation, but this usually settles with continued treatment.

Other information: Should be taken at least 2 days, and preferably 1 week, before travelling and for 4 weeks after returning. Care should be taken to avoid being bitten by mosquitoes; use mosquito repellents, wear long sleeves and trousers after dusk, avoid swamps and marshy areas and to use mosquito nets around the bed. Do not take antacids or indigestion remedies within 3 hours of taking proguanil. Tablets should be taken after meals at approximately the same time each day.

PROMETHAZINE

Brand name: Avomine, Phenergan, Sominex

Type of drug: Antihistamine

Uses: Treating nausea, various skin allergies, Meniere's disease and travel sickness. Due to its sedative effects it is often also given as a premedication before surgery.

How it works: Blocks the action of histamine – a chemical released by the body in response to allergies. Histamine causes the majority of symptoms associated with allergies such as runny nose, itchy eyes and sneezing. Promethazine also stops the actions of acetylcholine, a chemical messenger in the brain, which together with histamine, are responsible for nausea and vomiting.

Availability: In over-the-counter preparations.

Possible adverse effects: Drowsiness, dry mouth and blurred vision. This medicine may also cause a reaction to sunlight, so avoid direct sunlight and sunlamps.

Other information: As this medicine may cause drowsiness, it is best taken at night. For motion sickness take promethazine a couple of hours before the journey starts.

CAUTION

Children: It may be prescribed for children over 2 years of age.

Alcohol: Should not be consumed whilst taking this medicine

Driving and operating machinery: As this drug can cause blurred vision and drowsiness, patients receiving this medication should not drive or perform skilled tasks until they are certain they are not experiencing these, or any other side effects.

PROPAFENONE

Brand name: Arythmol

Type of drug: Anti-arrhythmic

Uses: Treating disorders of heart rhythm.

How it works: Exactly how this drug works is not fully understood though propafenone regulates the heartbeat and allows normal rhythm.

Availability: POM

Possible adverse effects: Constipation, stomach problems, blurred vision, dizziness, dry mouth, unusual tastes in the mouth, nausea, vomiting and fatigue. It can make the symptoms of asthma worse. If breathlessness or wheezing occurs, stop this medicine and consult your doctor or pharmacist.

Other information: Should be taken after meals. Patient should report any signs of infection.

CAUTION

Driving and operating machinery: As this drug can cause dizziness, blurred vision and drowsiness, patients receiving this medication should not drive or perform any skilled tasks until they are certain they are not experiencing these side effects.

PROPRANOLOL

Brand name: Inderal, Inderal-LA

Type of drug: Beta-blocker

Uses: Treating high blood pressure, heart disorders, symptoms associated with an overactive thyroid and severe anxiety. May also be used to prevent migraine.

How it works: Slows the heart rate, reducing its workload and making it more efficient. A reduced heart rate is also thought to help lower the blood pressure. However, in the brain propranolol may act to constrict the blood vessels and so stop migraines.

Availability: POM

Possible adverse effects: Cold hands and feet, dizziness or light-headedness when standing up, confusion, problems sleeping, nightmares, headaches, changes in dreams and breathlessness have all been reported. If there is any breathlessness, wheezing or trouble with breathing, inform the doctor immediately as this drug can make asthma worse. Tiredness and nausea have also been reported with this medicine, but usually go away if patients continue treatment.

Other information: Patients with asthma should check with the doctor or pharmacist before taking this medicine.

CAUTION

Alcohol: Can cause a large fall in blood pressure so should only be consumed in moderation.

Driving and operating machinery: As this drug can cause dizziness and drowsiness, patients receiving this medication should not drive or perform skilled tasks until they are certain they are not experiencing these or any other side effects.

PROPYLTHIOURACIL

Brand name: Propylthiouracil

Type of drug: Anti-thyroid

Uses: Management of an overactive thyroid.

How it works: Stops the production of thyroid hormones, and so reduces the symptoms of an overactive thyroid gland.

Availability: POM

Possible adverse effects: Skin rashes and itches, hair loss, joint and muscle pain and stomach problems.

Other information: Regular blood tests will monitor the effect on thyroid function and also on the blood.

PSEUDOEPHEDRINE

Brand name: Sudafed

Type of drug: Sympathomimetic

Uses: Decongestant

How it works: Narrows the blood vessels in the nose, making them smaller. This allows more air through the nose, and relieves the feeling of congestion

Availability: In over-the-counter preparations.

Possible adverse effects: Excitation, increased heart rate and problems sleeping.

Other information: Patients with high blood pressure should consult the doctor, or pharmacist before taking this medicine.

CAUTION

Children: It may be prescribed for children over 2 years of age.

PYRAZINAMIDE

Brand name: Rifater (a combination of pyrazinamide, rifampicin and isoniazid)

Type of drug: Antibacterial

Uses: Treating tuberculosis.

How it works: The precise way this medicine works is unknown, but it is thought that it stops the bacteria producing chemicals needed to maintain its cell walls, without which the bacteria die.

Availability: POM

Possible adverse effects: May affect the liver leading to fever and generally feeling unwell, which should be reported to the doctor as soon as possible. It also causes nausea, vomiting, muscleand joint pain and gout.

Other information: Usually prescribed for several months together with other drugs to fight TB. It should be taken an empty stomach, which means 30 minutes before meals or 2 hours after.

PYRIDOSTIGMINE

Brand name: Mestinon

Type of drug: Anticholinesterase

Uses: Treatment of myasthenia gravis.

How it works: Stops the breakdown of a chemical messenger in the brain and nerves called acetylcholine, which allows better control over the muscles in myasthenia.

Availability: POM

Possible adverse effects: Abdominal cramps, excessive saliva, dizziness, drowsiness, nausea, headache, vomiting, blurred vision and diarrhoea.

Other information: Tablets should be swallowed whole, not chewed or crushed. Patients are usually taught to how to evaluate any changes in muscle strength.

CAUTION

Driving and operating machinery: As this drug can cause dizziness and drowsiness, patients receiving this medication should not drive or perform skilled tasks until they are certain they are not experiencing these or any other side effects.

QUETIAPINE

Brand name: Seroquel

Type of drug: Antipsychotic

Uses: Control the symptoms of schizophrenia and other related disorders.

How it works: Schizophrenia and related disorders are thought to be due to an excessive amount of the chemical messengers dopamine in the brain. Quetiapine reduces dopamine levels; it also has effects upon other messengers in the brain.

Availability: POM

Possible adverse effects: Drowsiness, sedation, dry mouth, constipation, anxiety, stomach upsets and weight gain. Dizziness and light-headedness may occur when first standing up.

Other information: This medicine is associated with fewer side effects than traditional antipsychotic medication.

CAUTION

Alcohol: Should be avoided because of an increased risk of drowsiness that is associated with the combination.

Driving and operating machinery: As this drug can cause drowsiness and dizziness, patients receiving this medication should not drive or perform such tasks until they are certain they are not experiencing any side effects.

QUINAPRIL

Brand name: Accupro

Type of drug: Anti-hypertensive, ACE inhibitor

Uses: The treatment of high blood pressure and heart failure.

How it works: It enables the blood vessels to relax, which allows them to increase in size. This reduces the pressure of the blood flowing through them.

Availability: POM

Possible adverse effects: Chest pain, nausea, indigestion, abdominal pains, headache, insomnia and blurred vision. A dry cough may occur when first taking the medicine, but this side effect usually lessens with continued use. Any cough that does not lessen should be reported to the pharmacist or doctor.

Other information: This should be used with caution in patients with kidney problems. Blood tests are usually carried out to monitor the levels of potassium. Patients should avoid salt substitutes containing potassium, and should take care in hot weather, or if taking exercise, to avoid over-heating and dehydration.

CAUTION

Alcohol: Should only be consumed in strict moderation whilst taking this medicine because the combination may cause a large fall in blood pressure.

Driving and operating machinery: As this drug can cause blurred vision, patients receiving this medication should not drive or perform such tasks until they are certain they are not experiencing any side effects.

QUININE

Brand name: Quinine

Type of drug: Anti-malarial

Uses: Treating malaria and it is also used to treat nocturnal leg cramps.

How it works: Kills the malaria parasite before it can reproduce.

Availability: POM

Possible adverse effects: Tinnitus, headache, nausea, visual problems, confusion. Hot, itchy and flushed skin can also occur.

Other information: Quinine is effective treatment of falciparum malaria, which tends to be the most severe form of malaria. When used for leg cramps this medicine may take at least 4 weeks to have an effect.

CAUTION

Children: This medicine may be prescribed for the treatment of malaria.

Driving and operating machinery: As this drug can cause confusion and visual problems, patients receiving this medication should not drive or perform skilled tasks until they are certain they are not experiencing any side effects.

RABEPRAZOLE

Brand name: Pariet

Type of drug: Ulcer healing drugs

Uses: Treatment and prevention of stomach and intestinal ulcers, and acid reflux causing heartburn

How it works: Reduces the production of stomach acid which may cause or worsen gut irritation or ulceration.

Availability: POM

Possible adverse effects: Dry mouth, headache, nausea and diarrhoea. Occasionally it can affect blood cells. If allergic symptoms occur such as wheezing or an itchy rash, the patient should stop taking the medication and seek urgent medical advice.

Other information: The tablets should not be crushed or chewed but swallowed whole. This medicine should be taken in the morning, 30 minutes before breakfast.

RALOXIFENE

Brand name: Evista

Type of drug: Selective oestrogen receptor modulator

Uses: Treatment and prevention of osteoporosis in women who have gone through menopause.

How it works: Following menopause, levels of oestrogen lessen. This has many effects, including increasing the likelihood of osteoporosis. Raloxifene increases the effectiveness of the remaining oestrogen that delays the progression of osteoporosis, but not other symptoms of the menopause.

Availability: POM

Possible adverse effects: Flushing of the skin, cramping pains in the legs, flu-like symptoms and fluid retention which may cause breast tenderness. May also increase the risk of blood clots in the leg veins or lungs. If chest pain and shortness of breath or leg pain and swelling that cannot be explained occur then seek urgent medical advice. Bleeding from the uterus should be reported to your doctor.

Other information: To be taken for a long time and must be taken as prescribed.

RAMIPRIL

Brand name: Tritace

Type of drug: Anti-hypertensive, ACE inhibitor

Uses: Treatment of high blood pressure and heart failure, and to prevent heart attacks, stroke and related problems.

How it works: It allows the blood vessels to relax, which enables them to increase in size. This reduces the pressure of the blood flowing through them.

Availability: POM

Possible adverse effects: Chest pain, loss of appetite, indigestion, abdominal pains, headache, anxiety, dizziness and skin rash. A dry cough may occur when first taking this medicine, but this side effect usually lessens with continued use. A cough that does not go away should be reported to the doctor or pharmacist.

Other information: Should be used with caution in patients with kidney problems. Blood tests are usually carried out to monitor the levels of potassium. Patients should avoid salt substitutes containing potassium, and should take care in hot weather, or if taking exercise, to avoid over-heating and dehydration.

CAUTION

Alcohol: Should only be consumed in strict moderation because the combination may cause a large fall in blood pressure.

Driving and operating machinery: As this drug can cause dizziness and confusion, patients receiving this medication should not drive or perform such tasks until they are certain they are not experiencing any side effects.

RANITIDINE

Brand name: Zantac, Pyloric

Type of drug: Ulcer healing drugs

Uses: Treatment and prevention of stomach and duodenal ulcers and acid reflux. It may also be used in other stomach conditions where stomach acid increases the risk of irritation or ulceration such as *Helicobacter Pylori* infection.

How it works: This drug reduces the production of gastric acid and pepsin, an enzyme that helps in the digestion of protein. Gastric acid, although necessary for digestion of food, can cause stomach and gut irritation and ulceration.

Availability: OCM

Possible adverse effects: The most commonly reported side effects are rashes. It can also cause darkening of the tongue and breast enlargement in men.

Other information: Patient must swallow medication whole with water, preferably before meals.

REBOXETINE
Brand name: Edronax
Type of drug: Antidepressant
Uses: Treatment of depression.
How it works: Stops the breakdown of a chemical messenger in the brain called noradrenaline. An increased level of noradrenaline in the brain is thought to improve mood, and allow the patient to live a more balanced daily life.
Availability: POM
Possible adverse effects: Problems sleeping and with vision, a feeling of disorientation, dry mouth, constipation, changes in appetite, dizziness, sweating and chills.
Other information: It may take between 2 and 4 weeks to see the beneficial effects of this medication.
CAUTION
Alcohol: Should be avoided whilst taking this medicine, because the combination may reduce the effectiveness of reboxetine.
Driving and operating machinery: As this drug can cause dizziness and visual problems, patients should not drive or perform skilled tasks until they are certain they are not experiencing any side effects.

REPAGLINIDE
Brand name: Novonorm
Type of drug: Antidiabetic
Uses: Management of non-insulin dependent diabetes, for example, in cases where the pancreas is still producing some insulin.
How it works: Increases the amount of insulin secreted by the pancreas which in turn reduces the levels of sugar in the blood.
Availability: POM
Possible adverse effects: May cause abdominal pain, diarrhoea and vomiting. Can also cause blood sugar levels to become very low which requires urgent correction.

Other information: This medicine should be taken before main meals. A healthy diet, exercise programme and weight loss where appropriate are also important as well as specific recommendations from the doctor, diabetic nurse or pharmacist. Intermittent glucose and blood testing is required.

RIFAMPICIN
Brand name: Rifadin, Rimactane
Type of drug: Antibiotic
Uses: Treatment of tuberculosis (TB), leprosy and other infections. It is given to people who have come into contact with certain forms of meningitis.
How it works: Stops the production of chemicals essential to the survival of the bacteria, which kills them.
Availability: POM
Possible adverse effects: Headache, fatigue, weight loss, abdominal pain, and orange-red coloured urine and tears. Soft contact lenses may be permanently stained from using this medicine.
Other information: May render oral contraceptives ineffective and disrupt the menstrual cycle. It is recommended that alternative methods of contraception are used during, and preferably for 8 weeks after a course of treatment. Take 30 minutes before or 2 hours after food. It is usually given in combination with at least 1 other antibiotic for the treatment of tuberculosis, and prolonged treatment is usually necessary. It should be taken regularly as prescribed, and the course completed. May be used in children to treat or prevent some infections.

RISPERIDONE
Brand name: Risperdal
Type of drug: Antipsychotic
Uses: Treatment of schizophrenia and related disorders.
How it works: Schizophrenia and related disorders are thought to be due to an excess of the chemical messenger dopamine in the brain. Risperidone reduces dopamine levels; it also has effects upon other messengers in the brain.

Availability: POM

Possible adverse effects: Insomnia, anxiety, headache, drowsiness, blurred vision, constipation, nausea and vomiting and poor concentration.

Other information: If used for a long time, movement disorders may occur. Any unintentional movements should be reported to the doctor.

CAUTION

Children: This medicine may be used in children over 15 years of age.

Alcohol: Should be avoided because of the increased risk of drowsiness associated with the combination.

Driving and operating machinery: As this drug can cause drowsiness and blurred vision, patients receiving this medication should not drive or perform such tasks until they are certain they are not experiencing any side effects.

ROPINIROLE

Brand name: Requip

Type of drug: Dopaminergic

Uses: Treatment of some of the symptoms of Parkinson's disease.

How it works: Parkinson's disease is believed to be due to low levels of the chemical messenger, dopamine, in the brain . Ropinirole is capable of mimicking dopamine, and this helps to counteract the symptoms of Parkinson's disease.

Availability: POM

Possible adverse effects: Nausea, drowsiness, vomiting, abdominal pains, sleepiness and fluid retention.

Other information: The patient should be warned to rise slowly immediately after sitting or lying down to avoid becoming dizzy. Nausea will be minimised if this drug is taken with food.

CAUTION

Alcohol: Avoid alcohol while taking it.

Driving and operating machinery: As this drug can cause excessive daytime drowsiness that may appear suddenly, it is recommended that patients receiving this medication do not drive or perform such tasks.

ROSIGLITAZONE

Brand name: Avandia

Type of drug: Thiazolidinedione

Uses: Treatment of non-insulin dependent diabetes.

How it works: This medication works by increasing the sensitivity of the body to insulin. This means that sugar is taken up more readily by cells, and sugar producing processes are turned off in the presence of smaller amounts of insulin.

Availability: POM

Possible adverse effects: Weight gain, a reduced number of red cells in the blood and raised amounts of cholesterol and fats in the blood. Can also cause blood sugar levels to become very low requiring urgent correction.

Other information: A healthy diet, exercise and weight loss (where appropriate) are also important, as well as any specific recommendations given to them by the doctor, diabetic nurse or pharmacist.

CAUTION

Alcohol: Should only be consumed in strict moderation while taking this medicine as the combination may affect the levels of sugar in the blood.

ROSUVASTATIN

Brand name: Crestor

Type of drug: Lipid lowering drug

Uses: Treatment of high cholesterol and prevention of coronary heart disease.

How it works: Stops an enzyme in the liver called HMG-CoA Reductase from producing cholesterol. This then reduces the amount of cholesterol in the blood.

Availability: POM

Possible adverse effects: Headache, dizziness, nausea, constipation and stomach pains. It may also cause muscle pain or weakness which should be reported to the doctor.

Other information: This medicine should be taken in combination with a diet advised by the doctor or pharmacist.

CAUTION

Driving and operating machinery: As this medicine may cause dizziness, patients should not drive or perform skilled tasks until they are certain they are not experiencing this or any other side effects.

SALBUTAMOL

Brand name: Salamol, Ventolin, Volma
Type of drug: Bronchodilator
Uses: To treat asthma and other lung diseases. It is also used to stop premature labour.
How it works: Widens the airways, which makes it easier to breathe.
Availability: POM
Possible adverse effects: Muscle tremor, anxiety, increased heart rate and restlessness have all been reported. Low blood potassium levels can occur with repeated use.
Other information: It is important to use the correct inhaler technique as taught and described in the leaflet supplied with the medicine. If requiring more than eight puffs in 24 hours, consult your doctor. This medicine may be prescribed for children of any age.

SALICYLIC ACID

Brand name: Occlusal, and used as an ingredient in many preparations
Type of drug: Salicylate
Uses: Treatment of a variety of skin conditions including warts.
How it works: It removes the top layers of skin and prevents infection.
Availability: OTC
Possible adverse effects: As this medicine is usually only used on the skin there are very few adverse effects associated with it. The main complaint is an irritation of the skin surrounding the area where the medicine is applied, which can be relieved by only applying the medicine exactly where it is required.
Other information: Patients who are allergic to aspirin should not use this medicine. Diabetic patients should only use this medicine after consulting a doctor.

SALMETEROL

Brand name: Serevent

Type of drug: Bronchodilator

Uses: To prevent asthma and other lung diseases.

How it works: Salmeterol relaxes the muscles that control the diameter of the lungs. This makes the airways larger and makes it easier to breathe properly.

Availability: POM

Possible adverse effects: Tremor, headaches and dizziness. If wheezing or chest tightness and pain worsens, stop taking the medicine and seek medical advice.

Other information: Salmeterol should not be used more than twice daily and must be used regularly for several days for the full effect to become apparent. It is also important to use the correct inhaler technique as taught

CAUTION

Children: This medicine may be used to treat asthma in children over 4 years of age.

Driving and operating machinery: As this drug can cause dizziness and drowsiness, patients receiving this medication should not drive or perform skilled tasks until they are certain they are not experiencing these, or any other side effects.

SAQUINAVIR

Brand name: Invirase

Type of drug: Antiviral

Uses: To treat HIV infection.

How it works: Prevents the HIV virus from reaching maturity and multiplying.

Availability: POM

Possible adverse effects: Nausea, vomiting, headache, diarrhoea and abdominal discomfort.

Other information: The drug is best taken two hours after a full meal. This drug will usually be given in conjunction with other antiretroviral drugs. This medicine may be prescribed for patients over 16 years of age.

CAUTION

Driving and operating machinery: As this medicine may affect the ability to drive or any perform skilled tasks, patients must ensure they are free from any of these effects before attempting to drive or undertake such tasks.

SELEGILINE
Brand name: Eldepryl, Zelapar
Type of drug: Monoamine-oxidase-B Inhibitor
Uses: Treatment of the symptoms of Parkinson's disease.
How it works: Parkinson's disease is thought to be due to a decreased amount of a chemical messenger called dopamine in the brain. Selegiline stops the breakdown of dopamine in the body, and so relieves the symptoms of the disease.
Availability: POM
Possible adverse effects: Problems sleeping, confusion, dry mouth, uncontrolled and unintentional movement, feelings of disorientation, feeling dizzy or light-headed when standing up and nausea.
Other information: This medicine may be used alone or with other medicines.
CAUTION
Driving and operating machinery: As this drug can cause dizziness and drowsiness, patients receiving this medication should not drive or perform skilled tasks until they are certain they are not experiencing these or any other side effects.

SENNA
Brand name: Senokot
Type of drug: Stimulant laxatives
Uses: Treatment of constipation.
How it works: Stimulates contraction of the bowel and enhances propulsion of faeces.
Availability: Senna is available in some over-the-counter preparations.
Possible adverse effects: Diarrhoea, and stomach pain.
Other information: This medicine may change the colour of the stools, but this is normal when taking senna. It is not usually used for prolonged periods of time. It is important to increase the amount of water consumed

during the day whilst taking this medicine. Senna may be used in pregnancy and whilst breastfeeding.

CAUTION

Children: It may be prescribed for children over 2 years of age.

SERTRALINE

Brand name: Lustral

Type of drug: Selective serotonin re-uptake inhibitor

Uses: Treatment of depression and obsessive compulsive disorders.

How it works: Sertraline improves the mood, increases energy and stimulates an interest in day-to-day living without the sedative effects of similar drugs.

Availability: POM

Possible adverse effects: Nausea, upset stomach and heartburn, dry mouth, sweating and diarrhoea.

Other information: This medicine is usually only taken once each day.

CAUTION

Alcohol: Should be avoided while taking this medicine as it may make the condition worse.

Driving and operating machinery: As this drug may impair the ability to perform skilled tasks, patients receiving this medication should be certain they are not experiencing any side effects.

SIBUTRAMINE

Brand name: Reductil

Type of drug: Appetite suppressant

Uses: To aid weight loss in obese patients – working in combination with other measures.

How it works: Acts in the brain to increase the feeling of fullness or satiety. This stops the brain sending the urge to eat, allowing weight loss when used with exercise and a strictly controlled diet.

Availability: POM

Possible adverse effects: Constipation, dry mouth, insomnia, flushing, nausea, feeling light-headed, headache, feeling anxious and sweating more than usual.

Other information: Treatment will be reviewed after three months to see if it is working. Must be used in conjunction with other advice given on diet and exercise by a doctor or pharmacist. This medicine is best taken in the morning. Treatment will usually only last for a maximum of 12 months.

CAUTION

Alcohol: Should be avoided while taking this medicine

Driving and operating machinery: Patients receiving this medication should not drive or perform skilled tasks until they are certain they are not experiencing these or any other side effects.

SILDENAFIL

Brand name: Viagra

Type of drug: Phosphodiesterase inhibitor

Uses: Treatment of erectile dysfunction.

How it works: Enables impotent men to attain and maintain an erection.

Availability: POM

Possible adverse effects: Indigestion, headache, flushing, dizziness, visual disturbances and nasal congestion.

Other information: Should not be used at the same time as other impotence treatments or by people with heart problems. This drug will not be prescribed on the NHS unless the problem is caused by a medical disorder. This medicine should be taken about an hour before sexual activity and on an empty stomach.

CAUTION

Driving and operating machinery: As this drug can cause dizziness and visual problems, patients receiving this medication should not drive or perform skilled tasks until they are certain they are not experiencing these or any other side effects.

SIMVASTATIN

Brand name: Zocor

Type of drug: HMG-CoA Reductase inhibitor

Uses: Treatment of high cholesterol and to prevent problems with the heart.

How it works: Stops an enzyme in the liver, HMG-CoA Reductase, from producing cholesterol. This will reduce the amount of cholesterol in the blood.

Availability: Available in an over-the-counter preparation.

Possible adverse effects: Although rare, nausea and diarrhoea have been reported. Any joint or muscle pain, weakness, or cramp that cannot be attributed to any other activity should be reported to the doctor immediately and no further doses of the medicine taken, as it can cause inflammation of the muscles.

Other information: Tests to assess liver function and cholesterol levels may be performed. This medicine should be taken at night.

SIROLIMUS

Brand name: Rapamune

Type of drug: Calcineurin inhibitor

Uses: To prevent rejection of transplanted kidneys.

How it works: This medicine stops the activation of the immune system in response to something the body does not recognise. This stops the body attacking the transplanted organ, and so allows it to function normally.

Availability: POM

Possible adverse effects: Nausea, stomach pain, diarrhoea, anaemia, increased susceptibility to infection, joint pain, acne and rashes. Any sign of warmth or pain in the legs, sore throat, mouth ulcers, or unexplained bruising and bleeding should be reported to the doctor immediately.

Other information: This medicine is only given in hospital under the supervision of a doctor experienced in treating cancer. Avoid grapefruit juice while taking this medicine. The doctor will ask for regular blood tests to be carried out whilst this medicine is being taken, and regular assessment of kidney function will be undertaken.

CAUTION

Driving and operating machinery: Patients receiving this medication should not drive or perform skilled tasks until they are certain they are not experiencing these or any other side effects.

SODIUM AUROTHIOMALATE

Brand name: Myocrisin

Type of drug: Disease modifying anti-rheumatic drug

Uses: To treat rheumatoid arthritis in both adults and children.

How it works: The precise way that this medicine works is not totally understood. However this medicine seems to stop the condition becoming more serious, and improves patients' quality of life.

Availability: POM

Possible adverse effects: The most commonly reported side effects are a rash and itching after the injection is given. However, very serious side effects such as changes in the number of cells in the blood and problems with the lungs have also been reported. A potentially fatal allergic reaction can occur in a small minority of patients. This will appear as weakness, flushing, abdominal pain and difficulty with breathing. If this occurs, then a doctor should be consulted immediately. Patients should also report a sore throat, mouth ulcers, fever, any type of infection, and rashes, immediately.

Other information: The drug can take several months to reach full effectiveness. Specialists usually start this medicine in hospitals. The doctor may ask for X-rays to be conducted to check for any chest problems resulting from treatment.

SODIUM CROMOGLICATE

(Formerly known as: sodium chromoglycate)

Brand name: Intal, Opticrom, Rynacrom

Type of drug: Anti-inflammatory

Uses: Treatment of allergies and asthma.

How it works: Stops the release of histamine by the body. This reduces the severity of any allergic reaction.

Availability: Available in some over-the-counter preparations.

Possible adverse effects: When used as an inhaler, coughing, wheezing and throat irritation have been reported as side effects. When used as eye drops the only reported adverse effect is blurred vision for a short period of time.

Other information: This medicine is available as inhalers, nasal sprays and eye drops. It is not effective for the relief of an asthmatic attack, and it may take up to six weeks for benefits to be felt. When used for asthma it is important to use the medication regularly as prescribed by the doctor. This medicine may be prescribed to treat children.

SODIUM PICOSULFATE

(Formerly known as sodium picosulphate)
Brand name: Laxoberal, Dulco-Lax Liquid
Type of drug: Stimulant laxative
Uses: Relief of constipation.
How it works: Speeds the passage of content through the gut, relieving constipation.
Availability: POM
Possible adverse effects: Stomach pain and diarrhoea.
Other information: The instructions given with this medicine should be strictly adhered to. It is usually prescribed in short courses, and not taken for long-term problems. Plenty of fluid should also be taken. This medicine may be prescribed for children of any age.

SODIUM VALPROATE

Brand name: Epilim
Type of drug: Anti-epileptic
Uses: Treatment of epilepsy.
How it works: An epileptic fit (or seizure) is thought to occur when the nerves in the brain become overactive. Sodium valproate acts to stop this over activity, and so reduces the chances of a seizure occurring.
Availability: POM
Possible adverse effects: There can be some nausea, vomiting and stomach upsets at the start of treatment. Weight gain, reduced levels of platelets, hair loss and drowsiness have also been reported.
Other information: Blood tests may be performed to monitor drug levels and to check the liver. This medicine should be taken after food to try and minimise any stomach upset.
CAUTION
Children: This medicine is used to treat epilepsy in children.

Alcohol: Must not be consumed while taking this medicine.

Driving and operating machinery: The DVLA has special requirements for epileptics who wish to drive; the latest information should be consulted before driving.

SOMATROPIN

Brand name: Genotropin

Type of drug: Pituitary hormone

Uses: Treatment of growth problems caused by a deficiency in the growth hormone produced by the pituitary gland.

How it works: A synthetic form of growth hormone, it performs the same function – promoting normal growth and development. It stimulates skeletal, bone, muscle and organ growth.

Availability: POM

Possible adverse effects: Muscle stiffness, joint and muscle pain, rashes where the medicine is injected and fluid retention in adults.

Other information: When used in children, treatment will continue throughout childhood until an acceptable height is reached. Treatment may be stopped for a few months and then restarted depending on rate of growth. This medicine is commonly used to treat growth problems in children.

SOTALOL

Brand name: Beta-cardone, Sotacor

Type of drug: Beta-blocker

Uses: Treatment of disorders of heart rhythm.

How it works: Slows the rate at which the heart beats, bringing it back to normal.

Availability: POM

Possible adverse effects: Fluid retention, nausea, vomiting, diarrhoea, stomach pain, indigestion, flatulence, cramps, tiredness, dizziness, headache, problems sleeping, changes in mood and problems with vision. If chest pain or tightness or difficulty breathing occurs after taking this medicine, it should be discontinued and the advice of a doctor sought immediately.

Other information: This medicine should be taken as directed until told to stop by the doctor. Asthmatics should consult the doctor or pharmacist before taking this medicine.

CAUTION

Alcohol: Should only be consumed in strict moderation whilst taking this medicine because the combination can cause a greater than expected drop in blood pressure.

Driving and operating machinery: As this drug can cause dizziness and fatigue, patients receiving this medication should not drive or perform skilled tasks until they are certain they are not experiencing these or any other side effects.

SPIRONOLACTONE

Brand name: Aldactone

Type of drug: Potassium-sparing diuretic

Uses: Treatment of excess fluid in heart failure, liver and kidney disease and pre-menstrual syndrome.

How it works: Acts on the kidneys to encourage the expulsion of excess fluid. Unlike many diuretics, potassium is not lost into the urine.

Availability: POM

Possible adverse effects: Nausea, stomach upsets, drowsiness and tiredness. Breast growth and tenderness in males has also been reported with this medicine

Other information: Blood tests may be taken to monitor the kidneys. This medicine may be prescribed to treat children.

SUCRALFATE

Brand name: Antepsin

Type of drug: Ulcer-healing

Uses: Promotes the healing of stomach and duodenal ulcers.

How it works: Forms a barrier over the ulcer which protects it from further attack by stomach acid and gives it the opportunity to heal.

Availability: POM

Possible adverse effects: Constipation, diarrhoea, nausea, indigestion, upset stomach.

Other information: This medication should be taken on an empty stomach at least one hour before meals. Indigestion remedies should not be taken within 30 minutes either side of taking sucralfate.

CAUTION

Driving and operating machinery: Patients receiving this medication should not drive or perform skilled tasks until they are certain they are not experiencing any side effects.

SULFASALAZINE

(Formerly known as: sulphasalazine)

Brand name: Salazopyrin

Type of drug: Aminosalicylate

Uses: Treatment of Crohn's disease and ulcerative colitis. This medicine has also been found to be beneficial in the treatment of rheumatoid arthritis.

How it works: Related to aspirin, this medicine is believed to work by stopping the production of chemicals which cause inflammation in the bowel. It is likely that a similar process occurs within the joints in rheumatoid arthritis.

Availability: POM

Possible adverse effects: Nausea, appetite loss, headache, skin rashes and joint pain. May cause orange or yellow urine. This medicine may have an effect on the immune system, and any sign of bleeding, or bruising which cannot be explained, sore throat, or generally feeling unwell should be reported to the doctor immediately.

Other information: Patients allergic to aspirin or indomethacin may also be allergic to acemetacin and should not take this medicine without advice from the doctor or pharmacist. Treatment will be long-term. Patients should not wear contact lenses whilst taking this medicine because they may be stained. Sulfasalazine may be used in pregnancy, or whilst breast-feeding a child.

CAUTION

Children: This medicine may be used to treat children over the age of 2 years old.

SULFINPYRAZONE

(Formerly known as: sulphinpyrazone)

Brand name: Anturan

Type of drug: Drug for prevention of gout

Uses: To prevent attacks of gout.

How it works: Gout is thought to be caused by a waste product, urate, being deposited in the joints. This causes inflammation and swelling leading to gout. Sulfinpyrazone stops urate being reabsorbed by the body once it is excreted into the urine.

Availability: POM

Possible adverse effects: Nausea, vomiting and diarrhoea.

Other information: Sulfinpyrazone must be taken all the time and only stopped upon the advice of a doctor. It is best taken with or after meals, and should not be taken with aspirin.

CAUTION

Alcohol: Should only be consumed in strict moderation, as this can cause an attack of gout.

SULINDAC

Brand name: Clinoril

Type of drug: Non-steroidal anti-inflammatory

Uses: Treatment of arthritis, gout, and other related problems.

How it works: Inhibits the actions of an enzyme called cyclo-oxygenase. This enzyme produces chemical messengers that start, and continue the inflammatory process.

Availability: POM

Possible adverse effects: Stomach pain, nausea, vomiting, indigestion, diarrhoea or constipation, dizziness, headache, ringing in the ears and rashes. Report any sign of chest pain, tightness, or difficulty breathing to the doctor immediately.

Other information: Should be taken with or after meals. Patients who are allergic to, or taking, aspirin or related medicines should consult a pharmacist, or doctor before using the medicine.

CAUTION

Driving and operating machinery: As this drug can cause dizziness, patients receiving this medication should not drive or perform skilled tasks until they are certain they are not experiencing this or any other side effects.

SULPIRIDE

Brand name: Dolmatil, Sulpitil

Type of drug: Anti-psychotic

Uses: Treatment of schizophrenia.

How it works: Schizophrenia and other similar disorders are believed to occur when too much dopamine, a chemical messenger, is present in certain parts of the brain. Sulpiride stops the action of dopamine, and so reduces the severity of the symptoms associated with schizophrenia.

Availability: POM

Possible adverse effects: Drowsiness – which may last into the next day, symptoms of Parkinson's disease such as tremor, uncontrolled and involuntary movements, and increased salivation and weight gain.

CAUTION

Children: Sulpiride may be prescribed for children over 14 years of age

Alcohol: Must not be consumed while taking this medicine.

Driving and operating machinery: As this drug can cause dizziness and drowsiness, patients receiving this medication should not drive or perform skilled tasks until they are certain they are not experiencing these or any other side effects.

SUMATRIPTAN

Brand name: Imigran

Type of drug: Anti-migraine

Uses: Relieves acute migraine attacks.

How it works: Migraine appears to result from spasms within the blood vessels of the brain. Sumatriptan enhances the actions of the chemical messenger serotonin, which acts on the blood vessels.

Availability: POM

Possible adverse effects: Tingling sensations, feeling hot, dizziness, flushing and the arms, chest or head may feel heavy.

Other information: Sumatriptan is only used to stop attacks once they have occurred – it will not prevent them from recurring.

CAUTION

Driving and operating machinery: As this drug can cause dizziness, patients receiving this medication should not drive or perform skilled tasks until they are certain they are not experiencing this or any other side effects.

TACALCITOL

Brand name: Curatoderm

Type of drug: Vitamin D analogue

Uses: Treatment of certain types of psoriasis.

How it works: Acts in the same way as natural vitamin D. When applied to the skin it slows down the rate at which certain types of cells in the skin multiply. This stops the formation of plaques of skin, which characterises the condition.

Availability: POM

Possible adverse effects: Irritation of the skin including burning and itching sensations.

Other information: Wash hands immediately after use and avoid contact with the eyes.

TACROLIMUS

Brand name: Prograf

Type of drug: Calcineurin inhibitor

Uses: When taken orally, it is used to prevent rejection of kidney and liver transplants. When applied to the skin it is used to treat eczema and other skin conditions.

How it works: Stops the production of cells within the immune system that cause inflammation and damage in autoimmune and inflammatory diseases; these cells are responsible for organ rejection after transplant surgery.

Availability: POM

Possible adverse effects: When taken as capsules the body's ability to fight infection will be reduced so any sign of sore throat, mouth ulcers, raised temperatures, bleeding or bruising that cannot be explained, or generally feeling unwell should be reported to the doctor immediately.

Dehydration, tremor, headache, problems sleeping, dizziness, confusion, changes in mood, uncoordinated movement, problems with hearing, problems breathing (which should be reported to the doctor immediately), diarrhoea, nausea, and vomiting, stomach upset and pain, weight changes, itchy sweaty skin, muscle cramps and pain.

When used as an ointment stinging and burning sensations when the product is applied are common and itching may also occur. The area the cream is applied to may also become reddened with a feeling of warmth.

Other information: Capsules should be swallowed whole and not chewed, and should be taken about one hour before, or two to three hours after food. Patients must not stop taking this medicine unless told to do so by the doctor. This medicine is only given in hospital under the supervision of a doctor experienced in treating cancer. Regular blood tests are required to assess the effects and to monitor the blood levels of the drug. Patients should avoid direct sunlight and not use sun lamps. If going into the sun use a total sun block, wear a long-sleeved top, wide-brimmed hat and sunglasses.

Patients should not drink grapefruit juice whilst taking this medicine. The ointment should be applied sparingly over the affected areas. Once the condition is cleared, stop using the ointment. It usually takes at least 1 week before any effect is noticed. When using the ointment, hands should be washed if not being treated and the product should not be applied to the eyes, nose or mouth. It may be prescribed for patients over the age of 16 years old for dermatitis.

CAUTION

Children: It may be prescribed to children for prevention of transplant rejection.

Pregnancy: The effectiveness of the contraceptive pill may be reduced as a result of using this medicine.

Alcohol: Should be avoided whilst taking this medicine. This also applies to those using the ointment where facial flushing and further irritation of the skin have occurred.

Driving and operating machinery: As this drug can cause problems with vision, patients receiving this medication should not drive or perform skilled tasks until they are certain they are not experiencing these or any other side effects.

TADALAFIL

Brand name: Cialis
Type of drug: Phosphodiesterase inhibitor
Uses: Treatment of impotence in men.
How it works: Enables impotent men to achieve and maintain an erection.
Availability: POM
Possible adverse effects: Headache, dizziness, flushing, indigestion and muscle pain.
Other information: Tadalafil should not be used more than once each day, because its effects may last for longer than 24 hours. Patients who are receiving medicines for heart or circulation should consult the doctor before using this medicine. Do not drink grapefruit juice whilst taking this medicine as it may alter its effectiveness.

TAMOXIFEN

Brand name: Nolvadex
Type of drug: Anti-cancer
Uses: Treatment of breast cancer.
How it works: It is thought to block the action of some hormones that cancer cells require for survival.
Availability: POM
Possible adverse effects: Nausea, vomiting, diarrhoea, irregularities in the menstrual cycle, hot flushes and vaginal discharges. Liver damage can also occur. This medication is also associated with an increased risk of clots in the legs and lungs and raised lipids in the blood.
Other information: This treatment may be given for up to 5 years. This drug should not be discontinued unless advised by a doctor
CAUTION
Pregnancy: A barrier contraceptive is recommended during treatment. If patients suspect that they may be pregnant, the doctor must be informed straight away.

Driving and operating machinery: Patients receiving this medication should not drive or perform skilled tasks until they are certain they are not experiencing any side effects.

TAMSULOSIN

Brand name: Flomax MR

Type of drug: Alpha-blocker

Uses: Treatment of benign prostate hyperplasia.

How it works: It relaxes the muscles in the bladder neck, with the result that urine flow is improved.

Availability: POM

Possible adverse effects: Dizziness, headache, decrease in blood pressure (which may be experienced as a feeling of dizziness), or light-headedness when standing up, blurred vision, and palpitations.

Other information: The capsules should be taken after meals at approximately the same time each day. They should not be chewed or crushed. Patients should get up slowly from the bed or chairs at the beginning of therapy to prevent the light-headedness or dizzy feeling that might result in their falling over.

CAUTION

Driving and operating machinery: As this drug can cause dizziness and problems with vision, patients should not drive or perform any skilled tasks until they are certain that they are not experiencing these or any other side effects.

TEMAZEPAM

Brand name: Available only as a generic medicine

Type of drug: Benzodiazepine

Uses: Treatment of short-term insomnia.

How it works: Stops the transmission of messages through the nerves in the brain. This has the effect of relieving anxiety, and encouraging sleep.

Availability: POM

Possible adverse effects: Drowsiness, which may continue into the next day, confusion, headache, tiredness and double vision. When this medicine is stopped it may cause you to become more anxious and you may have trouble sleeping.

Other information: Should only be taken for short periods of time as it can be habit-forming. A maximum course of 4 weeks is usually prescribed.

CAUTION

Alcohol: Should be avoided with this medicine because the combination may increase the effect of drowsiness during the day.

Driving and operating machinery: As this drug can cause drowsiness – that may continue into the next day, patients receiving this medication should not drive or perform skilled tasks until they are certain that they are not experiencing these or any other side effects.

TENOXICAM

Brand name: Mobiflex

Type of drug: Non-steroidal anti-inflammatory

Uses: To treat pain in arthritis, and other muscular disorders.

How it works: Tenoxicam works by inhibiting the actions of an enzyme called cyclo-oxygenase. This enzyme produces chemical messengers that start and continue the inflammatory process.

Availability: POM

Possible adverse effects: This drug irritates the stomach, so can cause nausea, diarrhoea, indigestion and stomach pain. Occasionally bleeding can occur from the stomach, which is seen as darkened stools and severe stomach pain. Any sign of these should be reported to a doctor immediately. Patients who are allergic to aspirin may also be allergic to tenoxicam and should not take this medicine without advice from the doctor or pharmacist.

Other information: This medicine should be taken with or after meals to reduce the effects on the stomach. Before taking any pain relief bought over the counter, seek the advice of a pharmacist. Asthmatic patients should consult the doctor or pharmacist before taking this medicine as it can make asthma worse.

TERAZOSIN

Brand name: Hytrin

Type of drug: Alpha-blocker

Uses: To treat mild to moderate raised blood pressure and benign prostate hyperplasia.

How it works: Relaxes blood vessels causing them to widen, which improves blood flow and decreases blood pressure. When used for benign prostate hyperplasia, terazosin relaxes the muscles at the exit of the bladder making it easier to pass urine.

Availability: POM

Possible adverse effects: Dizziness, light-headedness, low blood pressure, headache, fatigue, problems with vision and fluid retention.

Other information: Dizziness and fainting may occur with the first dose. It should not be stopped abruptly, and must be taken until advised otherwise by a doctor.

CAUTION

Alcohol: Should only be consumed in moderation whilst taking this medicine, because the combination may further reduce the blood pressure, or increase any drowsiness that may be experienced.

Driving and operating machinery: Terazosin may cause drowsiness and dizziness in some patients, which may impair the ability to drive or perform skilled tasks. Patients should ensure that they are not affected before attempting to drive or undertake such tasks. Patients must wait at least 12 hours after taking the first dose of treatment before driving.

TERBINAFINE

Brand name: Lamisil

Type of drug: Anti-fungal

Uses: Treatment of fungal skin infections.

How it works: Stops the production of chemicals essential for the maintenance of the cell wall of the fungus.

Availability: Terbinafine is available as a cream and spray over-the-counter.

Possible adverse effects: When taken as tablets, the more common adverse effects are upset stomach, nausea, indigestion, headache and a skin rash. If a rash occurs, consult the doctor or pharmacist as soon as possible. This drug can also cause liver damage. When using a cream, the area where it is applied may become red, itchy and painful.

Other information: When using the cream avoid contact with the eyes, nose and mouth. The infection should clear up within a couple of weeks, but the cream should be applied for as long as prescribed even if the infection appears to have cleared up. The tablets should be taken regularly, and the prescribed course completed. The course of tablets may last from several weeks to several months depending on where the infection is.

CAUTION

Children: When prescribed as tablets, this may be used for children.

Driving and operating machinery: Patients receiving this medication should not drive or perform skilled tasks until they are certain they are not experiencing any side effects.

TERBUTALINE

Brand name: Bricanyl

Type of drug: Bronchodilator

Uses: Treatment of asthma and other lung problems.

How it works: Acts on the muscles within the lungs expanding the small airways. This makes it easier to get air in and out of the lungs so eases breathing.

Availability: POM

Possible adverse effects: Nausea, headache, tremor, sore throat and cramping pains.

Other information: The tablets should be swallowed whole and not crushed or chewed. It is important to use the correct inhaler technique as taught and described in the leaflet supplied with the medicine.

CAUTION

Children: This medicine is used in the treatment of asthma in children.

Driving and operating machinery: Patients receiving this medication should not drive or perform skilled tasks until they are certain they are not experiencing any side effects.

TETRACYCLINE

Brand name: Achromycin, Topicycline

Type of drug: Tetracycline antibiotic

Uses: Treatment of infections and acne.

How it works: Tetracycline stops the production of chemicals which are essential for the successful multiplication of the bacteria. As the bacteria cannot reproduce it allows the body's immune system a better chance to clear the infection.

Availability: POM

Possible adverse effects: When taken by mouth nausea, vomiting, diarrhoea, headache and dizziness. Any rash or difficulty in breathing should be reported to the doctor immediately. When applied to the skin there may be redness, itching and pain where it's applied. Tetracycline applied to the skin may leave a yellow residue that can stain clothes and bedding. An unusual side effect seen with this medicine on prolonged use is discolouration of the teeth, which turns them yellow, grey, or brown. There may be a reduction in the amount of enamel on the teeth. It can also cause a rash to develop on exposure to sunlight.

Other information: This medicine should not be taken at the same time of day as milk, indigestion remedies, or medicines containing zinc or iron. It should be taken regularly throughout the prescribed course and the full course completed. Tetracycline should be taken before food, on an empty stomach with a glass of water.

CAUTION

Children: This medicine should not be used in children under the age of 12 years old.

Pregnancy and breastfeeding: Patients should not take this medicine if pregnant or breastfeeding.

Driving and operating machinery: This medicine may cause headache, dizziness and problems with vision in some patients, which may impair the ability to drive or perform skilled tasks. Patients should ensure that they are not affected before attempting to drive or undertake such tasks.

THEOPHYLLINE
Brand name: Nuelin, Theo-Dur, Uniphyllin Continus
Type of drug: Bronchodilator

Uses: Treatment and prevention of asthma and other lung diseases.

How it works: This medicine allows the airways to expand, thus making breathing easier. It also reduces some of the inflammation that can be associated with the airways.

Availability: In some over-the-counter medicines as a decongestant.

Possible adverse effects: Headache, nausea, stomach upsets, vomiting and anxiety.

Other information: The tablets should be taken with or after meals. Modified release tablets should be swallowed whole and not chewed or crushed. Patients should not smoke whilst taking this medicine because it will have a marked effect on the way the body responds to it. Blood tests may be carried out to monitor the drug and potassium levels. This medicine may be prescribed for children of any age.

CAUTION

Alcohol: Should be avoided while taking this medicine, as it will have a marked affect on the way the body responds to the medicine.

Driving and operating machinery: Patients receiving this medication should not drive or perform skilled tasks until they are certain they are not experiencing any side effects.

TIBOLONE

Brand name: Livial

Type of drug: Hormone replacement

Uses: Treatment of the symptoms of menopause and to prevent osteoporosis.

How it works: Replaces hormones, which are depleted after either a naturally occurring menopause or one brought on by surgical treatment.

Availability: POM

Possible adverse effects: Weight gain, stomach pain, vaginal bleeding, rashes and itching. The risk of breast cancer is also increased from using this medicine.

Other information: This medicine is only used to prevent osteoporosis if no other medicines can be used, or have worked. It is usually started 12 months after the last menstrual period. The tablets should be swallowed whole and not crushed or chewed.

CAUTION

Driving and operating machinery: Patients receiving this medication should not drive or perform skilled tasks until they are certain they are not experiencing any side effects.

TIMOLOL

Brand name: Betim, Timoptol

Type of drug: Beta-blocker

Uses: Treatment of high blood pressure (hypertension), heart attack, glaucoma and to prevent migraine.

How it works: Slows the rate at which the heart beats, which reduces its workload and makes it more efficient. This is also thought to help lower the blood pressure. In the brain, timolol may act to constrict the blood vessels and so stop migraines from occurring. When used as eye drops timolol stops the production of fluid in the eye which reduces pressure and alleviates the symptoms of glaucoma.

Availability: POM

Possible adverse effects: When using eye drops the side effects include: burning, stinging, and pain in the eye. The eyes may also feel dryer and coldness of the hands and feet have been reported. When used as tablets, tiredness, blurred vision, headache, coldness of the extremities, stomach pain, nausea, vomiting, headache, dizziness and problems sleeping do occur. In patients with asthma, this drug can worsen the symptoms.

Other information: Patients should not wear soft contact lenses whilst using the eye drops as the preservative in this medicine may damage them. This medicine should be used regularly until you are told to stop taking it by a doctor.

CAUTION

Alcohol: Avoid alcohol because the combination may lead to an increased effect of the medicine.

Driving and operating machinery: As this drug can cause headache, dizziness and problems with vision, patients receiving this medication should not drive or perform skilled tasks until they are certain they are not experiencing these or any other side effects.

TIOCONAZOLE

Brand name: Trosyl Nail Solution
Type of drug: Anti-fungal
Uses: To treat fungal infections of the nails.
How it works: Tioconazole stops the production and repair of the fungal cell membrane which in turn leads to death of the fungus.
Availability: POM
Possible adverse effects: Although rare, they include irritation of the skin surrounding the nails being treated. This will be seen as a burning or stinging sensation, redness and swelling or a drying of the skin.
Other information: This medicine will need to be used for at least 6 months to be effective. It may be used in the treatment of children.

TIOTROPIUM

Brand name: Spiriva
Type of drug: Anti-muscarinic
Uses: Treatment of chronic lung disease.
How it works: Holds airways open longer which eases breathing.
Availability: POM
Possible adverse effects: Dry mouth, constipation, sinusitis and irritation and inflammation of the throat.
Other information: It is important to use the correct inhaler technique as taught. This product should be taken regularly and this leads to reduced number of attacks overall.

TOLBUTAMIDE

Brand name: Available only as a generic medicine
Type of drug: Sulphonylurea
Uses: Treatment of non insulin dependent diabetes.
How it works: Tolbutamide increases the sensitivity of cells in the pancreas to glucose in the blood stream. The cells then increase their production of insulin, which is required for glucose in the blood to enter cells. This leads to a decrease in the level of glucose in the blood.
Availability: POM
Possible adverse effects: Stomach upsets, a reduced number of cells in

the blood, and tinnitus may occur with this medicine. Report any sign of sore throat, bleeding or bruising that cannot be explained, or if you are generally feeling unwell to the doctor immediately.

Other information: Should be taken in conjunction with a diet recommended by the doctor, diabetic nurse or pharmacist. Blood or urine should be tested regularly for sugar. Tablets should be taken before the first main meal of the day. These tablets must not be taken on an empty stomach. Seek medical advice immediately if patient takes too many tablets.

CAUTION

Alcohol: Must not be consumed while taking this medicine because it can cause a serious reaction.

Driving and operating machinery: The DVLA has special requirements for diabetics who wish to drive; the latest information should be consulted before driving.

TOLTERODINE

Brand name: Detrusitol

Type of drug: Anti-spasmodic

Uses: Treatment of incontinence.

How it works: Reduces the symptoms of incontinence by stopping the contraction of the muscle at the exit of the bladder, allowing the bladder to fill to a greater capacity before the need to pass urine occurs.

Availability: POM

Possible adverse effects: Dizziness, nervousness, dry eyes, problems with vision, stomach pain, indigestion, stomach upsets, constipation and tiredness.

Other information: The capsules should be swallowed whole and not chewed.

CAUTION

Driving and operating machinery: As this drug can cause drowsiness, dizziness and problems with vision, patients receiving this medication should not drive or perform skilled tasks until they are certain they are not experiencing these, or any other side effects.

TOPIRAMATE

Brand name: Topamax

Type of drug: Anticonvulsant

Uses: Treatment of epilepsy.

How it works: An epileptic fit (or seizure) is thought to occur when the brain receives too many signals via the nervous system. Topiramate acts to stop some of those signals getting through, and so reduces the chances of a seizure occurring.

Availability: POM

Possible adverse effects: Drowsiness, headache, tiredness, weight changes, dizziness, nausea and vomiting, stomach pain, problems with memory, a shortened attention span and changes in mood.

Other information: Tablets should be swallowed whole and not crushed or chewed. Patients must continue to take this medicine unless told otherwise by the doctor.

CAUTION

Children: This medicine may be given to children over 2 years of age.

Alcohol: Avoid while taking this medicine.

Driving and operating machinery: Topiramate may cause drowsiness, which will impair the ability to drive. The DVLA has information for epileptic patients who wish to drive, the latest version of this should be consulted.

TRAMADOL

Brand name: Zydol

Type of drug: Opioid analgesic

Uses: Treatment of moderate pain.

How it works: The sensation we attribute to pain is only felt once signals from the body reach the brain. Tramadol stops those signals reaching the brain by blocking their transmission through the spinal cord.

Availability: POM

Possible adverse effects: Nausea and vomiting, dry mouth, constipation, dizziness, headache, drowsiness and sweating more than usual.

Other information: Modified release tablets and capsules should be swallowed whole and not chewed. The medicine may cause drowsiness, which can persist into the next day.

CAUTION

Children: This medicine may be given to children over 12 years of age

Alcohol: Should be avoided while taking this medicine.

Driving and operating machinery: As this drug can cause dizziness and drowsiness, patients receiving this medication should not drive or perform skilled tasks until they are certain they are not experiencing these, or any other side effects.

TRANDOLAPRIL

Brand name: Gopten

Type of drug: ACE inhibitor

Uses: To treat raised blood pressure, and after a heart attack.

How it works: It allows the blood vessels to relax, which enables them to increase in size. This reduces the pressure of the blood flowing through them.

Availability: POM

Possible adverse effects: Headache, dizziness, cough and a general weakness.

Other information: Patient should report immediately any signs of infection, sore throat, swelling or difficulty in breathing. Salt substitutes containing potassium should be avoided whilst taking this medicine, as should high potassium foods. A cough may occur during the initial stages of treatment, but this usually disappears without having to stop treatment.

CAUTION

Alcohol: Should only be consumed in strict moderation because the combination can cause a greater than expected drop in blood pressure.

Driving and operating machinery: Although there are not usually any problems with driving while taking this medicine, there may be some impairment on the ability to drive after the first few doses, so patients should not drive or perform skilled tasks until they are certain they are not experiencing any side effects.

TRANEXAMIC ACID

Brand name: Cykolkapron

Type of drug: Anti-fibrinolytic

Uses: The treatment of bleeding in various forms, such as menstrual periods and tooth extractions.

How it works: Promotes the clotting mechanism of the blood.

Availability: POM

Possible adverse effects: Nausea, vomiting and diarrhoea. Report any problems with colour vision to the doctor immediately.

CAUTION

Children: This medicine is licensed for use in children over 15 years of age. However it is frequently used in specialist haemophilia centres for younger children.

TRAZODONE

Brand name: Molipaxin

Type of drug: Antidepressant

Uses: Treatment of depression, particularly for people who have difficulty in sleeping.

How it works: The precise way this medicine works is not known at the moment. However it can lift the mood, and allow the patient a more balanced life.

Availability: POM

Possible adverse effects: Drowsiness, dizziness, headache, stomach upsets, weight loss, constipation, dry mouth and problems with vision.

Other information: Trazodone should be taken with or after meals to reduce the chances of an upset stomach. This medicine may take several weeks for the effect to become apparent.

CAUTION

Alcohol: Should be avoided while taking the medicine.

Driving and operating machinery: As this drug can cause dizziness and drowsiness, patients receiving this medication should not drive or perform skilled tasks until they are certain they are not experiencing these or any other side effects.

TRETINOIN

Brand name: Retin-A

Type of drug: Vitamin A derivative

Uses: Treatment of acne.

How it works: Halts the production of sebaceous cells in the skin, which stops the formation of comedones or spots.

Availability: POM

Possible adverse effects: Skin irritation and sensitivity, including peeling, redness, stinging and drying of the skin when applying gel or lotion These effects seem to decrease as treatment progresses.

Other information: Tretinoin will cause a reddening and stinging of the skin when it is applied correctly. It may take 6 to 8 weeks for the effects of treatment to become apparent. Avoid excessive exposure to the sun, and wear a total sun block during treatment. Follow the instructions included with the product carefully. This medicine should not be applied to the eyes, nose or mouth.

TRIAMCINOLONE ACETONIDE

Brand name: Adcortyl, Kenalog, Nasacort

Type of drug: Corticosteroid

Uses: Treatment of mouth ulcers and similar conditions, relief from swelling of the joints associated with rheumatoid and osteoarthritis, long term relief from severe allergies and relief from hay fever.

How it works: Steroids work by suppressing the production of cells, chemicals and enzymes that cause inflammation.

Availability: POM

Possible adverse effect: When used as a cream, ointment or paste adverse effects are usually rare and disappear when treatment is stopped; a doctor should be consulted before doing this. When triamcinolone acetonide is used as a nasal spray, a headache, runny nose and irritation of the throat may occur. When it is given by injection, patients may be at increased risk of infections and any sign of sore throat, mouth ulcers, raised temperature or generally feeling unwell should be reported to the doctor immediately. Other adverse effects when used by injection include fluid retention, muscle loss, tiredness, wounds may not heal quickly, thinning of the skin, bruising, sweating, stomach upsets, an irregular menstrual cycle, the suppression of growth in children, weight gain and pain where the injection is given.

Other information: A steroid card will be given to patients receiving the injections. This should be shown to anybody who treats the patient in order to allow an appropriate choice of treatment to be made. The paste which is used for mouth ulcers should be applied after meals.

CAUTION

Children: Those over 6 years of age may use the nasal spray or receive the injection. The growth of children will be monitored whilst they are receiving triamcinolone to ensure they are developing normally.

Driving and operating machinery: Patients receiving this medication should not drive or perform skilled tasks until they are certain they are not experiencing any side effects.

TRIHEXYPHENIDYL

(Formerly known as: benzhexol)

Brand name: Broflex

Type of drug: Anti-muscarinic

Uses: To control tremor found in both Parkinson's disease, and as a side effect of some medication for psychiatric disorders.

How it works: Tremor is due to an imbalance between two transmitters in the brain – acetylcholine and dopamine. Trihexyphenidyl stops the actions of acetylcholine, responsible for the tremor, and allows the levels of dopamine to effectively rise.

Availability: POM

Possible adverse effects: Dry mouth, nausea, dizziness and blurred vision are the most commonly reported side effects. These are usually mild and will decrease with time as tolerance to them develops. Occasionally it can affect the bladder, making it difficult to pass water, in which case medical advice should be sought immediately.

Other information: Regular checks will be made on blood pressure, eyes and heart whilst taking this drug to ensure both its effectiveness and absence of side effects.

CAUTION

Driving and operating machinery. As this drug can cause drowsiness and dizziness patients receiving this medication should not drive or perform skilled tasks until they are certain they are not experiencing these, or any other side effects.

TRIMEPRAZINE – See Alimenazine

TRIMETHOPRIM
Brand name: Monotrim suspension, and available as a generic medicine
Type of drug: Antibiotic
Uses: Treatment of infections, particularly of the urinary tract and respiratory tract.
How it works: This medicine stops bacteria producing a chemical called tetrahydrofolate, which is an active form of folic acid. Without this the bacteria cannot survive and the infection is cleared.
Availability: POM
Possible adverse effects: Although rare, adverse effects include rashes, nausea and vomiting.
Other information: When this medicine is used for urine infections, patients should ensure they drink plenty of fluids during the day.
CAUTION
Children: This medicine may be given to children over 6 weeks of age.

URSODEOXYCHOLIC ACID
Brand name: Destolit, Ursofalk
Type of drug: Bile acid preparation
Uses: Treatment of gallstones when surgery is not possible.
How it works: Reduces the amount of cholesterol made by the liver and passed out in the bile. As the gallstones are composed of cholesterol, this allows the gallstones to dissolve.
Availability: POM
Possible adverse effects: Adverse effects are uncommon but can include diarrhoea, nausea and vomiting
Other information: Ultrasound examinations may be carried out to check progress of treatment. It may take many months or years to achieve its effect. Ursodeoxycholic acid should be used in conjunction with a low calorie, low cholesterol diet. Advice on these can be obtained from the doctor or pharmacist.
CAUTION
Pregnancy: The contraceptive pill may be stopped during treatment in

order to allow faster removal of the gallstones. It is therefore essential that alternative contraceptive measures be taken.

VENLAFAXINE
Brand name: Efexor
Type of drug: Serotonin and noradrenaline reuptake inhibitor
Uses: To treat depression and anxiety.
How it works: Venlafaxine increases the chemical messengers, serotonin and noradrenaline, in the brain, which results in a heightening of mood.
Availability: POM
Possible adverse effects: Nausea, dizziness – especially on standing, lethargy, blurred vision, constipation, dry mouth, nervousness, and sweating and weight loss. Report any bleeding or bruising that cannot be explained, sore throat, raised temperature, or a general feeling of being unwell to the doctor.
Other information: Patients should consult a pharmacist before buying any over-the-counter preparations. It may take at least 2 weeks before any effect is noticed. The modified release capsules should not be crushed or chewed, but swallowed whole with water at approximately the same time each day.
CAUTION
Alcohol: Avoid while taking it because it may reduce the effectiveness of the venlafaxine.
Driving and operating machinery: Patients receiving this medication should not drive or perform skilled tasks until they are certain they are not experiencing side effects.

VALACICLOVIR
Brand name: Valtrex
Type of drug: Antiviral
Uses: Treatment of viral infections caused by herpes, including herpes simplex (cold sores and genital infections), and varicella-zoster (chickenpox and shingles). Also used to prevent of cytomegalovirus infection in transplant patients.
How it works: Stops the virus multiplying, enabling the immune system to deal with the infection more easily.

Availability: POM

Possible adverse effects: Nausea, headache, stomach pain and discomfort, vomiting, diarrhoea, headaches and mood changes have all been reported.

Other information: Patients taking this medicine to prevent infection may need very long courses of treatment. Always complete the full course.

CAUTION

Children: May be used in children over 12 years of age.

VALDECOXIB

Brand name: Bextra

Type of drug: Non-steroidal anti-inflammatory

Uses: Treatment of rheumatoid arthritis, osteoarthritis and also period pains.

How it works: Inhibits the actions of the enzyme cyclo-oxygenase, which triggers the inflammatory process leading to pain and swelling.

Availability: POM

Possible adverse effects: Indigestion, stomach pain, diarrhoea, dry mouth, problems sleeping, cough and a sore throat. Gastrointestinal ulceration and/or bleeding may occur, so if you suffer severe stomach pain, or there is blood in your stools then seek urgent medical advice. If allergic symptoms occur such as wheezing or swelling of the face, the patient should stop taking the medication and seek urgent medical advice.

Other information: Should be taken with or after meals to reduce problems with the stomach.

CAUTION

Driving and operating machinery: As this drug can cause dizziness and drowsiness, patients receiving this medication should not drive or perform skilled tasks until they are certain they are not experiencing these or any other side effects.

VALSARTAN

Brand name: Diovan

Type of drug: Angiotensin 2 receptor antagonist

Uses: Treatment of high blood pressure.

How it works: A chemical naturally found in the body which causes the blood vessels to constrict or become narrower, thus increasing blood pressure. Valsartan prevents the actions of Angiotensin 2 allowing blood vessels to relax and reducing blood pressure.

Availability: POM

Possible adverse effects: Headache, diarrhoea, joint and muscle pain and tiredness.

Other information: Should be taken with food to reduce stomach irritation.

CAUTION

Alcohol: This should only be consumed in moderation because the combination can cause a large drop in blood pressure.

Driving and operating machinery: As this drug can cause headaches and drowsiness, patients should not drive or perform any other skilled tasks until they are certain they are not experiencing these, or any other side effects.

VERAPAMIL

Brand name: Cordilox, Securon, Univer

Type of drug: Calcium channel blocker

Uses: Treatment of high blood pressure and angina.

How it works: Relaxes the blood vessels in the circulatory system allowing blood to flow more easily, so reducing blood pressure. For angina it relaxes the blood vessels of the heart and allows more blood and oxygen to reach the heart muscle. This allows it to pump more effectively and relieves the pain associated with angina.

Availability: POM

Possible adverse effects: Headache and dizziness may occur due to a fall in blood pressure. Rashes, leg or ankle swelling, constipation, nausea, slowed heartbeat and facial flushing can also occur.

Other information: Verapamil should not be discontinued unless advised by a doctor but any side effects should be reported. Do not take this medication with grapefruit juice. The tablets should be swallowed whole, and not chewed or crushed.

CAUTION

Alcohol: Can increase the likelihood of experiencing side effects and so should be avoided or consumed in moderation.

Driving and operating machinery: As this drug can cause dizziness and headache, patients should not drive or perform skilled tasks until they are certain they are not experiencing these, or any other side effects.

VIGABATRIN

Brand name: Sabril

Type of drug: Anticonvulsant

Uses: Treatment of epilepsy.

How it works: An epileptic fit (or seizure) is thought to occur when the brain receives too many or abnormal signals. Vigabatrin acts by reducing the number of signals that the brain receives.

Availability: POM

Possible adverse effects: Drowsiness, dizziness, problems with vision, weight gain, changes in mood, nausea, stomach pain and fatigue. Report any problems with vision to the doctor immediately as the effects may be permanent if left for a prolonged period of time.

Other information: Vigabatrin is generally used together with other anticonvulsants, although it is used alone to treat infantile spasms.

CAUTION

Alcohol: Avoid while taking this medicine.

Driving and operating machinery: As this drug can cause drowsiness, dizziness and visual problems, patients should not drive or perform skilled tasks until they are certain they are not experiencing the side effects. The DVLA offers guidance for people with epilepsy who wish to drive, and the latest version of this should be consulted.

WARFARIN

Brand name: Marevan and many generic formulations available

Type of drug: Anti-coagulant

Uses: To prevent blood clots forming.

How it works: Many clotting proteins use vitamin K. Warfarin prevents vitamin K from working and so reduces the production of clotting factors.

Availability: POM

Possible adverse effects: Excessive bleeding. Patients should also consult a doctor if they experience unexplained bruising, nosebleeds, bleeding gums, or red or black coloured urine or stools.

Other information: Regular blood tests are required to assess the effects of warfarin; these are performed at a hospital clinic or your GP surgery. Caution must be taken to avoid any injuries, as these could cause excessive bleeding. Patients are usually given a booklet detailing what dose they must take and precautions to be observed. They should always show this booklet to doctors, dentists, pharmacists and any other person who treats them so that medicines and procedures that are compatible with warfarin can be chosen. Patients must not take aspirin, ibuprofen, or other over-the-counter medicines unless advised by a doctor or pharmacist. Any changes in medicines being taken should be reported to the clinic, as many medicines can affect how warfarin works. Diet must not be significantly altered as this too can affect how well warfarin works.

There are standard colours for warfarin tablets in the UK which are; white for 500microgram tablets, brown for 1mg tablets, blue for 3mg tablets and pink for 5mg tablets. Patients must ensure the dose is taken at approximately the same time each day and that they do not take too many tablets. If a dose is missed then the date should be recorded and this brought to the attention of the clinic at the next visit.

CAUTION

Pregnancy: Contraception must be used, but if you become pregnant while on this medicine, inform your doctor as soon as possible.

Alcohol: Should only be consumed in strict moderation.

Driving and operating machinery: Patients receiving this medication should not drive or perform skilled tasks until they are certain they are not experiencing any side effects.

ZAFIRLUKAST

Brand name: Accolate

Type of drug: Leukotriene receptor antagonist

Uses: Treatment of asthma.

How it works: Stops the actions of chemical messengers leukotrienes, which are partly responsible for the inflammatory process and halts the inflammation of the airways that lead to an asthma attack.

Availability: POM

Possible adverse effects: Nausea, vomiting and stomach pain. It can cause liver problems so if symptoms such as weight loss, stomach pains, rashes, yellowing of the skin and itching develop, patients should stop taking this medicine and consult a doctor as soon as possible.

Other information: Used to prevent asthma rather than given during an acute attack so should be taken regularly. Smoking increases the dose required for effect.

CAUTION

Children: May be prescribed for children over 12 years of age.

Driving and operating machinery: Patients receiving this medication should not drive or perform skilled tasks until they are certain they are not experiencing any side effects.

ZALEPLON

Brand name: Sonata

Type of drug: Hypnotic

Uses: Treatment of insomnia.

How it works: Stops transmission of signals through the nerves in the brain, reducing anxiety and allowing sleep.

Availability: POM

Possible adverse effects: Diarrhoea, nausea and vomiting, disorientation, headache, hallucinations, drowsiness that may continue into the next day, changes to the menstrual cycle, and dizziness. May cause sleeping problems when you stop taking the drug; this will only last for a short time while the body adjusts.

Other information: Not normally be used for longer than 2 weeks.

CAUTION

Alcohol: Avoid while taking this medicine.

Driving and operating machinery: As this drug can cause drowsiness, patients receiving this medication should not drive or perform skilled tasks until they are certain they are not experiencing this or other side effects.

ZOLPIDEM

Brand name: Stilnoct

Type of drug: Hypnotic

Uses: Treatment of insomnia.

How it works: Zolpidem stops transmission of signals through the nerves. This reduces anxiety, and allows sleep to occur.

Availability: POM

Possible adverse effects: Diarrhoea, nausea, vomiting, disorientation, headache, dizziness and drowsiness – which may continue into the next day have all been reported. Zolpidem may cause sleeping problems when you stop taking the drug, but this will only last for a short time while the body adjusts.

Other information: Will not normally be used for longer than 4 weeks. This medicine should be taken with or after food, so ideally just before going to bed.

CAUTION

Alcohol: Avoid while taking this medicine.

Driving and operating machinery: As this drug can cause dizziness and drowsiness, patients receiving this medication should not drive or perform skilled tasks until they are certain they are not experiencing these or any other side effects.

ZOPICLONE

Brand name: Zimovane

Type of drug: Hypnotic

Uses: Treatment of insomnia

How it works: Stops transmission of signals through the nerves. This reduces anxiety and allows sleep to occur.

Availability: POM

Possible adverse effects: A bitter taste in the mouth, and the feeling of sleepiness during the day. It may also cause sleeping problems when you stop taking the drug, but this will only last for a short time while the body adjusts.

Other information: The medicine will not usually be prescribed for longer than 4 weeks.

CAUTION
Alcohol: Should be avoided while taking this medicine.

Driving and operating machinery: As this drug can cause dizziness and drowsiness, patients receiving this medication should not drive or perform skilled tasks until they are certain they are not experiencing these or any other side effects.

ZUCLOPENTHIXOLE
Brand name: Clopixol

Type of drug: Antipsychotic

Uses: Treatment of schizophrenia and related disorders.

How it works: Schizophrenia and related disorders are thought to be due to an excessive amount of one of the chemical messengers, dopamine, in the brain. Zuclopenthixole reduces dopamine levels; it also effects other messengers in the brain.

Availability: POM

Possible adverse effects: Drowsiness, tiredness, blurred vision, urine retention, visual problems, tremors, uncontrolled movements, uncoordinated movements and weight gain have all been reported with this treatment. Sedation is common and may be a desired effect in agitated patients. Dizziness, drowsiness, a dry mouth, anxiety, constipation, a rash that develops when skin is exposed to sunlight, stomach upsets, and weight gain may also occur. Some dizziness and light-headedness can also occur when standing up. Unwanted effects include abnormal, involuntary movements such as uncontrolled or repetitive tongue movement, stiffness, restlessness and a condition that is like Parkinson's disease, which should be all reported to your doctor.

Other information: Treatment is usually started and monitored by specialists. Sunlight should be avoided where possible, especially between the hours of 11:00 and 14:00 when the sun is as its strongest as a skin rash may occur. Sensible precautions to prevent this skin reaction to sunlight include applying a total sun block, covering the arms and legs in long clothes, wearing a wide-brimmed hat and sunglasses and not using sunlamps.

CAUTION

Alcohol: This should be avoided because of an increased risk of drowsiness associated with the combination.

Driving and operating machinery: As this drug can cause dizziness, drowsiness and blurred vision, patients receiving this medication should not drive or perform skilled tasks until they are certain they are not experiencing these, or any other side effects.

Over-the-counter Medicines

Over-the-counter (OTC) medicines are those which can be bought from either a pharmacist or other retail outlet, without the need for a prescription from a doctor.

Medicines which are available OTC are designed to help with the treatment of minor ailments at home. Many of the available products are not 'cures' but aim to relieve the symptoms of the problem so that the illness can run its course. For example, the many cold remedies available OTC do not attack the virus that causes colds, but relieve the sufferer of the discomfort of symptoms, such as sore throat or headache.

The minor conditions which are generally suitable for treatment with OTC medicines include: aches and pains, constipation and diarrhoea, coughs and colds, travel sickness, tummy upsets, skin conditions and low-grade infections such as thrush and cystitis.

However, as with all types of medicines, OTC products can be harmful or simply ineffective if they are not used, stored and disposed of properly. For this reason they should be treated with the same care as prescription medicines or any other dangerous chemicals you may keep in the house.

When buying OTC preparations the advice of a pharmacist should be sought. Pharmacists are trained, independent professionals who are willing to answer questions or give advice about the suitability of the medicines they sell. When you are discussing the suitability of a particular treatment with a pharmacist, ensure that you tell them about any prescription drugs you are taking or any other illnesses or allergies you, or the patient, may have. The pharmacist may refer you to a doctor to have a more thorough investigation of a problem, and may also refuse to sell products if they are not the right ones for the patient, or the condition being treated.

When you are preparing to take the medicine, or to give it to someone else, always ensure that you read the packet carefully, taking note of how much you should take, when, and any other specific instructions such as whether it should be taken with food. Do not take any medication when you are pregnant or breastfeeding without first taking advice. Take extra care when giving medicines to children – they are not mini adults and their doses need to be carefully calculated by experts. Follow the advice on the packet or, if in doubt, ask your pharmacist.

Finally, remember to dispose of any unused medicines carefully and safely.

HOW TO USE THIS SECTION

The aim of this section is to give some basic information about the range of over-the-counter preparations available. The information is intended as guidance only and does not provide all you need to know about a product before deciding whether or not to use it. Most importantly, it should not be used as a substitute for talking to a qualified professional. Any queries you may have about a particular medicine should be addressed to your pharmacist. Some OTC medicines should not be used by certain groups of people – for example, children of various age groups or people with long-standing conditions such as asthma, epilepsy, heart disease, or diabetes. Patients with these conditions should always seek the advice of a pharmacist before taking any medicines.

The most commonly used OTC products are listed below in alphabetical order with the information arranged as follows:

Name: The branded name under which the product is sold.
Use: A brief description of the disorder the product treats and how it works.
Dose: The frequency and amount of each dose or, in the case of creams and lotions, each application.

AAA SPRAY
Use: An aerosol spray for soothing sore throats. It contains benzocaine, a local anaesthetic.

Dose: Adults should apply 2 sprays every 2-3 hours. The maximum dose is 16 sprays over 24 hours. For children over 6 years, half the adult dose should be given, with a maximum of 8 sprays over 24 hours. This treatment is not recommended for children under 6 years.

ACRIFLEX CREAM
Use: This is a cream for the treatment of minor burns, cuts and grazes, containing chlorhexidine, an antiseptic.
Dose: The cream should be smoothed onto the affected area and can be applied several times a day if required.

ACTAL
Use: Available in tablet form for relieving indigestion and settle digestive discomfort. The tablets contain an antacid.
Dose: 1-2 tablets should be taken as required. The maximum dose is 16 tablets over 24 hours. This treatment is not recommended for children under 12 years.

ACTIFED
Use: These are tablets for hayfever that contain triprolidine, an anti-histamine, and pseudoephedrine, a decongestant.
Dose: 1 tablet should be taken up to 4 times a day. This treatment is not recommended for children under 12 years.

ACTIFED COMPOUND LINCTUS
Use: This is a liquid remedy for the treatment of coughs, containing dextromethorphan, a cough suppressant, pseudoephedrine, a decongestant and triprolidine, an antihistamine.
Dose: Adults should take 10ml every 4-6 hours. Children (6-12 years) should be given 5ml every 4-6 hours. Children (2-5 years) should be given 2.5ml every 4-6 hours. Take a maximum of 4 doses in 24 hours. This treatment is not recommended for children under 2 years.

ACTIFED EXPECTORANT
Use: A liquid remedy for the treatment of coughs. It contains guaiphenesin,

an expectorant, pseudoephedrine, a decongestant and an antihistamine.

Dose: Adults should take 10ml every 4-6 hours. Children (6-12 years) should be given 5ml every 4-6 hours. Children (2-5 years) should be given 2.5ml every 4-6 hours. This treatment is not recommended for children under 2 years.

ACTIFED SYRUP

Use: A liquid remedy for relieving cold, flu and hayfever symptoms. It contains triprolidine, an antihistamine, and pseudoephedrine, a decongestant.

Dose: Adults should take 10ml every 4-6 hours, with a maximum of 4 doses over 24 hours. Children (2-12 years) should be given 2.5-10ml, according to age. Always read the label. This treatment is not recommended for children under 2 years. This product is also available in tablet form.

ADCORTYL IN ORABASE

Use: Available in the form of a paste for the treatment of mouth ulcers, containing triamcinolone, a corticosteroid.

Dose: The paste should be applied to the affected area up to 3 times a day after meals and then once at night. The treatment can be used for up to 5 days.

ADULT MELTUS DRY COUGH ELIXIR

Use: A liquid remedy for the treatment of coughs, containing dextromethorphan, a suppressant, and pseudoephedrine, a decongestant.

Dose: Adults should take 5-10ml 4 times a day. This treatment is not recommended for children under 12 years.

ADULT MELTUS EXPECTORANT

Use: A liquid remedy for the treatment of coughs, containing guaiphenesin, an expectorant, cetylpyridinium, an antiseptic, purified honey and sucrose.

Dose: Adults should take 5-10ml every 3-4 hours. This treatment is not recommended for children under 12 years.

ADULT MELTUS EXPECTORANT WITH DECONGESTANT

Use: A liquid remedy for the treatment of coughs, containing guaiphenesin, an expectorant, and pseudoephedrine, a decongestant.

Dose: 10ml should be taken 4 times a day. This treatment is not recommended for children under 12 years.

AFRAZINE NASAL SPRAY

Use: This is a spray for clearing nasal congestion caused by a cold, sinusitis or hayfever. It contains oxymetazoline, a decongestant.

Dose: Adults and children over 5 years should apply 2-3 sprays into each nostril morning and night. The spray should not be used continuously for more than 1 week. This treatment is not recommended for children under 5 years.

AFTER BITE

Use: A pen that dispenses ammonia for soothing bites, stings and irritated or itchy skin.

Dose: The pen should be applied as often as required. This treatment is not recommended for children under 2 years.

ALGESAL

Use: This cream can be applied to the skin to alleviate muscular aches and pains. It contains a rubefacient and salicylate, an aspirin derivative.

Dose: The cream should be massaged into the affected part of the body up to 3 times a day. This treatment is not recommended for children under 6 years.

ALKA-SELTZER

Use: Effervescent tablets which contain an antacid and an analgesic for the relief of headache and upset stomach caused by excess alcohol or over-eating. The tablets contain aspirin, sodium bicarbonate and citric acid.

Dose: 2 tablets should be dissolved in water every 4 hours. The maximum dose is 8 tablets over 24 hours. This treatment is not recommended for children under 16 years.

ALKA-SELTZER XS

Use: Effervescent tablets containing an antacid and an analgesic for the relief of headache, upset stomach and general pain caused by excess alcohol or over-eating. The tablets contain aspirin, paracetamol, sodium bicarbonate, citric acid and caffeine.

Dose: 1-2 tablets should be dissolved in water. The maximum dosage is 8 tablets over 24 hours. This treatment is not recommended for children under 16 years.

ALPHOSYL SHAMPOO 2-IN-1

Use: This is a medicated shampoo for the treatment of dandruff. It contains coal tar and a hair conditioner.

Dose: Apply as an ordinary shampoo once or twice every week.

ALPKA KERI BATH OIL

Use: This is an emollient bath additive containing various oils, including lanolin, for the relief and treatment of eczema and dermatitis.

Dose: 5-20ml should be added to bath water.

ALTACITE PLUS

Use: A liquid for the relief of indigestion and heartburn. It contains dimeticone to aid the release of trapped wind.

Dose: Adults should take 10ml between meals and at bedtime. Children (8-12 years) should take 5ml between meals and 1 at bedtime. This treatment is not recommended for children under 8 years.

ALUDROX

Use: These are antacid tablets for the relief of indigestion and heartburn.

Dose: Adults should take 1-2 tablets 4 times a day and at bedtime. Children (6-12 years) should take 1 tablet 2-3 times a day. This treatment is not recommended for children under 6 years. The product is also available in liquid form.

ANACAL RECTAL OINTMENT

Use: An ointment for the treatment and relief of piles. It contains mucopolysaccharide, which is thought to strengthen tissue in the anus.

Dose: The ointment should be applied to the affected area 1-4 times a day. This treatment is not recommended for children under 12 years.

ANACAL SUPPOSITORIES

Use: A treatment for piles available in the form of a suppository. It contains mucopolysaccharide, which is thought to strengthen the tissue in the anus.

Dose: Insert 1 suppository once or twice a day. This treatment is not recommended for children.

ANADIN & ANADIN MAXIMUM STRENGTH

Use: Analgesic tablets which can be used for general pain relief, they contain aspirin and caffeine.

Dose: Adults should take 1-2 tablets every 4 hours. The maximum dose is 12 tablets over 24 hours. This treatment is not recommended for children under 16 years.

ANADIN EXTRA

Use: Analgesic tablets which can be used for general pain relief, they contain aspirin and paracetamol.

Dose: Adults should take 2 tablets every 4 hours. There is a maximum dose of 8 tablets over 24 hours. This treatment is not recommended for children under 16 years. The product is also available in the form of soluble tablets with caffeine.

ANADIN IBUPROFEN, ANADIN IBUPROFEN GEL CAPSULES

Use: Analgesic tablets for general pain relief, they contain ibuprofen.

Dose: Adults should take 1-2 tablets 2-3 times a day. There is a maximum dose of 6 tablets over 24 hours. This treatment is not recommended for children under 12 years.

ANADIN PARACETAMOL

Use: Analgesic tablets which can be used for general pain relief, they contain paracetamol.

Dose: Adults should take 2 tablets every 4 hours. There is a maximum dose of 8 tablets over 24 hours. Children (6-12 years) should take ½ to 1 tablet every 4 hours with a maximum of 4 tablets in 24 hours. This treatment is not recommended for children under 6 years.

ANBESOL

Use: This treatment is available in liquid form for the relief and treatment of mouth ulcers and teething pain. It contains lidocaine, an anaesthetic, and chlorocresol and cetylpyridinium, which are antiseptics.

Dose: 2 applications to the affected area, allowing at least 30 minutes between applications. Use a maximum of 8 applications over 24 hours.

ANBESOL TEETHING GEL

Use: This is a gel for the relief and treatment of mouth ulcers. It contains lidocaine, an anaesthetic, and chlorocresol and cetylpyridinium, which are antiseptics.

Dose: Adults should apply the gel up to 4 times a day for 1 week. This treatment is not recommended for children under 6 months.

ANDREWS ANTACID

Use: Available in tablet form for relieving the symptoms of upset stomach, indigestion and heartburn. The tablets contain various antacids.

Dose: Adults should take 1-2 tablets as needed. The maximum dose is 12 tablets over 24 hours. This treatment is not recommended for children under 12 years. The product is available in a variety of flavours.

ANDREWS SALTS

Use: Available in powder form for relieving an upset stomach. It contains antacids and sodium.

Dose: Adults should take 1 teaspoon or 1 sachet dissolved in water. Take a maximum of 4 doses over 24 hours. Children over 3 years should be given half the adult dose. This treatment is not recommended for children under 3 years.

ANETHAINE

Use: Available in the form of a cream for the treatment and relief of itching and irritation caused by bites and stings, it contains a mild anaesthetic.

Dose: The cream should be applied to the affected area 2-3 times a day for up to 3 days. This treatment is not recommended for children under 3 years, or be applied to areas where the skin is broken.

ANODESYN OINTMENT

Use: This is an ointment for the treatment of piles, containing benzocaine, a mild local anaesthetic, and allantoin, an astringent.

Dose: Adults should use the ointment twice a day and after each bowel movement. This treatment is not recommended for children under 12 years. The cream should not be used for more than 1 week unless advised otherwise by a doctor.

ANODESYN SUPPOSITORIES

Use: A suppository for the treatment and relief of piles, containing lignocaine, a mild local anaesthetic, and allantoin, an astringent.

Dose: Insert 1 suppository in the morning and 1 in the evening and after each bowel movement. This treatment is not recommended for children under 12 years. The suppositories should not be used for more than 2 weeks unless advised otherwise by a doctor.

ANTHISAN CREAM

Use: A cream for the treatment and relief of itching and irritation caused by bites and stings, containing an antihistamine.

Dose: The cream should be applied to the affected area 2-3 times a day for up to 3 days. This treatment is not recommended for children under 3 years.

ANTHISAN PLUS STING RELIEF SPRAY

Use: A spray with a metered dose for the treatment and relief of itching and irritation caused by stings, rashes and bites. It contains an antihistamine and a mild anaesthetic.

Dose: To deliver a single dose, the nozzle head should be pressed once. Do this 2 or 3 times per day to the affected part. This treatment is not recommended for children under 3 years.

ANUSOL OINTMENT AND CREAM

Use: Available in cream and ointment form for the treatment and relief of piles, containing bismuth, balsam of Peru and zinc oxide, all of which are astringents.

Dose: Should be applied at night and in the morning and after each bowel movement. This treatment is not recommended for children under 12 years.

ANUSOL SUPPOSITORIES

Use: A suppository for the treatment and relief of piles, containing bismuth, balsam of Peru and zinc oxide, all of which are astringents.

Dose: 1 suppository should be inserted into the anus at night and 1 in the morning and after each bowel movement. This treatment is not recommended for children under 12 years.

ANUSOL PLUS HC OINTMENT

Use: This is an ointment for the treatment and relief of piles, containing similar ingredients to those in the suppositories with the added ingredient of hydrocortisone, a steroid.

Dose: The ointment should be applied sparingly to the affected area at night and in the morning and after each bowel movement. This treatment is not recommended for those under 18 years of age. Ointment should not be used for more than 7 days. The product is also available in suppository form.

AQUA-BAN

Use: Available in tablet form to relieve pre-menstrual water retention. It is a mild diuretic and contains caffeine.

Dose: 2 tablets should be taken 3 times a day for the 4-5 days before a period is due. The tablets should not be taken for more than 5 days in 1 month.

ARRET

Use: Available in capsule form to stop diarrhoea. It contains loperamide.
Dose: Take 2 capsules initially and then 1 capsule after every loose bowel movement. Take a maximum of 8 capsules over 24 hours. This treatment is not recommended for children under 12 years.

ASILONE ANTACID LIQUID

Use: A liquid remedy for the relief of indigestion, heartburn and upset stomach. It contains antacids, and dimethicone, an anti-flatulent.
Dose: 5-10ml should be taken after meals and at bedtime or as required. Take a maximum of 40ml over 24 hours. This treatment is not recommended for children under 12 years.

ASILONE ANTACID TABLETS

Use: These tablets are for the relief of indigestion, heartburn, excess gas and an upset stomach, containing antacids.
Dose: 1-2 tablets should be taken before meals and at bedtime. This treatment is not recommended for children under 12 years.

ASKIT POWDERS

Use: An analgesic powder, which can be used for general pain relief. The powder contains aspirin, aloxiprin and caffeine.
Dose: 1 sachet of powder should be mixed with water and taken every 4 hours. Take a maximum of 6 sachets over 24 hours. This treatment is not recommended for children under 16 years.

ASPRO CLEAR

Use: These are effervescent analgesic tablets for the relief of general pain, and contain aspirin.
Dose: 2-3 tablets should be dissolved in water every 3 hours. Take a maximum of 13 tablets over 24 hours. This treatment is not recommended for children under 16 years.

ATKINSON AND BARKER'S INFANT GRIPE MIXTURE

Use: A liquid remedy for the relief of colic and wind in infants, containing sodium bicarbonate, an antacid, dill and caraway oils.

Dose: 2.5-10ml should be given every 4 hours depending on age. Always read the label. This treatment is not recommended for babies under 1 month.

AUDAX EAR DROPS

Use: These are drops for softening earwax. The drops contain a mild analgesic and an ingredient to soften the wax.

Dose: The ear should be filled with the liquid and plugged with cotton wool. Repeat this treatment twice a day for 4 days. This treatment is not recommended for children under 1 year. This medicine should also not be used by those allergic to aspirin.

AVOCA WART & VERRUCA SET

Use: This treatment is available as a kit for the removal of warts and verrucae. The kit contains a caustic pencil, an emery file, dressings and protector pads.

Dose: The pencil should be applied to the wart or verruca for 1-2 minutes and re-applied after 24 hours if required. Protect with the dressings provided. Use a maximum of 3 treatments for warts and 6 for verrucae.

AVOMINE

Use: Available in tablet form for the relief of travel sickness, containing promethazine, an antihistamine.

Dose: To prevent travel sickness, adults and children over 10 years should take 1 tablet the night before a long journey or 2 hours before a shorter one.

BABY MELTUS COUGH LINCTUS

Use: This is a liquid remedy for the treatment of coughs. It contains acetic acid, a soothing ingredient.

Dose: Babies (3-12 months) should be given 2.5 ml every 2 to 3 hours. Babies (13-30 months) should be given 5 ml every 2-3 hours. Babies over 30 months should be given 10ml every 2-3 hours. This treatment is not recommended for babies under 3 months.

BALMOSA CREAM

Use: This is a cream rub for the relief of muscular aches and pains, containing rubefacients and a salicylate, an aspirin derivative.

Dose: The cream should be massaged into the affected area as required. This treatment is not recommended for children under 6 years.

BAZUKA GEL

Use: A gel for the treatment of corns, calluses, warts and verrucae that comes with an applicator and an emery board containing salicylic acid. The gel dries to form a water-resistant barrier over the affected area.

Dose: 1-2 drops should be applied to the corn or callus each night, then the area should be rubbed down once a week with the emery board. This treatment is not recommended for children under 6 years. The product is also available in Extra Strength form.

BECONASE ALLERGY

Use: Available in the form of a nasal spray for easing the congestion caused by hayfever. It contains beclomethasone, a steroid.

Dose: 2 sprays should be applied into each nostril morning and evening. This treatment is not recommended for children under 18 years.

BEECHAMS ALL-IN-ONE

Use: This treatment is available in liquid form to alleviate the symptoms of colds and flu. It contains paracetamol, phenylephrine, a decongestant and guaiphenesin, an expectorant.

Dose: 20ml should be taken every four hours as necessary, with a maximum of 4 doses in 24 hours. This treatment is not recommended for children under 12 years.

BEECHAMS FLU-PLUS CAPLETS

Use: These are tablets for treatment of the symptoms of colds and flu, containing paracetamol, phenylephrine, a decongestant and caffeine.

Dose: 2 capsules should be taken every 4-6 hours if required. Take a maximum of 8 capsules over 24 hours. This treatment is not recommended for children under 12 years.

BEECHAMS FLU-PLUS DRINKS

Use: Available in the form of sachets of powder for relieving the symptoms of colds and flu. Each sachet contains paracetamol, phenylephrine, a decongestant and vitamin C.

Dose: 1 sachet should be dissolved in a mug of hot water every 4-6 hours. Take a maximum of 4 sachets over 24 hours. Treatment is not recommended for children under 12 years.

BEECHAMS POWDERS

Use: These are sachets of powder that contain aspirin and caffeine for relieving the symptoms of colds and flu.

Dose: 1 sachet should be dissolved in hot water and taken every 3-4 hours. Take a maximum of 6 sachets over 24 hours. This treatment is not recommended for children under 16 years.

BEECHAMS POWDERS CAPSULES

Use: These are capsules for relieving the symptoms of colds and flu. They contain paracetamol, phenylephrine, a decongestant and caffeine.

Dose: Adults should take 2 capsules every 3-4 hours if required. Take a maximum of 12 capsules over 24 hours. Children (6-12 years) should take 1 capsule every 3 to 4 hours, with a maximum dose of 6 capsules in 24 hours. This treatment is not recommended for children under 6 years.

BENADRYL ALLERGY RELIEF

Use: Available in capsule form for easing the symptoms of hayfever. Each capsule contains acrivastine, an antihistamine.

Dose: 1 capsule should be taken up to 3 times a day. This treatment is not recommended for children under 12 years, or for the elderly over 65 years.

BENYLIN CHESTY COUGHS

Use: This is a liquid remedy for the treatment of coughs, containing diphenhydramine, an antihistamine and menthol.

Dose: Adults should take 10ml 4 times a day. Children (6-12 years) should take 5 ml 4 times a day. This treatment is not recommended for children under 6 years. A non-drowsy version is also available.

BENYLIN CHILDREN'S CHESTY COUGHS

Use: A liquid remedy for the treatment of chesty coughs, containing guaiphenesin, an expectorant.

Dose: Children (6-12 years) should be given 10ml 4 times a day, with a maximum of 4 doses a day. Children (1-5 years) should be given 5ml 4 times a day, with a maximum of 4 doses a day. This treatment is not recommended for babies under 1 year.

BENYLIN CHILDREN'S COUGHS AND COLDS

Use: This is a sugar- and colour-free liquid remedy for treatment of the symptoms of coughs and colds. It contains dextromethorphan, a cough suppressant and triprolidine, an antihistamine.

Dose: Children (6-12 years) should take 10ml 3-4 times a day. Children (2-5 years) should be given 5ml 3-4 times a day. Children (1-2 years) should be given 2.5ml 3-4 times a day. This treatment is not recommended for children under 1 year.

BENYLIN CHILDREN'S DRY COUGHS

Use: A liquid remedy used for the treatment of dry coughs, it contains pholcodine, a cough suppressant.

Dose: Children (6-12 years) should be given 10-15ml 3 times a day. Children (1-5 years) should be given 5ml 3 times a day. This treatment is not recommended for children under 1 year.

BENYLIN CHILDREN'S NIGHT COUGHS

Use: A liquid remedy for the treatment of coughs. It contains diphenhydramine, an antihistamine, and menthol.

Dose: Children (6 years and over) should take 10ml no more than 4 times a day. Children (1-5 years) should take 5ml no more than 4 times a day. This treatment is not recommended for children under 1 year.

BENYLIN COUGH AND CONGESTION

Use: This is a liquid remedy for the treatment of coughs, containing diphenhydramine, an antihistamine, dextromethorphan, a cough suppressant, pseudoephedrine, a decongestant and levomenthol.

Dose: Adults should take 10ml no more than 4 times a day. Children (6-12 years) should take 5ml no more than 4 times a day. This treatment is not recommended for children under 6 years.

BENYLIN DAY AND NIGHT COLD TREATMENT

Use: These are tablets for the treatment of colds and flu. The white tablets should be taken in the day and contain paracetamol and phenyl-propanolamine, a decongestant. The blue night time tablets contain paracetamol and diphenhydramine, an antihistamine.

Dose: 1 white tablet should be taken 3 times a day and 1 blue tablet should be taken at night. This treatment is not recommended for children under 6 years.

BENYLIN DRY COUGHS

Use: A liquid remedy for the treatment of dry coughs, containing dextromethorphan, a cough suppressant, diphenhydramine, an anti-histamine and menthol.

Dose: Adults should take 10ml 4 times a day. Children (6-12 years) should take 5ml 4 times a day. This treatment is not recommended for children under 6 years. A non-drowsy version is also available which doesn't contain the antihistamine.

BENYLIN FOUR FLU LIQUID

Use: A liquid remedy for relieving the symptoms of colds and flu. The liquid contains pseudoephedrine, a decongestant, diphenhydramine, an antihistamine and paracetamol.

Dose: Adults should take 20ml 4 times a day. Children (6-12 years) should take 10ml 4 times a day. This treatment is not recommended for children under 6 years. Hot drink and tablet forms are also available.

BENYLIN WITH CODEINE

Use: This is a liquid remedy for the treatment of coughs, containing codeine, a cough suppressant and diphenhydramine, an antihistamine.

Dose: Adults should take 10ml 4 times a day. Children (6-12 years) should be given 5ml 4 times a day. This treatment is not recommended for children under 6 years.

BETADINE SKIN CLEANSER

Use: This is a liquid facial wash for the treatment of acne and spots. It contains povidone iodine, an anti-microbial.

Dose: The liquid should be applied with a damp sponge, lathered and left on for 3-5 minutes; the skin should then be rinsed with warm water and dried. Repeat this twice a day. This treatment is not recommended for children under 2 years. Read the label for warnings about povidone iodine.

BETADINE SPRAY

Use: A dry powder spray for the treatment of minor burns, scalds, cuts and grazes. It contains povidone iodine, an anti-microbial.

Dose: The spray should be applied onto the affected area once or twice a day as required and covered with a clean dressing. This treatment is not recommended for children under 2 years.

BIRLEY'S ANTACID POWDER

Use: An antacid powder remedy for relieving the symptoms of indigestion and heartburn.

Dose: Adults should take 5ml in water after each meal, or twice a day. Check the label for the correct dosage for children.

BISODOL INDIGESTION RELIEF POWDER

Use: A remedy for indigestion and heartburn available in powder form, containing antacids.

Dose: 5ml of the powder should be dissolved in water after meals. This treatment is not recommended for children. The product is also available in tablet form.

BISODOL HEARTBURN RELIEF TABLETS

Use: These are tablets for relieving the symptoms of indigestion and heartburn, containing antacids and sodium.

Dose: Adults should chew 1-2 tablets as required. Children (6-12 years) should chew 1 tablet after meals and at bedtime. This treatment is not recommended for children under 6 years.

BLISTEZE
Use: This is a cream for the treatment of cold sores. It contains ammonia, a soothing ingredient.
Dose: The cream should be applied to the affected area every 2 hours or as required.

BONJELA
Use: This is a gel for the treatment of cold sores and mouth ulcers. It contains choline salicylate, an aspirin derivative, and cetalkonium, an antiseptic.
Dose: A small quantity of the gel should be applied to the affected area every 3 hours. Use a maximum of 6 applications in 24 hours.

BONJELA TEETHING GEL
Use: A gel for easing teething pain in babies, containing choline salicylate and an antiseptic.
Dose: The gel should be applied to the gums every 3 hours. Use a maximum of 6 applications over 24 hours. This treatment is not recommended for babies under 4 months.

BRADOSOL
Use: Lozenges for relieving sore throats, containing benzalkonium chloride, an antibacterial.
Dose: 1 lozenge should be sucked as required. This treatment is not recommended for children under 5 years. Available in various flavours.

BROLENE EYE DROPS
Use: Eye drops for the treatment of infections of the eye, containing propamidine, an anti-microbial.
Dose: 1-2 drops should be applied into the affected eye up to 4 times a day.

BROLENE EYE OINTMENT

Use: This is an ointment for the treatment of eye infections, including conjunctivitis and styes, containing dibromopropamidine, an anti-microbial.

Dose: The ointment should be applied to the infected eye/s twice a day.

BURNEZE

Use: A spray for the treatment of minor burns and scalds. It contains benzocaine, an anaesthetic.

Dose: The spray should be applied onto the affected area and then again after 15 minutes if required.

BUSCOPAN TABLETS

Use: These are tablets containing an antispasmodic for relieving period pains.

Dose: 1-2 tablets should be taken up to 4 times a day when necessary.

BUTTERCUP SYRUP (ORIGINAL)

Use: A liquid remedy for relieving coughs, containing capsicum and squill, both expectorants.

Dose: Adults should take 10ml 3 times a day. Children over 2 years should be given 5ml. This treatment is not recommended for children under 2 years. The product is also available in honey and lemon flavour.

BUTTERCUP INFANT COUGH SYRUP

Use: A liquid remedy for relieving coughs, containing ipecacuanha, an expectorant, menthol and liquid glucose.

Dose: Children (1-5 years) should be given 5ml 3-4 times a day. This treatment is not recommended for children under 1 year.

CALADRYL CREAM

Use: A cream containing an antihistamine for relieving bites, stings, rashes and sunburn.

Dose: The cream should be applied to the affected part 2-3 times a day as required. The product is also available as a lotion.

CALGEL TEETHING GEL

Use: A gel for relieving teething pains in babies, containing lignocaine, an anaesthetic, and an antiseptic.

Dose: The cream should be applied up to 6 times a day, leaving a minimum of 20 minutes between applications. This treatment is not recommended for babies under 3 months.

CALIFIG CALIFORNIA SYRUP OF FIGS

Use: A liquid remedy for the treatment of constipation, containing senna, a stimulant laxative.

Dose: 7.5-30ml (depending on age) should be taken at bedtime. Read the label for the correct dosage. This treatment is not recommended for children under 1 year.

CALIMAL ANTIHISTAMINE TABLETS

Use: Tablets for relieving the symptoms of hayfever, containing chlorpheniramine, an antihistamine.

Dose: Adults should take 1 tablet 3-4 times a day. Children (6-12 years) should take half a tablet 3-4 times a day. This treatment is not recommended for children under 6 years.

CALPOL INFANT SUSPENSION

Use: A strawberry flavoured analgesic liquid for general pain relief, containing 120mg of paracetamol in every 5ml.

Dose: A maximum of 4 doses can be taken over 24 hours. Babies (3-12 months) should be given 2.5ml every 4 hours if required, with no more than 20ml in 24 hours. Children (1-5 years) should be given 5-10ml every 4 hours. This treatment is not recommended for babies under 3 months. This medicine should not be taken with any other paracetamol containing product and the dosage must not be exceeded.

CALPOL SIX PLUS SUSPENSION

Use: A strawberry flavoured analgesic that is sugar- and colour-free. It contains 250mg of paracetamol in every 5ml.

Dose: A maximum of 4 doses can be taken in 24 hours. Adults can take

10-20ml 4 times day when required. Children (6-12 years) should be given 5-10ml every 4 hours if required. For children under 6 years use Calpol Infant Suspension. This medicine should not be taken with other products containing paracetamol and the stated dosage must not be exceeded.

CANESTEN 1% CREAM

Use: A cream treatment for the treatment of nappy rash, containing clotrimazole, an antifungal.

Dose: The cream should be massaged gently into clean, dry skin 2-3 times a day.

CANESTEN 2% CREAM

Use: This is a cream for the treatment of thrush infections, it contains clotrimazole, an antifungal.

Dose: The cream should be applied sparingly 2 to 3 times each day. This preparation can damage the latex in condoms and diaphragms.

CANESTEN AF CREAM

Use: An antifungal cream containing clotrimazole for the treatment of athlete's foot.

Dose: The cream should be rubbed gently into the affected area 2-3 times a day and should be used for 4 weeks.

CANESTEN AF POWDER

Use: A powder treatment for athlete's foot, containing clotrimazole.

Dose: The powder should be sprinkled onto the affected area 2-3 times a day. It is also advisable to dust the inside of socks and footwear each day. This treatment may be continued for 4 weeks.

CANESTEN AF SPRAY

Use: A spray treatment for athlete's foot, containing clotrimazole, an antifungal ingredient.

Dose: The feet should be washed and dried, particularly between the toes. The product should then be sprayed thinly all over the affected area 2-3 times a day. The treatment should be continued for 1 month.

CANESTEN COMBI

Use: A combination treatment for thrush comprising of a cream and pessary that both contain clotrimazole. Pack includes applicator.

Dose: The pessary should be inserted into the vagina at night. The cream should be applied twice daily to the external area around the vagina and also applied to the partner's penis. These preparations can damage the latex in condoms and diaphragms.

CANESTEN HYDROCORTISONE

Use: A cream for the treatment of athlete's foot, containing clotrimazole, an antifungal, and a steroid.

Dose: The cream should be applied thinly to the affected area and rubbed in gently. The product should not be used for more than 7 days, or on the head, neck, face or genitals.

CANESTEN PESSARY

Use: A pessary for the treatment of thrush, containing clotrimazole, an antifungal drug. An applicator is included in the pack.

Dose: The pessary should be inserted into the vagina at night. This single-dose treatment can damage the latex in condoms and diaphragms.

CANESTEN 10% VAGINAL CREAM

Use: A cream for the treatment of thrush, containing 10 per cent clotrimazole, an antifungal drug. An applicator is included in the pack.

Dose: Should be applied once into the vagina. This is a single dose treatment. These preparations can damage the latex in condoms and diaphragms.

CANESTEN ORAL

Use: A capsule containing fluconazole for the treatment of vaginal thrush.

Dose: The single capsule is taken as a single dose.

CAPASAL SHAMPOO

Use: A shampoo remedy for the treatment of cradle cap in children, containing coal tar, coconut oil and salicylic acid.

Dose: Shampoo the baby's head, rinse and repeat. The treatment can be applied once daily if necessary.

CAPASAL THERAPEUTIC SHAMPOO

Use: A medicated shampoo for the treatment of dandruff, containing coal tar, salicylic acid and coconut oil.

Dose: Should be used as a shampoo when required.

CAPRIN

Use: Analgesic tablets which can be used for general pain relief, containing aspirin.

Dose: 1-3 tablets should be taken 3-4 times a day. Take a maximum of 12 tablets over 24 hours. This treatment is not recommended for children under 16 years.

CARBELLON

Use: Antacid tablets for relieving indigestion, heartburn and gastritis.

Dose: Adults should take 2-4 tablets 3 times a day. Children over 6 years should be given 2 tablets 3 times a day. This treatment is not recommended for children under 6 years.

CARNATION CALLUS CAPS

Use: A medicated plaster containing salicylic acid for the treatment of corns and calluses.

Dose: The plaster should be applied to the affected area and changed after 3 days. The callus can be removed after 6 days. This treatment is not recommended for children under 16 years.

CARNATION CORN CAPS

Use: Medicated plasters for the treatment of corns, containing salicylic acid.

Dose: The plaster should be applied and changed every 2 days. The corn can be removed after 6 days. This treatment is not recommended for children under 15 years unless advised otherwise by a doctor. Do not use for more than 10 days and do not use more than 5 caps in that time.

CARNATION VERRUCA CARE

Use: Medicated pads used for the removal of verrucae, containing salicylic acid.

Dose: The pad should be applied and changed every 2 days, for up to 10 days. The treatment can be repeated after a month. This treatment is not recommended for children under 6 years, unless advised otherwise by a doctor.

CEANEL CONCENTRATE

Use: A medicated shampoo for the treatment of dandruff, containing various anti-microbials.

Dose: Should be used as a shampoo 3 times a week for 1 week, then twice a week as required.

CEPTON

Use: A wash for the treatment of acne, containing chlorhexidine, an anti-microbial.

Dose: The wash should be applied to clean skin and left for 1 minute before rinsing off thoroughly. This treatment is not recommended for children under 15 years. The product is also available as a lotion.

CERUMOL EAR DROPS

Use: Ear drops for removing earwax, containing a mild analgesic and an ingredient for softening the wax.

Dose: 5 drops should be applied into the affected ear and left for 20 minutes. This should be repeated 2-3 times a day for 3 days.

CETAVLEX ANTISEPTIC CREAM

Use: A cream for the treatment of minor burns, scalds, cuts and grazes, containing cetrimide, an antiseptic.

Dose: The cream should be applied to the affected area as required.

CETRIMIDE CREAM

Use: An antiseptic cream for the treatment of minor wounds or irritations of the skin, containing cetrimide.

Dose: The cream should be applied to the affected area or smeared on a dressing to cover the wound.

CLARITYN ALLERGY EYE DROPS

Use: Eye drops for relieving irritated eyes caused by hayfever. They contain sodium cromoglycate, an anti-inflammatory.

Dose: 1-2 drops should be applied to each affected eye up to 4 times a day. This treatment is not recommended for children under 5 years.

CLARITYN ALLERGY

Use: Tablets for relieving the symptoms of hayfever, containing loratadine, an antihistamine.

Dose: 1 tablet should be taken daily. This treatment is not recommended for children under 12 years.

CLARITYN ALLERGY SYRUP

Use: A liquid remedy for relieving the symptoms of hayfever. It contains loratadine, an antihistamine.

Dose: Adults should take 10 ml once a day. Children (2-5 years) should be given half the adult dose. This treatment is not recommended for children under 2 years.

CLEARASIL

Use: A cream for the treatment of acne and spots, containing benzoyl peroxide.

Dose: The cream should be applied once a day for 1 week. Increase applications to twice a day after 1 week if there are no adverse effects. This treatment is not recommended for children under 12 years.

CLEARASIL TREATMENT CREAM (REGULAR)

Use: A cream treatment for acne and spots, containing triclosan, an anti-microbial, and sulphur.

Dose: The cream should be applied twice daily to clean skin. This treatment is not recommended for children under 15 years.

CLINITAR CREAM

Use: A cream for the treatment of dermatitis and eczema, containing coal tar.

Dose: The cream should be applied once or twice a day as required.

CLINITAR SHAMPOO

Use: A medicated shampoo for the treatment of dandruff, containing coal tar.

Dose: The shampoo should be used up to 3 times a week

COCOIS SCALP OINTMENT

Use: An ointment for the treatment of dandruff, containing coal tar.

Dose: The ointment should be applied to the scalp once a week as necessary. For severe conditions apply daily for 3 to 7 days. Shampoo the hair 1 hour after using the ointment. This treatment is not recommended for children under 6 years.

CODIS 500

Use: A soluble analgesic tablet that can be used for general pain relief. Each tablet contains aspirin and codeine phosphate.

Dose: 1-2 tablets should be dissolved in water and taken every 4 hours as required. A maximum of 8 tablets may be taken in 1 24 hour period. The treatment is not recommended for children under 16 years old.

COLOFAC IBS

Use: A tablet remedy for easing the symptoms of irritable bowel syndrome. The tablets contain mebeverine, an ingredient that helps to calm intestinal spasms.

Dose: 1 tablet should be taken 3 times a day, preferably 20 minutes before meals. This treatment is not recommended for children under 10 years.

COLPERMIN

Use: Capsules for irritable bowel syndrome, containing peppermint oil for calming intestinal spasms.

Dose: 1-2 capsules should be taken 3 times a day for up to 2 weeks. The capsules should be swallowed whole to prevent the peppermint oil irritating the throat. This treatment is not recommended for children under 15 years.

COLSOR CREAM

Use: A cream treatment for cold sores, containing tannic acid and phenol, astringents, and menthol, a soothing ingredient.
Dose: The cream should be applied as required. The product is also available in the form of a lotion.

COMPOUND W

Use: A liquid treatment for warts and verrucae, containing salicylic acid.
Dose: The liquid should be applied to the wart or verruca daily for up to 12 weeks. This treatment is not recommended for children under 6 years.

CONOTRANE CREAM

Use: A cream for the treatment of nappy rash, containing benzalkonium chloride - an antiseptic - and dimethicone, a soothing agent.
Dose: The cream should be applied after every nappy change.

CONTAC NON-DROWSY 12 HOUR RELIEF

Use: Capsules for relieving the symptoms of colds and flu, containing pseudoephedrine, a decongestant.
Dose: 1 capsule should be taken in the morning and another before bedtime. This treatment is not recommended for children under 12 years.

CORLAN PELLETS

Use: A pellet for the treatment of mouth ulcers, containing hydrocortisone, a corticosteroid.
Dose: 1 tablet should be dissolved near the site of the ulcer 4 times a day. This treatment is not recommended for children under 12 years, unless advised otherwise by a doctor or dentist.

CORSODYL MOUTHWASH

Use: This is a solution for the treatment of mouth infections, sore gums and bad breath. It contains chlorhexidine, an anti-microbial.

Dose: The mouth should be rinsed with 10ml of the mouthwash for 1 minute. This should be carried out daily for 1 month. This medicine may cause a discolouration of the tongue and teeth, which will disappear after patients no longer use the product. It may be prevented by regularly cleaning the teeth and mouth.

CORSODYL DENTAL GEL

Use: A gel for the treatment of mouth infections such as thrush and mouth ulcers, containing chlorhexidine, an antiseptic.

Dose: The gel should be applied directly onto the affected area once or twice a day and left for 1 minute.

COVONIA BRONCHIAL BALSAM

Use: A liquid remedy for the treatment of coughs, containing dextromethorphan - a cough suppressant - and menthol.

Dose: Adults should take 10ml every 4 hours. Children (6-12 years) should be given 5ml every 4 hours. This treatment is not recommended for children under 6 years. The elderly should check with their pharmacist prior to use.

COVONIA MENTHOLATED COUGH MIXTURE

Use: A liquid remedy for the treatment of coughs, containing squill and liquorice - both expectorants - and menthol.

Dose: Adults should take 5-10ml every 4 hours. Children (5-12 years) should be given 5ml every 4 hours. This treatment is not recommended for children under 5 years.

COVONIA NIGHT TIME FORMULA

Use: A liquid remedy for the treatment of coughs, containing dextro-methorphan, a cough suppressant, and diphenhydramine, an antihistamine.

Dose: 15ml should be taken before bedtime. This treatment is not recommended for children under 5 years.

CRAMPEX

Use: A tablet for dispelling cramps, it contains nicotinic acid, which improves the circulation.

Dose: 1-2 tablets should be taken before bedtime. This treatment is not recommended for children.

CREMALGIN

Use: A cream rub for relieving muscular aches and pains, containing rubefacients and a salicylate, an aspirin derivative.

Dose: The cream should be massaged into the affected area 2-3 times a day. This treatment is not recommended for children under 6 years.

CUPLEX

Use: A gel containing salicylic acid for the treatment of calluses, corns, warts and verrucae.

Dose: This gel should be applied at night to the affected part. When it is dry, Cuplex produces a protective film, which should be removed in the mornings. This treatment may take between 6 and twelve weeks before it shows a result. The product is not recommended for young children.

CUPROFEN

Use: Analgesic tablets which can be used for general pain relief, containing ibuprofen.

Dose: 1-2 tablets should be taken after food. 1-2 tablets can be taken every 4 hours if required. Take a maximum of 6 tablets in 24 hours. This treatment is not recommended for children under 12 years.

CUPROFEN MAXIMUM STRENGTH

Use: Analgesic tablets which can be used for general pain relief, containing ibuprofen.

Dose: 1 tablet should be taken with food every 8 hours. Take a maximum of 3 tablets in 24 hours. Not recommended for children under 12 years.

CYMALON

Use: Granules containing sodium citrate and sodium bicarbonate for relieving the symptoms of cystitis.

Dose: 1 sachet of the granules should be dissolved in water and taken 3 times a day for 2 days.

CYMEX CREAM

Use: A cream treatment for cold sores, which contains cetrimide, an antiseptic, and urea, a soothing ingredient.

Dose: The cream should be applied sparingly every hour if necessary.

CYSTOPURIN

Use: Sachets of granules for the treatment of cystitis, containing potassium citrate.

Dose: 1 sachet of granules should be dissolved in water 3 times a day for 2 days.

DAKTARIN DUAL ACTION CREAM

Use: This is a cream for the treatment of athlete's foot, containing the antifungal ingredient, miconazole.

Dose: The cream should be applied twice a day to the affected area. Continue this treatment for a further 10 days after the infection has cleared up.

DAKTARIN DUAL ACTION POWDER

Use: This is a spray-on treatment for athlete's foot. The powder contains miconazole, an antifungal ingredient.

Dose: The powder should be applied to the affected area twice a day. Continue with this treatment for a further 10 days after the infection has cleared up.

DAKTARIN ORAL GEL

Use: This is a gel treatment for oral thrush, containing miconazole, an antifungal.

Dose: A small amount of the gel should be applied and held in the mouth for as long as possible and then spat out. Repeat this 4 times a day. The dosage for children varies according to age. Always read the label. Continue treatment for 2 days after the infection has cleared up.

DAY NURSE

Use: A liquid remedy for relieving the symptoms of colds and flu, containing paracetamol, pseudoephedrine, a decongestant and dextromethorphan, a cough suppressant.

Dose: Adults should take 30ml every 4 hours. Take a maximum of 120ml over 24 hours. This treatment is not recommended for children under 12 years. The product is also available in capsule form.

DDD MEDICATED CREAM

Use: A medicated antiseptic cream that is used for the treatment of minor wounds and skin irritations. It contains thymol, menthol, salicylic acid, chlorbutol and titanium dioxide.

Dose: The cream should be applied morning and evening until the problem has cleared up.

DDD MEDICATED LOTION

Use: A medicated antiseptic lotion that can be used for the treatment of minor wounds and skin irritations, containing thymol, menthol, salicylic acid, chlorobutol, methyl salicylate, glycerin and ethanol.

Dose: The cream should be applied to the affected area as needed.

DEEP FREEZE

Use: This is a cooling, spray treatment for relieving muscular aches.

Dose: The treatment should be sprayed onto the affected area as required but no more than 3 times in 24 hours. This treatment is not recommended for children under 6 years.

DEEP FREEZE COLD GEL

Use: A gel for soothing muscular pain and stiffness, cramps and bruises, which contains cooling ingredients.

Dose: The gel should be rubbed into the affected area 3-4 times a day. This treatment is not recommended for children under 5 years.

DEEP HEAT MASSAGE LINIMENT

Use: A liniment for the treatment of muscular aches and pains, containing rubefacients and a salicylate, an aspirin derivative.

Dose: The cream should be rubbed into the affected area 3-4 times a day. This treatment is not recommended for children under 5 years.

DEEP HEAT MAXIMUM STRENGTH

Use: A cream for relieving muscular aches and pains, containing a rubefacient and a salicylate, an aspirin derivative.

Dose: The product should be massaged into the affected area 2-3 times a day. This treatment is not recommended for children under 5 years.

DEEP HEAT RUB

Use: A cream rub treatment for relieving muscular aches and pains, containing rubefacients, and a salicylate, an aspirin derivative.

Dose: The product should be massaged into the affected area 2-3 times a day. This treatment is not recommended for children under 5 years.

DEEP HEAT SPRAY

Use: A spray for easing muscular aches and pains, containing rubefacients and a salicylate, an aspirin derivative.

Dose: The affected area should be sprayed with 2-3 short bursts as required. This treatment is not recommended for children under 5 years.

DEEP RELIEF

Use: A gel treatment for relieving muscular aches and pains, containing ibuprofen, a non-steroidal anti-inflammatory (NSAID).

Dose: The gel should be massaged into the affected area up to 3 times a day. This treatment is not recommended for children under 12 years.

DENTINOX CRADLE CAP TREATMENT SHAMPOO

Use: A shampoo for the treatment of cradle cap.

Dose: To be used as a normal shampoo until the condition clears up.

DENTINOX INFANT COLIC DROPS

Use: A liquid remedy for relieving colic in infants, containing dimethicone, an anti-wind ingredient.

Dose: 2.5ml should be given with or after each feed. A maximum of 6 doses can be given in 1 day. The product can be used from birth onwards.

DENTINOX TEETHING GEL
Use: A gel for soothing teething pain in babies, containing an antiseptic and lignocaine, an anaesthetic.
Dose: The gel should be applied every 20 minutes as required and is suitable for use from birth onwards.

DENTOGEN
Use: A gel for relieving toothache, containing clove oil.
Dose: The gel should be rubbed onto the affected tooth.

DEQUACAINE LOZENGES
Use: Lozenges for relieving sore throats, containing dequalinium, an antibacterial, and benzocaine, an anaesthetic.
Dose: 1 lozenge should be dissolved in the mouth every 2 hours or as required. Take a maximum of 8 lozenges in 24 hours. This treatment is not recommended for children under 12 years.

DERBAC M LIQUID
Use: A liquid treatment for head lice and other similar infestations, containing malathion.
Dose: For head lice, the liquid should be applied to the affected area, combed through the hair while wet, left to dry and finally washed out after 12 hours. For pubic lice, it should be left on for at least 1 hour, ideally overnight. For scabies, it should be applied to the whole body and left for 24 hours before washing off. This treatment is not recommended for babies under 6 months.

DERMACORT CREAM
Use: A cream for the treatment of bites, stings, hives, eczema and dermatitis, containing hydrocortisone, a steroid.
Dose: The product should be applied to the affected area once or twice a

day. This treatment is not recommended for children under 10 years. Do not use for more than 7 days.

DERMAMIST

Use: An emollient spray for the treatment of eczema and dermatitis, containing a mixture of oils.

Dose: The product should be sprayed onto the affected areas after a bathing.

DERMIDEX CREAM

Use: This is a cream for the treatment of bites, stings, eczema, dermatitis and hives, containing an anaesthetic and antiseptic.

Dose: The product should be applied to the affected part every 3 hours if necessary. Treatment is not recommended for children under 4 years.

DETTOL ANTISEPTIC PAIN RELIEF SPRAY

Use: A liquid antiseptic spray with a mild anaesthetic for the treatment of minor wounds and skin irritations, containing benzalkonium chloride and lidocaine hydrochloride.

Dose: The liquid should be sprayed onto the affected area as required.

DETTOL CREAM

Use: An antiseptic cream for the treatment of minor wounds or irritations of the skin, containing triclosan, chloro-xylenol and edetic acid.

Dose: The cream should be applied thinly onto the affected area.

DETTOL LIQUID

Use: A liquid antiseptic and disinfectant for the treatment of minor wounds and irritations of the skin, containing chloroxylenol.

Dose: The liquid should be diluted with water as appropriate for its intended use.

DIFFLAM

Use: A cream for relieving muscular aches and pains, containing benzydamine, a non-steroidal anti-inflammatory (NSAID).

Dose: The cream should be massaged into the affected area 3 times a day. This treatment is not recommended for children under 6 years.

DIFLUCAN ONE
Use: An oral capsule for the treatment of thrush, containing fluconazole.
Dose: 1 capsule should be taken orally. This is a single-dose treatment.

DIMOTANE CO ADULT
Use: A liquid remedy for the treatment of coughs that contains brompheniramine, an antihistamine, pseudoephedrine, a decongestant, codeine, a cough suppressant and ethanol (alcohol).
Dose: Adults should take 5-10ml up to 4 times a day. Children (4-12 years) should be given 5-7.5ml 3 times a day, depending on age. Read the label for the correct dosage. This treatment is not recommended for children under 2 years. The product is also available in a children's formula.

DIOCALM DUAL ACTION
Use: A remedy for stopping diarrhoea, containing morphine and attapulgite.
Dose: 2 tablets should be taken every 2 to 4 hours as required. Take a maximum of 12 tablets in 24 hours. Children (6-12 years) should be given 1 tablet every 2-4 hours, with a maximum of 6 tablets in 24 hours. This treatment is not recommended for children under 6 years.

DIOCALM ULTRA
Use: Capsules for stopping diarrhoea, containing loperamide.
Dose: 2 capsules should be taken at the start of the diarrhoea, followed by 1 capsule after every loose bowel movement. Take a maximum of 8 capsules in 24 hours. This treatment is not recommended for children under 12 years.

DIOCTYL
Use: Capsules for easing constipation, containing docusate, a stimulant laxative with a stool-softening action.

Dose: Adults can take up to 5 capsules through the day. The dosage should be reduced as the condition improves. This treatment is not recommended for children under 12 years. The product is also available as a solution and in a lower dose form for children.

DIORALYTE

Use: A powder remedy to help replace the salts and water lost during an attack of diarrhoea.

Dose: Adults should take 1-2 sachets of the powder in a measured amount of water after each loose bowel movement. Children should be given 1 sachet. Bottle-fed infants should be given a diluted solution instead of their feed - read the instructions on the packet for the correct dosage. Always consult a doctor before giving this treatment to babies under 1 year. This product is also available in other flavours.

DIORALYTE RELIEF

Use: A powder formula to replace salts and water lost from the body during an attack of diarrhoea.

Dose: 1 sachet should be dissolved in a measured quantity of water. Read the instructions on the packet. Take a maximum of 5 sachets in 24 hours. The product can be taken up to 3-4 days after loose bowel movements. Consult a doctor before giving the solution to babies under 1 year.

DIPROBASE

Use: An emollient cream for relieving the discomfort of eczema and dermatitis, containing a mixture of oils.

Dose: The cream should be applied when necessary.

DIPROBATH

Use: An emollient bath additive for relieving the discomfort of eczema and dermatitis, containing oil.

Dose: The liquid should be added to bathwater.

DISPRIN, DISPRIN DIRECT

Use: Soluble analgesic tablets, which can be used for general pain relief, disprin and disprin direct both contain aspirin.

Dose: 2-3 tablets should be taken every 4 hours. Take a maximum of 13 tablets in 24 hours. The disprin direct can be taken without water as it dissolves in the mouth. The treatment is not recommended for children under 16 years.

DISPRIN EXTRA

Use: A soluble analgesic tablet, which can be used for general pain relief, containing aspirin and paracetamol.

Dose: 1-2 tablets should be dissolved in water every 4 hours as required. Take a maximum of 6 tablets in 24 hours. This treatment is not recommended for children under 16 years.

DISPROL PARACETAMOL SUSPENSION

Use: A banana-flavoured, sugar-free analgesic liquid which can be used for general pain relief, containing 120mg of paracetamol in every 5ml.

Dose: Babies (3-12 months) should be given 2.5-5ml every 4 hours if required, with a maximum of 4 doses in 24 hours. Children (1-6 years) should be given 5-10ml every 4 hours if required, with a maximum of 4 doses in 24 hours. The treatment is not recommended for babies under 3 months. This medicine should not be given with any other paracetamol containing medicines such as calpol, and the stated doages must not be exceeded.

This medicine is also available as tablets, with 1 tablet equal to 5ml of the suspension.

DO-DO CHESTEZE

Use: Tablets for the treatment of coughs, containing ephedrine, a decongestant, theophylline, a bronchodilator, and caffeine.

Dose: Adults should take no more than 1 tablet in 4 hours. Take a maximum of 4 tablets in 24 hours. Children over 12 years should be given a maximum of 3 tablets in 24 hours. This treatment is not recommended for children under 12 years.

DOLVAN TABLETS

Use: Tablets for the treatment of colds and flu, containing paracetamol, diphenhydramine, an antihistamine, ephedrine, a decongestant and caffeine.

Dose: Adults should take 1-2 tablets 3 times a day. The elderly should take 1 tablet 3 times a day. This treatment is not recommended for children under 12 years.

DRAPOLENE CREAM

Use: A cream which can help soothe sunburn and nappy rash, containing the antiseptics, benzalkonium chloride and cetrimide.

Dose: The cream should be applied as required.

DUBAM SPRAY

Use: A spray treatment for easing muscular aches and pains, containing rubefacients and a salicylate, an aspirin derivative.

Dose: The product should be sprayed onto the affected area for 2 seconds, up to 4 times a day. This treatment is not recommended for children under 6 years. Use with caution if asthmatic or allergic to aspirin.

DULCO-LAX SUPPOSITORIES

Use: A suppository for alleviating constipation, containing the stimulant laxative, bisacodyl.

Dose: 1 suppository should be applied in the morning. This treatment is not recommended for children under 10 years. A lower strength version is also available for children.

DULCO-LAX TABLETS

Use: Tablets for relieving constipation. They contain bisacodyl, a stimulant laxative.

Dose: 1-2 tablets should be taken at bedtime. This treatment is not recommended for children under 10 years. The product is also available in liquid form and as a children's lower strength version.

DUOFILM

Use: A liquid remedy for the treatment of warts and verrucae, containing salicylic acid and lactic acid.

Dose: The liquid should be applied once or twice a day. Allow 6-12 weeks for it to take effect. Discuss with a doctor before using the product on children.

DUPHALAC SOLUTION
Use: A liquid remedy for relieving constipation, containing lactulose, an osmotic laxative.
Dose: Adults should take 15ml twice a day. Children (5-10 years) should be given 10ml twice a day. Children (1-5 years) should be given 5ml twice a day. Check dosage with a pharmacist if administering to babies under 1 year.

E45 CREAM
Use: An emollient cream for the treatment of eczema and dermatitis, which contains a mixture of oils including hypoallergenic lanolin.
Dose: The cream should be applied to the affected area 2-3 times a day as required.

EAREX EAR DROPS
Use: Ear drops for softening and removing earwax, which contain various oils including peanut oil.
Dose: 4 drops of the liquid should be applied into the affected ear and a cotton wool plug applied. Repeat morning and evening for 4 days until the wax clears.

EAREX PLUS DROPS
Use: Ear drops for the removal of earwax, containing a mild analgesic and an ingredient for softening wax.
Dose: The ear should be filled with the liquid and plugged with cotton wool. Use twice a day for 4 days. This treatment is not recommended for babies under 1 year.

ECOSTATIN
Use: This is a cream for the treatment of athlete's foot, containing econazole, an antifungal ingredient.
Dose: Apply this product twice a day to the affected area.

EFFERCITRATE TABLETS

Use: An effervescent tablet that helps to reduce the acidity that causes cystitis, containing citric acid and potassium citrate
Dose: 2 tablets should be dissolved in water and taken up to 3 times a day after meals.

EFFICO TONIC

Use: A liquid tonic for general fatigue, containing caffeine, Vitamin B1 and nicotinamide.
Dose: Adults should take 10ml 3 times a day after food. Children should be given 2.5-5ml, according to age, 3 times a day after food.

ELECTROLADE

Use: A powder solution for replacing the fluids and salts lost from the body during an attack of diarrhoea.
Dose: Adults should take 1-2 sachets dissolved in a measured amount of water (see instructions on the packet for correct measurements) after every loose bowel movement. Up to 16 sachets can be taken in 24 hours. Children should be given 1 sachet after every loose bowel movement, with up to 12 sachets in 24 hours. Consult a doctor before using this treatment on babies under 2 years. The product is available in a range of flavours.

ELLIMAN'S UNIVERSAL EMBROCATION

Use: An lotion for easing muscular aches and pains, containing rubefacients.
Dose: The product should be applied to the affected area every 3 hours on the first day, then twice a day until the pain eases. This treatment is not recommended for children under 12 years.

ELUDRIL MOUTHWASH

Use: A mouthwash for the treatment of bad breath, sore gums and general infections of the mouth. It contains chlorhexidine, an anti-microbial.
Dose: The mouth should be rinsed with 10-15ml of the mouthwash diluted with water, 2-3 times a day, taking care not to swallow the liquid.

This treatment is not recommended for children. The product is also available as a spray.

EMULSIDERM EMOLLIENT
Use: An emollient bath additive for relieving the discomfort of eczema and dermatitis, containing various oils and an antiseptic.
Dose: The product can be added to bath water or applied directly onto the skin.

ENO
Use: A powder remedy for relieving indigestion, heartburn and gastritis, containing an antacid.
Dose: 1 sachet or 1 teaspoon should be dissolved in water every 2-3 hours or as required. Take a maximum of 6 doses in 24 hours. This treatment is not recommended for children under 12 years. The product is also available in lemon flavour.

ESKAMEL CREAM
Use: A cream for the treatment of acne and spots, containing resorcinol and sulphur.
Dose: The cream should be applied once a day. This treatment is not recommended for children under 15 years.

EURAX CREAM
Use: This is a cream containing crotamiton for relieving itching caused by stings, bites, hives, eczema, dermatitis and sunburn.
Dose: The product should be applied 2-3 times a day. The product is also available as a lotion.

EURAX HC CREAM
Use: This cream contains crotamiton and the steroid, hydrocortisone, for the treatment of eczema, dermatitis, stings, bites and hives.
Dose: The cream should be applied sparingly up to twice a day for a maximum of 1 week. This treatment is not recommended for children under 10 years.

EX-LAX SENNA

Use: Chocolate tablets for easing the discomfort of constipation, containing senna, a stimulant laxative.

Dose: Adults should take 1 tablet of chocolate at bedtime. Children over 6 years should be given half to 1 tablet at bedtime. This treatment is not recommended for children under 6 years.

EXTEROL EAR DROPS

Use: Ear drops for removing earwax, containing softening ingredients.

Dose: 5 drops should be applied into the affected ear once or twice a day, for 3-4 days.

FELDENE P GEL

Use: This is a gel for the treatment of muscular aches and pains, containing piroxicam, which is a non-steroidal anti-inflammatory (NSAID).

Dose: The product should be applied to the affected area up to 4 times a day for 7 days. This treatment is not recommended for children under 12 years.

FEMINAX

Use: A tablet remedy for relieving period pain, containing paracetamol, codeine, caffeine and an antispasmodic.

Dose: 1-2 tablets should be taken every 4 hours when necessary. Take a maximum of 6 tablets in 24 hours.

FENBID GEL

Use: A gel containing ibuprofen, a non-steroidal anti-inflammatory (NSAID), for the treatment of muscular aches and pains.

Dose: The gel should be massaged into the affected area up to 4 times a day. This treatment is not recommended for children under 14 years. The product is also available as a cream.

FENOX NASAL DROPS

Use: Nasal drops for relieving nasal congestion caused by sinusitis or hayfever, containing phenylephrine, a decongestant.

Dose: Adults should take 4-5 drops into each nostril morning and night and every 4 hours if required. Children (5-12 years) should take 2 drops in each nostril night and morning and every 4 hours if required. This treatment is not recommended for children under 5 years. Do not use longer than 7 days. The product is also available as a spray.

FIERY JACK CREAM

Use: A cream for alleviating muscular aches and pains, containing rubefacients.

Dose: The product should be applied to the affected area twice a day. This treatment is not recommended for children under 12 years.

FRADOR

Use: A liquid treatment for mouth ulcers, containing antiseptic and astringent ingredients.

Dose: The liquid should be applied to the ulcer with the applicator provided, 4 times a day after meals and before bed. This treatment is not recommended for children.

FULL MARKS LIQUID

Use: A liquid treatment for head lice containing phenothrin.

Dose: The liquid should be rubbed into the scalp and the hair combed whilst wet, then allowed to dry naturally. The treatment should be left in for at least 12 hours, then washed out. This treatment is not recommended for babies under 6 months.

FULL MARKS LOTION

Use: A lotion for the treatment of head lice, containing phenothrin and alcohol.

Dose: The lotion should be rubbed into dry hair and left in for 2 hours or overnight. Wash and comb through hair while it is wet. This treatment is not recommended for babies under 6 months.

FYBOGEL

Use: These are granules for the treatment of constipation and irritable bowel syndrome, containing ispaghula husk, which is a bulking agent.

Dose: Adults should dissolve 1 sachet of the granules in water and drink after a meal, twice a day. The product should be taken with plenty of liquid and not before bedtime. This treatment is not recommended for children under 12 years. The product is available in various flavours.

GALENPHOL ADULT LINCTUS

Use: A liquid remedy for the relief of dry or tickly coughs, containing pholcodine, a cough suppressant.

Dose: 10-15ml 3-4 times a day, children (6-12 years) 5ml 4 times a day, (1-5 years) 2.5-5ml 3-4 times a day.

GALENPHOL PAEDIATRIC LINCTUS

Use: A liquid remedy for the relief of dry, or tickly coughs, containing pholcodine, a cough suppressant.

Dose: Children (1-5 years) 5-10ml 3 times a day, (6-12 years) 10ml 3 times a day.

GALLOWAY'S COUGH SYRUP

Use: A liquid remedy for coughs, containing ipecacuanha and squill, both expectorants.

Dose: Adults and children over 10 years old should take 10 ml 3 to 4 times a day. Children under 10 years should be given half the adult dose. Read the label for the correct dosage.

GALPSEUD (AKA GALSUD)

Use: Tablets for the treatment of sinusitis, containing pseudoephedrine, a decongestant.

Dose: Adults should take 1 tablet 4 times a day. This treatment is not recommended for children under 12 years. The product is also available as a liquid.

GASTROCOTE LIQUID

Use: A liquid remedy for the treatment of upset stomachs, indigestion and heartburn, containing sodium, an antacid and an alginate.

Dose: 5-15ml should be taken 4 times a day after meals and on retiring. This treatment is not recommended for children under 6 years. The product is also available in tablet form.

GAVISCON 250

Use: A tablet remedy for indigestion and heartburn, containing an antacid, sodium and an alginate.

Dose: 2 tablets should be chewed as needed. This treatment is not recommended for children under 12 years. The product is also available in liquid form, Gaviscon liquid, and an extra strength liquid, Gaviscon Advance.

GERMOLENE ANTISEPTIC WIPES

Use: Cleansing wipes for the treatment of minor wounds and skin irritations, impregnated with an antiseptic. The wipes contain benzalkonium chloride and chlorhexidine gluconate.

Dose: Use to clean wounds as required.

GERMOLENE CREAM

Use: An antiseptic cream for the treatment of minor wounds and irritations of the skin, containing phenol and chlorhexidine gluconate.

Dose: The cream should be applied to the affected area and covered with a dressing if necessary.

GERMOLENE NEW SKIN

Use: A liquid that forms a water- and germ-proof barrier to protect minor wounds.

Dose: The liquid should be applied to the cut or graze and allowed to dry.

GERMOLENE OINTMENT

Use: An antiseptic ointment for the treatment of minor wounds and irritations of the skin. It contains zinc oxide, methyl salicylate, phenol lanolin and octaphonium chloride.

Dose: The product should be applied to the affected area or smeared onto a dressing.

GERMOLOIDS CREAM

Use: A cream treatment for piles, containing lidocaine, a mild local anaesthetic, and zinc oxide, an astringent.

Dose: The product should be applied to the affected area twice a day and after each bowel movement, with no more than 4 applications in 1 day. This treatment is not recommended for children under 12 years. The product is also available as suppositories and as an ointment.

GLUTAROL

Use: A liquid treatment for warts and verrucae, containing glutaraldehyde.

Dose: The product should be applied to the wart or verruca twice a day.

GODDARD'S EMBROCATION

Use: An liniment for relieving muscular aches and pains, containing a rubefacient.

Dose: The product should be applied to the affected area once or twice a day or as required. This treatment is not recommended for children under 6 years.

GOLDEN EYE OINTMENT

Use: Eye ointment for treating infections of the eye including conjunctivitis and styes. It contains dibromopropamidine, an anti-microbial.

Dose: The product should be applied to the affected eye once or twice a day.

HAYMINE

Use: Tablets for relieving the symptoms of hayfever, containing chlorpheniramine, an antihistamine, and ephedrine, a decongestant.

Dose: 1 tablet should be taken in the morning and another tablet can be taken at night if necessary.

HC45 HYDROCORTISONE CREAM

Use: A hydrocortisone cream for the treatment of eczema, dermatitis, stings, bites and hives.

Dose: The product should be applied to the affected area sparingly once or twice a day, for no longer than 7 days. This treatment is not recommended for children under 10 years.

HEDEX
Use: Analgesic tablets that can be used for general pain relief, containing paracetamol.
Dose: Adults should take 2 tablets up to 4 times a day. Take a maximum of 8 tablets in 24 hours. Children (6-12 years) should be given half of 1 tablet every 4 hours, with a maximum of 4 tablets over 24 hours. This treatment is not recommended for children under 6 years.

HEDEX EXTRA
Use: Analgesic tablets which can be used for general pain relief, containing paracetamol and caffeine.
Dose: 2 tablets should be taken up to 4 times a day. Take a maximum of 8 tablets in 24 hours. This treatment is not suitable for children under 12 years.

HEDEX IBUPROFEN
Use: Analgesic tablets for general pain relief, containing ibuprofen.
Dose: 1-2 tablets should be taken up to 3 times a day. Take a maximum of 6 tablets in 24 hours. This treatment is not recommended for children under 12 years.

HEMOCANE CREAM
Use: A cream treatment for the treatment of piles, containing lignocaine, a mild local anaesthetic and zinc oxide, an astringent.
Dose: The cream should be applied morning and night and after each bowel movement. This treatment is not recommended for children under 12 years.

HILL'S BALSAM CHESTY COUGH LIQUID
Use: A liquid remedy for the treatment of coughs, containing guaiphenesin, an expectorant.

Dose: 5-10ml should be taken every 2 to 4 hours. Take a maximum of 60ml in 24 hours. This treatment is not recommended for children under 12 years.

HILL'S BALSAM CHESTY COUGH LIQUID FOR CHILDREN

Use: A liquid sugar-free remedy for relieving coughs, containing ipecacuanha, citric acid and capsicum, all expectorants, and benzoin, saccharin and orange oil.

Dose: 2.5-5ml should be given 3 times a day and at bedtime, according to age. Read the label for the correct dosage.

HILL'S BALSAM DRY COUGH LIQUID

Use: A liquid remedy for the treatment of coughs, containing pholcodine, a cough suppressant.

Dose: 5ml should be taken 3-4 times a day. This treatment is not recommended for children under 12 years.

HILL'S BALSAM EXTRA STRONG 2-IN-1 PASTILLES

Use: Herbal pastilles for soothing the symptoms of colds and flu, containing ipecacuanha, menthol and peppermint.

Dose: 1 pastille should be dissolved in the mouth as required, with a maximum of 10 pastilles in 24 hours. Children over 12 years should be given a maximum of 7 pastilles in 24 hours. This treatment is not recommended for children under 12 years.

HIRUDOID CREAM

Use: A cream to aid the healing of minor bruises, containing heparinoid, an ingredient that helps resolve bruising.

Dose: Apply to the bruise 4 times a day. This treatment is not recommended for children under 5 years. The product is also available as a gel.

HYDROMOL CREAM

Use: An emollient cream for relieving the discomfort of eczema and dermatitis, containing a mixture of oils including peanut oil.

Dose: The cream should be applied liberally and used as often as required. This product is not suitable for those allergic to peanuts.

HYDROMOL EMOLLIENT
Use: An emollient bath additive for relieving the discomfort of eczema and dermatitis, containing a mixture of oils.
Dose: 1-3 capfuls of the liquid should be added to a shallow bath.

IBULEVE GEL, IBULEVE SPORTS GEL
Use: A gel for the treatment of muscular aches and pains, containing ibuprofen, a non-steroidal anti-inflammatory (NSAID).
Dose: The gel should be massaged into the affected area up to 3 times a day. This treatment is not recommended for children under 12 years. The product is also available in a spray and as a mousse.

IBUSPRAY
Use: A spray for relieving muscular aches and pains, containing ibuprofen, a non-steroidal anti-inflammatory (NSAID).
Dose: The product should be sprayed onto the affected part and massaged in 3-4 times a day.

IMODIUM CAPSULES
Use: Capsules to help stop diarrhoea, containing loperamide.
Dose: 2 capsules should be taken at the start of an attack of diarrhoea, and then 1 capsule after every loose bowel movement. Take a maximum of 8 capsules in 24 hours. This treatment is not recommended for children under 12 years. The product is also available in liquid form.

IMUDERM THERAPEUTIC OIL
Use: An emollient bath additive for the treatment of eczema and dermatitis, containing various oils.
Dose: 15-30ml of the oil can be added to the bath water or applied directly to the skin.

INADINE
Use: A non-stick dressing to be applied to minor burns and scalds, containing povidone iodine - an anti-microbial.
Dose: The product should be applied as required.

INFACOL

Use: A liquid remedy for relieving wind and colic in babies, containing simethicone, an anti-wind ingredient. A measure is supplied.

Dose: 1 measured dose of 0.5ml should be given before each feed. The liquid can be used from birth onwards.

INFADROPS

Use: An analgesic liquid for general pain relief, containing 100mg of paracetamol in 1ml. A measuring pipette is supplied.

Dose: A maximum of 4 doses can be given in 24 hours. Babies (3-12 months) should be given 0.8ml. Babies (1-2 years) should be given 1.2ml. Children (2-3 years) should be given 1.6ml. This treatment is not recommended for babies under 3 months.

ISOGEL

Use: A granule remedy for relieving the symptoms of constipation, diarrhoea and irritable bowel syndrome. The granules contain ispaghula husk, a bulking laxative.

Dose: Adults should take 10ml dissolved in water once or twice a day. Children (6-12 years) should be given 5ml once or twice a day. The granules should be taken with plenty of fluid and it is advisable not to take the treatment at bedtime. This treatment is not recommended for children under 6 years.

JACKSON'S ALL FOURS EXTRA STRENGTH

Use: A liquid remedy for the treatment of coughs, containing guaiphenesin, a cough suppressant.

Dose: 5-10ml should be taken at bedtime or every 4 hours if necessary. This treatment is not recommended for children under 12 years.

JACKSON'S LITTLE HEALERS

Use: A tablet for treating of coughs, containing ipecacuanha, an expectorant.

Dose: Adults should take 2 tablets 3 times a day. Children (5-12 years) should take 1 tablet. This treatment is not recommended for children under 5 years.

J COLLIS BROWNE'S MIXTURE

Use: This is a liquid remedy for the treatment of diarrhoea and digestive upsets, containing morphine.

Dose: Adults should take 10-15ml every 4 hours. Children (6-12 years) should be given 5ml every 4 hours. This treatment is not recommended for children under 6 years. The product is also available in tablet form.

JELONET

Use: A sterile gauze dressing for the treatment of burns and scalds. It is impregnated with soft paraffin which prevents fibres from sticking to the burn.

Dose: The product should be applied to the affected area as required.

JOY-RIDES

Use: Tablets for the prevention of travel sickness, containing hyoscine, an anti-spasmodic.

Dose: Adults should take 2 tablets 20 minutes before the start of a journey or at the onset of nausea. The dose may be repeated after 6 hours if necessary. Children over 3 years should be given half to 2 tablets depending on age, with a maximum of 2 doses in 24 hours. Check instructions on the label for the correct dosage. This treatment is not recommended for children under 3 years.

JUNGLE FORMULA BITE AND STING RELIEF CREAM

Use: This is a cream for the treatment of bites and stings. It contains hydrocortisone, which is a steroid.

Dose: The product should be applied sparingly to the affected area once or twice a day. Do not use for more than 7 days. This treatment is not recommended for children under 10 years.

JUNIOR KAO-C

Use: A liquid remedy for stopping diarrhoea in children, containing kaolin.

Dose: Children should be given 5-20ml according to age, 3 times a day. Check the label for the correct dosage. This treatment is not recommended for babies under 1 year.

JUNIOR MELTUS EXPECTORANT

Use: A liquid remedy for the treatment of coughs, containing guaiphenesin, an expectorant, cetylpyridinium, an antiseptic, purified honey and sucrose.
Dose: Children over 6 years should be given 10ml 3-4 times a day. Children (1-6 years) should be given 5ml 3-4 times a day. This treatment is not suitable for children under 1 year. Sugar- and colour-free versions are also available.

KAMILLOSAN BABY CREAM

Use: This is an ointment for the treatment of nappy rash, containing lanolin and camomile extract.
Dose: The cream should be applied to clean dry skin at each nappy change.

KARVOL DECONGESTANT TABLETS /CAPSULES

Use: Capsules for relieving the symptoms of colds and flu, containing various decongestant oils.
Dose: For babies over 3 months, children, adults and the elderly, the capsules contents should be squeezed onto a pillow or bed sheets. Adults can also squeeze a capsule into a bowl of hot water and inhale. For young children a capsule can be squeezed onto a handkerchief or clothing.

KOLANTICON GEL

Use: A liquid gel solution for relieving gastritis, indigestion and heartburn, containing antacid and an antispasmodic.
Dose: 10-20ml should be taken every 4 hours. This treatment is not recommended for children under 12 years.

KWELLS

Use: Tablets for preventing travel sickness, containing hyoscine, an anti-spasmodic.
Dose: Adults should take 1 tablet every 6 hours. Take a maximum of 3 tablets in 24 hours. Children over 10 years should be given half the adult dose. This treatment is not recommended for children under 10 years. The product is also available as a children's version.

KY JELLY

Use: A lubricating gel for alleviating vaginal dryness.

Dose: A little of the gel should be applied to the vagina as required.

LABITON

Use: A liquid remedy for alleviating general fatigue, containing alcohol, caffeine, vitamin B1 and dried extract of kola nut.

Dose: 10-20ml should be taken twice a day. This treatment is not recommended for children under 12 years.

LABOSEPT PASTILLES

Use: Pastilles for relieving sore throats, containing dequalinium, an antibacterial.

Dose: 1 pastille should be sucked every 3-4 hours. Take a maximum of 8 pastilles in 24 hours. This treatment is not recommended for children under 10 years.

LACTO-CALAMINE LOTION

Use: A lotion for soothing sunburn, containing calamine and zinc oxide.

Dose: The lotion should be applied as required.

LANACANE CREAM

Use: A cream for relieving bites, stings and sunburn, containing a local anaesthetic.

Dose: The product should be applied to the affected area 3 times a day. This medicine should not be applied to large areas of the skin. This treatment is not recommended for children under 12 years.

LANACORT CREAM

Use: A cream for the treatment of eczema and dermatitis, containing hydrocortisone, a steroid.

Dose: The cream should be applied sparingly once or twice a day. This treatment is not recommended for children under 12 years and should not be used for longer than 1 week. The product is also available as an ointment.

LASONIL

Use: An ointment for the treatment of bruises containing heparinoid, an ingredient that helps to resolve bruising.

Dose: The product should be applied 2-3 times a day to the affected area and should not used on broken skin.

LAXOBERAL

Use: This is a liquid remedy for constipation, containing sodium picosulphate, a stimulant laxative.

Dose: 5-10 ml should be given at nightfor adults and children over 10 years old. This treatment is not recommended for children under 10 years without medical supervision.

LEMSIP BREATHE EASY

Use: Sachets of powder for relieving the symptoms of colds and flu, which contains paracetamol, phenylephrine, a decongestant, and vitamin C.

Dose: 1 sachet should be dissolved in hot water every 4 hours or as required. Take a maximum of 4 sachets in 24 hours. This treatment is not recommended for children under 12 years.

LEMSIP MAX COLD & FLU CAPSULES

Use: Capsules for relieving the symptoms of colds and flu, containing paracetamol, phenylephrine, a decongestant, and caffeine.

Dose: 2 capsules should be taken every 3-4 hours. Take a maximum of 8 capsules in 24 hours. This treatment is not recommended for children under 12 years.

LEMSIP MAX COLD & FLU

Use: A lemon flavoured powder in sachets, for relieving the symptoms of colds and flu. Each sachet contains paracetamol, phenylephrine, a decongestant, and vitamin C.

Dose: 1 sachet should be dissolved in hot water every 4-6 hours or as required. Take a maximum of 4 sachets in 24 hours. This treatment is not recommended for children under 12 years.

LEMSIP COLD & FLU

Use: A lemon flavoured powder for relieving the symptoms of colds and flu, containing paracetamol, phenylephrine, a decongestant and vitamin C.

Dose: 1 sachet should be dissolved in hot water every 4 hours or as required. Take a maximum of 4 sachets in 24 hours. This treatment is not recommended for children under 12 years.

LEMSIP MAX FLU

Use: A lemon flavoured powder in sachets for relieving the symptoms of colds and flu. Each sachet contains paracetamol, pseudoephedrine, a decongestant, and vitamin C.

Dose: 1 sachet should be dissolved in hot water every 4 hours if required. Take a maximum of 4 sachets in 24 hours. This treatment is not recommended for children under 12 years.

LEMSIP FLU 12 HOUR IBUPROFEN + PSEUDOEPHEDRINE

Use: Capsules for relieving the symptoms of colds and flu, containing ibuprofen and pseudoephedrine, a decongestant.

Dose: 2 capsules should be taken every 4 hours. Take a maximum of 4 capsules in 24 hours. This treatment is not recommended for children under 12 years.

LIQUFRUTA GARLIC (COUGH MEDICINE)

Use: A liquid remedy for the treatment of coughs, containing guaiphenesin, an expectorant.

Dose: Adults should take 10-15ml 3 times a day and at bedtime. Children (3-12 years) should be given 10ml. Children (1-3 years) should be given 5ml. This treatment is not recommended for children under 1 year.

LLOYDS CREAM

Use: A cream rub for the treatment of muscular aches and pains. It contains a rubefacient and a salicylate, an aspirin derivative.

Dose: The cream should be applied to the affected area up to 3 times a day. This treatment is not recommended for children under 6 years.

LYCLEAR CREME RINSE

Use: A lotion treatment containing permethrin for head lice and other similar infestations.

Dose: The lotion should be massaged into the hair and scalp after shampooing, then left for 10 minutes and washed out. The hair should be combed through while still wet. This treatment is not recommended for babies under 6 months.

LYPSYL COLD SORE GEL

Use: This is a gel for the treatment of cold sores. It contains lignocaine, a local anaesthetic, cetrimide, an antiseptic, and zinc sulphate, an astringent.

Dose: The cream should be applied to the cold sore 3-4 times a day.

MAALOX PLUS SUSPENSION

Use: A liquid remedy for relieving indigestion, heartburn and trapped wind. It contains an antacid and simethicone, an antiflatulent.

Dose: 5-10ml should be taken 4 times a day after meals and at bedtime. This treatment is not recommended for children under 12 years. The product is also available in tablet form.

MAALOX SUSPENSION

Use: A liquid for relieving indigestion and heartburn, containing antacids.

Dose: 10-20ml should be taken 4 times a day 20-60 minutes after meals and at bedtime. This treatment is not recommended for children under 12 years.

MACKENZIES SMELLING SALTS

Use: Liquid smelling salts for easing nasal congestion, containing ammonia with eucalyptus oil.

Dose: The vapour should be inhaled as required. This treatment is not recommended for babies under 3 months.

MAGNESIUM SULPHATE PASTE BP

Use: This is a non-brand name paste for 'drawing out' boils. It contains magnesium sulphate, phenol and glycerol.

Dose: The paste should be stirred and then applied to the boil. The area should then be covered with a clean, dry dressing.

MANEVAC

Use: A granular remedy for relieving constipation, containing fibre and senna, a stimulant laxative.

Dose: The granules should be placed on the tongue and swallowed with plenty of water, without chewing. Adults should take 5-10ml once or twice a day. Children (5-12 years) should be given 5ml once a day. Pregnant women should take 5-10ml every morning and evening. This treatment is not recommended for children under 5 years.

MAXIMUM STRENGTH ASPRO CLEAR

Use: An effervescent analgesic tablet for general pain relief, containing aspirin.

Dose: 1-2 tablets should be dissolved in water every 4 hours. Take a maximum of 8 tablets in 24 hours. This treatment is not recommended for children under 16 years.

MEDIJEL GEL

Use: A gel for the treatment of sore gums, bad breath and mouth ulcers, containing lidocaine, a local anaesthetic.

Dose: The gel should be applied every 20 minutes or as necessary.

MEDINOL OVER 6 PARACETAMOL ORAL SUSPENSION

Use: A strawberry flavoured analgesic liquid for general pain relief, which is sugar- and colour-free. It contains 250mg of paracetamol in every 5ml.

Dose: Take a maximum of 4 doses in 24 hours. Children (6-12 years) should be given 5-10ml every 4 hours if required. For children under 6 years, use Medinol Under 6.

MEDINOL UNDER 6 PARACETAMOL ORAL SUSPENSION

Use: A strawberry flavoured analgesic liquid for general pain relief, which is sugar- and colour-free. It contains 120mg of paracetamol in every 5ml.

Dose: Take a maximum of 4 doses in 24 hours. Babies (3-12 months) should be given 2.5-5 ml every 4 hours if required. Children (1-5 years) should be given 10 ml every 4 hours. Children over 5 years should be given 15-20 ml. This treatment is not recommended for babies under 3 months unless advised otherwise by a doctor.

MEDISED INFANT

Use: An analgesic liquid for general pain relief, containing 120mg of paracetamol in every 5ml, and diphenhydramine, an antihistamine.
Dose: Take a maximum of 4 doses in 24 hours. Children (1-6 years) should be given 10ml every 4 hours if required. Children (6-12 years) should be given 20ml every 4 hours. This treatment is not recommended for babies under 1 year.

MELTUS COUGH ELIXIR – See Adult Meltus Cough Elixir

MELTUS JUNIOR EXPECTORANT – See Junior Meltus Expectorant

MENTHOLATUM RUB

Use: An ointment for the treatment of muscular aches and pains, containing rubefacients and a salicylate, an aspirin derivative.
Dose: The product should be applied to the affected area 2-3 times a day. This treatment is not recommended for children under 1 year.

MEROCAINE LOZENGES

Use: Lozenges for relieving sore throats, containing cetylypridinium, an antiseptic and benzocaine, an anaesthetic.
Dose: 1 lozenge should be dissolved in the mouth every 2 hours. Take a maximum of 8 pastilles in 24 hours. This treatment is not recommended for children under 12 years.

MEROCETS LOZENGES

Use: Lozenges for relieving sore throats, containing cetylpyridinium, an antiseptic.
Dose: 1 lozenge should be dissolved in the mouth every 3 hours or as required. This treatment is not recommended for children under 6 years.

METANIUM OINTMENT

Use: An ointment for relieving nappy rash, containing titanium salts and an astringent.

Dose: Ointment should be applied to clean, dry skin at each nappy change.

METATONE

Use: A liquid remedy for alleviating fatigue, containing calcium, sodium, potassium, manganese and vitamin B1.

Dose: Adults should take 5-10ml 2-3 times a day. Children (6-12 years) should be given 5ml 2-3 times a day. This treatment is not recommended for children under 6 years.

METED SHAMPOO

Use: A medicated shampoo for the treatment of dandruff, contains salicylic acid.

Dose: Should be used as a shampoo twice a week.

MIGRALEVE

Use: The yellow tablets contain paracetamol, and codeine phosphate as painkillers. The pink tablets also contain buclizine hydrochloride, a sedative antihistamine to relieve the nausea associated with a migraine attack.

Dose: Adults should take 2 pink tablets as soon as an attack is about to start. Take a maximum of 2 tablets in 24 hours. 2 yellow tablets may then be taken up every 4 hours thereafter, to a maximum of 6 tablets in 24 hours. There is no need to take the pink tablets if there is no nausea. In which case the pink tablets may be swapped for yellow ones. Children (10-14 years) should be given only 1 pink tablet in 24 hours. This may be followed by 1 yellow tablet every 4 hours to a maximum of 3 yellow tablets in 24 hours. This treatment is not recommended for children under 10 years.

MILK OF MAGNESIA

Use: A liquid remedy for relieving indigestion, heartburn, upset stomachs and constipation. It contains magnesium hydroxide, an osmotic laxative.

Dose: For constipation adults should take 30-45ml at bedtime, and for indigestion 5-10ml as necessary to a maximum of 60ml. Children over 3 years should be given 5-10ml at bedtime. This treatment is not recommended for children under 3 years.

MIL-PAR
Use: A liquid remedy for easing constipation, containing magnesium sulphate, an osmotic laxative, and liquid paraffin, which helps to soften the stools.
Dose: Adults should take 15-30ml a day, mixed with water or milk before breakfast or bedtime. Children over 3 years should be given 5-15ml a day, depending on age. Read the label for the correct dosage. This treatment is not recommended for children under 3 years of age.

MINTEC
Use: These are capsules for the treatment of irritable bowel syndrome, containing peppermint oil, which can help to calm intestinal spasms.
Dose: 1 capsule should be taken 3 times a day just before a meal, swallowed whole to prevent the peppermint oil irritating the throat. This treatment is not recommended for children.

MOLCER EAR DROPS
Use: Ear drops containing softening ingredients for the removal of earwax.
Dose: The ear should be filled with the drops and plugged with cotton wool. Treatment should be repeated for 2 nights and then clear the wax out the ear.

MONPHYTOL PAINT
Use: This is a liquid treatment for athlete's foot, containing a mixture of antifungals.
Dose: The liquid should be applied to the affected area twice a day. The treatment should be repeated until the infection has cleared.

MOORLAND
Use: Antacid tablets for relieving indigestion and heartburn.

Dose: 2 tablets should be dissolved in the mouth as required, after meals and at bedtime. This treatment is not recommended for children under 6 years.

MORHULIN OINTMENT
Use: An emollient ointment relieving the discomfort of eczema, dermatitis and nappy rash, containing cod liver oil and zinc oxide, an astringent and an antiseptic.
Dose: The ointment should be applied to the affected area thinly. For nappy rash, apply after washing and drying baby's bottom.

MOTILIUM 10
Use: Tablets for easing digestive discomfort, containing domperidone, an ingredient to help speed up the digestive system.
Dose: 1 tablet should be taken 3 times a day and at night if required. This treatment is not recommended for children under 16 years.

MOVELAT RELIEF CREAM, MOVELAT RELIEF GEL
Use: A non-steroidal cream for the treatment of muscular aches and pains, containing salicylic acid, an aspirin derivative, and an ingredient for reducing swelling.
Dose: The product should be applied to the affected area up to 4 times a day. This treatment is not recommended for children under 16 years.

MU-CRON
Use: A tablet for easing the congestion of colds and catarrh, containing paracetamol and pseudoephedrine, a decongestant.
Dose: 1 tablet can be taken up to 4 times a day, allowing 4 hours between doses. Take a maximum of 4 tablets in 24 hours. This treatment is not recommended for children under 12 years.

MYCIL ATHLETE'S FOOT SPRAY
Use: This is a powder in a spray form for the treatment of athlete's foot. It contains tolnaftate, an antifungal ingredient.
Dose: The product should be applied morning and evening until the

symptoms clear and continued for a further 7 days.

MYCIL GOLD CLOTRIMAZOLE / MYCIL OINTMENT

Use: This is an ointment treatment for athlete's foot, containing the antifungal ingredient tolnaftate.

Dose: The product should be applied to the affected part morning and evening and continued for a further 7 days once the infection has cleared.

MYCIL POWDER

Use: This is a powder treatment for athlete's foot, containing the antifungal ingredient tolnaftate.

Dose: The powder should be sprinkled over the affected area morning and evening. Treatment should be continued for a further 7 days after the infection has cleared.

MYCOTA CREAM

Use: This is a cream treatment for athlete's foot, containing undecenoic acid, an antifungal ingredient.

Dose: Apply the cream to clean, dry skin. The treatment should be continued for a further 7 days after the infection has cleared.

MYCOTA POWDER

Use: This is a powder for the treatment of athlete's foot. It contains undecenoic acid and zinc undecenoate, both antifungal ingredients.

Dose: Sprinkle the powder over the affected area morning and evening. The treatment should be continued for a further 7 days after the infection has cleared up. This product is also available in spray form.

NASCIODINE

Use: A cream treatment for relieving muscular aches and pains, containing rubefacients and a salicylate, an aspirin derivative.

Dose: The cream should be massaged into the affected area 2-3 times a day. This treatment is not recommended for children under 6 years.

NEO BABY CREAM

Use: A cream for the treatment of nappy rash, containing cetrimide and benzalkonium, both antiseptics.

Dose: The product should be applied to clean dry skin as required.

NEO BABY MIXTURE

Use: A liquid remedy for relieving infant wind and colic, containing sodium bicarbonate, an antacid, dill oil and ginger.

Dose: 2.5ml, 3 times a day, for those under 1 month, 5ml for those from 1 month to 1 year of age.

NICORETTE

Use: A treatment for nicotine dependence (for those who smoke less than 20 cigarettes a day) in the form of chewing gum, containing 2mg of nicotine per gum piece.

Dose: 1 piece of gum should be chewed for 30 minutes. Take a maximum of 15 pieces in 24hours. After 3 months the dosage should be reduced. Nicorette Plus is also available, containing 4 mg of nicotine per piece of gum.

NICORETTE INHALER

Use: These are inhalable cartridges for nicotine dependence (for those who smoke more than 20 cigarettes a day). 1 cartridge contains 10mg of nicotine.

Dose: The cartridge should be fixed into the inhaler and sucked when an urge to have a cigarette arises. Use a minimum of 12 cartridges in 24 hours. The amount used should be stable over 8 weeks, then halved over the following 2 weeks, and reduced to zero by the twelfth week of treatment.

NICORETTE PATCH

Use: This is a skin patch for treating nicotine dependence.

Dose: These patches are available in 5mg, 10mg and 15mg strengths. 1 patch should be applied to the arm on waking and removed 16 hours later. The dose should be reduced gradually by using lower dosage patches.

NICOTINELL CHEWING GUM, NIQUITIN CQ GUM

Use: This is a chewing gum for treating nicotine dependence. Each piece of gum contains 2mg of nicotine.

Dose: 8-12 pieces of gum should be chewed a day. Take a maximum of 25 pieces in 24 hours. The number of pieces of gum should be reduced gradually over a 3-month period. The product is also available in 4mg pieces.

NICOTINELL TTS (PATCH)

Use: This is a skin patch treatment for reducing nicotine dependence.

Dose: There are 3 strength doses available according to cigarette consumption. The dosage should be reduced gradually over a 3-month period.

NIGHT NURSE

Use: A liquid remedy for easing cold and flu symptoms at night, containing paracetamol, promethazine, an antihistamine and dextromethorphan, a cough suppressant.

Dose: Adults should take 20ml just before retiring. Children (12 years and over) should be given 10ml just before bedtime. This treatment is not recommended for children under 12 years.

NIQUITIN CQ, NIQUITIN CQ CLEAR

Use: To aid patients wishing to stop smoking

Dose: The strength of the patch applied is related to the number of cigarettes smoked in a day. The initial patch strength will be used for 6 weeks, and then the strength reduced every 2 weeks until no patched are required.

NIQUITIN CQ LOZENGES

Use: To aid patients who wish to give up smoking.

Dose: Initially 1 lozenge should dissolve in the mouth every 1-2 hours for around 6 weeks, the interval between lozenges is then doubled every week until they are no longer required. No more than 15 lozenges should be used in a day, and preferably no more than 9.

NIZORAL DANDRUFF SHAMPOO

Use: A medicated shampoo for the treatment of dandruff, containing ketoconazole.

Dose: Should be used as a shampoo, left in for 3-5 minutes and then rinsed out. It should be used twice a week for 2-4 weeks, reducing use to once every 1-2 weeks as a preventive measure.

NUPERCAINAL

Use: A treatment for piles, containing cinchocaine, a mild local anaesthetic.

Dose: The ointment should be applied sparingly to the affected area up to 3 times a day. This treatment is not recommended for children under 12 years.

NUROFEN, NUROFEN LIQUID CAPSULES, NUROFEN MELTLETS, NUROFEN ORODISPERSIBLE, NUROFEN MIGRAINE PAIN

Use: Analgesic tablets for pain relief, containing ibuprofen.

Dose: 2 tablets should be taken initially and a further 1-2 tablets every 4 hours if required. Take a maximum of 6 tablets in 24 hours. This treatment is not recommended for children under 12 years.

NUROFEN COLD AND FLU, NUROFEN SINUS RELIEF

Use: These are tablets for relieving the symptoms of cold and flu. Each tablet contains ibuprofen and pseudoephedrine, a decongestant.

Dose: 2 tablets should be taken initially, followed by 1-2 tablets every 4 hours if required. Take a maximum of 6 tablets in 24 hours. This treatment is not recommended for children under 12 years.

NUROFEN FOR CHILDREN
NUROFEN FOR CHILDREN SACHETS

Use: An orange flavoured analgesic liquid for general pain relief, which is sugar- and colour-free.

Dose: Take a maximum of 4 doses in 24 hours. Babies (6-12 months) should be given 2.5ml up to 3 times in 24 hours. Babies (1-2 years) should be given 2.5ml every 4 hours if required. Children (3-7 years) should be given 5ml every 4 hours. Children (8-12 years) should be given 10ml every 4 hours. Not recommended for babies under 6 months.

NUROFEN PLUS
Use: Analgesic tablets for general pain relief containing ibuprofen and codeine phosphate.
Dose: 2 tablets should be taken initially and then 1-2 tablets every 4-6 hours if required. Take a maximum of 6 tablets in 24 hours. This treatment is not recommended for children under 12 years.

NURSE HARVEY'S GRIPE MIXTURE
Use: A liquid remedy for relieving infant colic and wind, containing sodium bicarbonate, an antacid, and dill and caraway oil.
Dose: 5-10ml should be given according to age, after or during feeds. Give a maximum of 6 doses in 24 hours. This treatment is not recommended for babies under 1 month.

NURSE SYKES BRONCHIAL BALSAM
Use: A remedy for relieving coughs, containing guaiphenesin, an expectorant.
Dose: 5-10ml should be taken every 4 hours and at bedtime. This treatment is not recommended for children under 12 years.

NURSE SYKES POWDERS
Use: An analgesic powder for general pain relief, containing aspirin, paracetamol and caffeine.
Dose: 1 powder should be dissolved in water and taken every 4 hours. Take a maximum of 6 powders in 24 hours. This treatment is not recommended for children under 12 years.

NYLAX
Use: A constipation remedy in the form of tablets. Each tablet contains senna, which is a stimulant laxative.
Dose: Adults should take 2 tablets on retiring. Children (5-12 years) should be given 1 tablet at bedtime. This treatment is not recommended for children under 5 years.

NYTOL

Use: A remedy for insomnia, containing diphenhydramine, an antihistamine.
Dose: 2 tablets should be taken 20 minutes before retiring. This treatment is not recommended for children under 16 years.

OCCLUSAL

Use: A liquid treatment for the removal of warts and verrucae, containing salicylic acid.
Dose: The product should be applied to the wart or verruca and allowed to dry. The treatment should be repeated daily. This treatment is not recommended for children under 6 years.

OILATUM EMOLLIENT

Use: An emollient liquid for the treatment of eczema and dermatitis, containing various oils.
Dose: The liquid can be added to the bath water, or applied to the skin directly and rinsed off afterwards. The product is also available as shower gel and hand gel.

OILATUM JUNIOR FLARE UP

Use: An emollient liquid for treating the discomfort of eczema and dermatitis in children, containing a mixture of oils and antiseptics.
Dose: The liquid should be added to bath water.

OILATUM PLUS

Use: An emollient liquid for relieving the discomfort of skin disorders such as eczema and dermatitis, containing a mixture of oils and antiseptics.
Dose: The liquid should be added to bath water.

OPAS

Use: Antacid tablets for easing indigestion and heartburn, containing sodium.
Dose: 1-2 tablets should be taken after each meal, or as required. This treatment is not recommended for children under 12 years.

OPAZIMES

Use: Tablets to help stop diarrhoea, containing kaolin, morphine and belladonna.

Dose: Adults should chew or suck 2 tablets every 4 hours, with a maximum of 8 tablets in 24 hours. Children over 6 years should chew or suck 1 tablet every 4 hours, with a maximum of 4 tablets in 24 hours. This treatment is not recommended for children under 6 years.

OPTICROM ALLERGY EYE DROPS

Use: Eye drops for relieving itchy eyes caused by hayfever, containing sodium cromoglycate, an anti-inflammatory.

Dose: 1-2 drops should be applied to each eye 4 times a day. This treatment is not recommended for children under 5 years.

ORALDENE

Use: This is a mouthwash for the treatment of mouth infections, sore gums and bad breath. It contains hexetidine, an anti-microbial.

Dose: 15 ml of the mouthwash should be rinsed or gargled 2-3 times a day. The product should not be diluted or swallowed. This treatment is not recommended for children under 5 years.

ORUVAIL

Use: This is a gel for the treatment of muscular aches and pains, containing ketoprofen, a non-steroidal anti-inflammatory (NSAID).

Dose: The gel should be massaged into the affected area 3 times a day. This treatment is not recommended for children under 12 years.

OTEX EAR DROPS

Use: Ear drops for the removal of earwax, containing softening ingredients.

Dose: 5 drops of the liquid should be put into the ear once or twice a day, for 3-4 days until the wax loosens.

OTRIVINE-ANTISTIN

Use: Eye drops for hayfever sufferers, containing xylometazeline, a decongestant and antazoline, a topical antihistamine.

Dose: Adults should take 1-2 drops into the affected eye/s, 2-3 times a day. Children over 5 years should be given 1 drop 2-3 times a day. This treatment is not recommended for children under 5 years.

OVEX TABLETS
Use: Tablets for the treatment of intestinal worms, containing mebendazole, an anti-worm ingredient.
Dose: For threadworms 1 dose of 1 tablet should be taken. This should be repeated after 2 weeks if the infestation is still present. Treatment is not recommended for children under 2 years.

OXY 5, OXY 10
Use: This is a lotion for the treatment of spots and acne, containing benzoyl peroxide.
Dose: The lotion should be applied once a day for 1 week. If no irritation occurs, it can be applied twice a day. The lower dose should be used first, progressing to the stronger version if required - Oxy 10. This treatment is not recommended for children under 15 years.

PANADOL, PANADOL CAPSULES, PANADOL SOLUBLE
Use: Analgesic tablets for general pain relief, containing paracetamol.
Dose: Adults should take 2 tablets every 4 hours. The soluble tablets should be dissolved in a glass of water before taking. Take a maximum of 8 tablets in 24 hours. Children (6-12 years) should be given ½-1 tablet every 4 hours, with a maximum of 4 tablets in 24 hours. This treatment is not recommended for children under 6 years.

PANADOL EXTRA, PANADOL EXTRA SOLUBLE
Use: Analgesic tablets for general pain relief containing paracetamol and caffeine.
Dose: 2 tablets can be taken every 4 hours if required. Take a maximum of 8 tablets in 24 hours. The soluble tablets should be dissolved in a glass of water. This treatment is not recommended for children under 12 years.

PANADOL NIGHT PAIN

Use: Analgesic capsules for general pain relief, containing paracetamol, and diphendydramine, an antihistamine.

Dose: 2 tablets should be taken 20 minutes before going to bed. Do not take for more than 7 consecutive nights. This treatment is not recommended for children under 12 years.

PANADOL ULTRA

Use: Analgesic tablets for general pain relief, containing paracetamol and codeine phosphate.

Dose: 2 tablets should be taken up to 4 times a day if required. Take a maximum of 4 tablets in 24 hours. This treatment is not recommended for children under 12 years.

PANOXYL ACNEGEL, AQUAGEL, CREAM, LOTION

Use: A medicine for the treatment of acne and spots available in 2 strengths, containing benzoyl peroxide.

Dose: The product should be applied to clean skin once a day, using the lower strength version first and then progressing to the higher strength version if necessary. This treatment is not recommended for children under 15 years.

PANOXYL WASH (10)

Use: A wash for the treatment of acne and spots, containing benzoyl peroxide.

Dose: The wash should be applied to wet skin, rinsed with alternate warm and cold water and patted dry. Use once a day in the morning. This treatment is not recommended for children under 15 years.

PARACETS, PARACETS CAPSULES

Use: Analgesic tablets for general pain relief, containing paracetamol.

Dose: Adults should take 2 tablets up to 4 times a day if required. Take a maximum of 8 tablets in 24 hours. Children (6-12 years) should be given $1/2$-1 tablet up to 4 times a day, with a maximum of 4 tablets in 24 hours. This treatment is not recommended for children under 6 years.

PARACODOL

Use: Analgesic capsules for general pain relief, containing paracetamol and codeine phosphate.

Dose: 1-2 capsules should be taken every 4-6 hours. Take a maximum of 8 capsules in 24 hours. This treatment is not recommended for children under 12 years. The product is also available in soluble tablet form.

PARAMOL

Use: Analgesic tablets for general pain relief, containing paracetamol and dihydrocodeine tartrate.

Dose: 1-2 tablets should be taken during or after meals, every 4-6 hours as required. Take a maximum of 8 tablets in 24 hours. This treatment is not recommended for children under 12 years.

PAVADOL D

Use: A sugar-free liquid remedy for relieving coughs, containing pholcodine, a cough suppressant.

Dose: Adults should take 5-10ml 4 times a day if required, up to 60ml a day. Children (1-12 years) should be given 2.5-5ml 3-5 times a day according to age. Read the label for the correct dosage. This treatment is not suitable for children under 1 year.

PAXIDORM TABLETS

Use: Tablets for insomnia, containing diphenhydramine, an antihistamine.

Dose: 1-2 tablets should be taken just before bedtime. This treatment is not recommended for children under 16 years.

PENTRAX SHAMPOO

Use: A medicated shampoo for the treatment of dandruff, containing coal tar.

Dose: The treatment should be used as an ordinary shampoo twice a week.

PEPCID AC

Use: Tablets for relieving general stomach discomfort, indigestion and heartburn, containing famotidine, a histamine H2 antagonist that helps reduce stomach acid.

Dose: 1 tablet should be taken 1 hour before eating. Take a maximum of 2 tablets in 24 hours. This treatment is not recommended for children under 16 years and should not be taken for more than 2 weeks.

PEPTO-BISMOL

Use: A liquid remedy for relieving indigestion, heartburn and general stomach discomfort. The liquid contains bismuth, an ingredient to coat the stomach lining.

Dose: Adults should take 30ml every 30 minutes to 1 hour. This treatment is not recommended for children under sixteen years.

PEVARYL

Use: This is a cream for the treatment of athlete's foot, containing econazole, an antifungal ingredient.

Dose: The cream should be applied twice a day for as long as it is needed. This product is also available in lotion and powder forms.

PHENERGAN

Use: Tablets for preventing travel sickness, containing promethazine, an antihistamine. The tablets are available in 2 strengths, 10mg and 25mg.

Dose: Adults and children over 10 years should take 1-2 10mg tablets, or 1 x 25mg tablet, the night before the journey. The dose should be repeated after 6 to 8 hours if necessary. Children (5-10 years) should be given 1 x 10mg tablet the night before the journey, and then again 6-8 hours later if necessary. The 25mg tablets are not suitable for children under 10 years. A liquid version is available for younger children (2-5 years). This treatment is not recommended for children under 2 years.

PHENERGAN NIGHTIME

Use: A tablet remedy for insomnia, containing promethazine, an anti-histamine.
Dose: 2 tablets should be taken at night. This treatment is not recommended for children under 16 years.

PHENSIC

Use: Analgesic tablets for general pain relief, containing aspirin and caffeine.
Dose: 2 tablets should be taken every 3-4 hours as required. Take a maximum of 12 tablets in 24 hours. This treatment is not recommended for children under 16 years.

PICKLE'S OINTMENT

Use: An ointment for treating corns and calluses, containing salicylic acid.
Dose: The product should be applied to the affected area at night for 4 nights. The skin should be allowed to fall off before reapplying the ointment.

PIRITON TABLETS

Use: A tablet for relieving hayfever symptoms, containing chlorpheniramine, an antihistamine.
Dose: Adults should take 1 tablet every 4-6 hours, with a maximum of 6 tablets in 24 hours. Children (6-12 years) should be given half a tablet every 4-6 hours, with a maximum of 3 tablets in 24 hours. This treatment is not recommended for children under 6 years.

PIRITON ALLERGY SYRUP

Use: A liquid remedy for relieving hayfever symptoms, containing chlorpheniramine, an antihistamine.
Dose: Adults should take 10ml every 4-6 hours. Children (1-12 years) should be given 2.5-5ml, according to age. Read the label for the correct dosage. This treatment is not recommended for babies under 1 year.

POLYTAR AF

Use: A liquid for the treatment of dandruff, containing peanut oil, zinc

Dose: The liquid should be massaged into the hair and scalp and left in for 2-3 minutes before rinsing out. Use 1-2 times a week.

POLYTAR LIQUID

Use: A liquid treatment for dandruff, containing coal tar and peanut oil.
Dose: The lotion should be applied to wet hair, massaged into the scalp and rinsed out. This should be carried out twice. The lotion should be used once or twice a week.

PREPARATION H OINTMENT

Use: An ointment for the treatment of piles, containing shark oil, a skin protectant.
Dose: The ointment should be applied morning and evening and after each bowel movement. This treatment is not recommended for children under 12 years. The product is also available in suppository form.

PR HEAT SPRAY

Use: A spray for relief of muscular pain, containing salicylates which are related to aspirin.
Dose: Spray should be applied to the affected area up to 3 times a day. This treatment is not recommended for children under 6 years of age.

PRIODERM CREAM SHAMPOO

Use: A shampoo for the treatment of head lice, containing malathion.
Dose: The treatment should be shampooed into the hair and left for 5 minutes, then rinsed out. This should be carried out twice. Repeat this twice more at 3-day intervals. The lotion can be used for treating pubic lice. This treatment is not recommended for babies under 6 months.

PRIODERM LOTION

Use: A lotion for the treatment of lice and scabies, containing malathion and alcohol.
Dose: For head or pubic lice, the lotion should be applied to the affected area and left to dry for at least 2 hours, but preferably for 12 hours if possible. The treatment should then be washed off and the hair combed

out while still wet. For scabies the lotion should be applied to the whole body and left on for 24 hours before washing off. This treatment is not recommended for babies under 6 months.

PRIPSEN MEBENDAZOLE TABLETS

Use: Tablets for removing intestinal worms, containing mebendazole, an anti-worm ingredient.

Dose: For threadworms 1 dose of 1 tablet should be taken. This can be repeated after 2 weeks if the infestation is still present. This treatment is not recommended for children under 2 years.

PRIPSEN PIPERAZINE PHOSPHATE POWDER

Use: A powder treatment for the removal of intestinal worms, containing piperazine phosphate, an anti-worm ingredient.

Dose: For threadworms and roundworms, adults and children over 6 years should take 1 sachet dissolved in a measured quantity of milk. Adults should take at bed-time and children in the morning. Children (1- 6 years) should be given 5ml of the sachet contents in the morning. For threadworms, a repeat dose should be taken 14 days after the first dose. For roundworms, additional doses can be taken each month to avoid re-infestation. This treatment is not recommended for babies under 1 year.

PROFLEX PAIN RELIEF CREAM

Use: A cream for the treatment of muscular pains, containing ibuprofen, a non-steroidal anti-inflammatory (NSAID).

Dose: The cream should be massaged into the affected area 3-4 times a day. This treatment is not recommended for children under 12 years.

PROPAIN

Use: Analgesic tablets for general pain relief, containing paracetamol, codeine phosphate, diphenhydramine and caffeine.

Dose: 1-2 tablets should be taken every 4 hours. Take a maximum of 10 tablets in 24 hours. This treatment is not recommended for children under 12 years.

PULMO BAILLY

Use: A liquid remedy for relieving coughs, containing guaicol, an expectorant and codeine, a cough suppressant.

Dose: Adults should take up to 10 ml diluted in water, before food. Take a maximum of 3 doses in 24 hours. Children (5-15 years) should be given 5 ml. This treatment is not recommended for children under 5 years.

PYRALVEX

Use: A liquid treatment for mouth ulcers, containing salicylic acid, an analgesic.

Dose: The liquid should be brushed onto the affected area 3-4 times a day. This treatment is not recommended for children under 12 years.

QUELLADA-M CREAM SHAMPOO

Use: A shampoo for the treatment for lice and scabies, containing malathion.

Dose: The shampoo should be applied to dry hair and scalp, and to the pubic area if necessary, left for 4 minutes, then lathered and rinsed off. This treatment is not recommended for babies under 6 months.

QUELLADA-M LOTION

Use: A lotion for the treatment of lice and scabies, containing malathion and alcohol.

Dose: For head or pubic lice, the lotion should be applied to the affected area and left to dry for 2-12 hours. It should then be washed off and the hair combed out while wet. For scabies, the lotion should be applied to the whole body and left on for 24 hours before washing off. This treatment is not recommended for babies under 6 months.

QUINODERM CREAM

Use: This is a cream for the treatment of acne and spots available in 2 strengths, containing benzoyl peroxide.

Dose: The cream should be massaged into the affected area 1-3 times a day, starting with the lower dose version and progressing to the stronger dose version if required. This treatment is not recommended for children under

RADIAN-B PUMP SPRAY, RADIAN-B LOTION

Use: A spray for relieving muscular aches and pains, containing rubefacients and a salicylate, an aspirin derivative.

Dose: The product should be sprayed onto the affected area and a second dose applied 15 minutes later. This can be repeated up to 3 times a day if required. The number of applications should be reduced as symptoms subside. This treatment is not recommended for children under 6 years.

RADIAN-B IBUPROFEN GEL

Use: A gel for the treatment of muscular aches and pains, containing ibuprofen, a non-steroidal anti-inflammatory (NSAID).

Dose: The product should be applied to the affected area and used every 4 hours if necessary, with a maximum of 4 applications in 24 hours. This treatment is not recommended for children under 14 years.

RALGEX CREAM

Use: A cream for alleviating muscular aches and pains, containing rubefacients and a salicylate, an aspirin derivative.

Dose: The cream should be applied to the affected area up to 4 times a day. This treatment is not recommended for children under 12 years. Do not apply onto broken skin, or near eyes or mouth.

RALGEX FREEZE SPRAY

Use: A cooling spray for relieving muscle pain, containing a salicylate, an aspirin derivative.

Dose: The product should be applied to the affected area up to 4 times a day. This treatment is not recommended for children under 5 years.

RALGEX HEAT SPRAY

Use: A spray for relieving muscular pain, containing rubefacients and a salicylate, an aspirin derivative.

Dose: 2 or 3 short bursts of spray should be applied to the affected area every 2 hours if required, no more than 4 times a day. This treatment is not recommended for children under 5 years.

RALGEX STICK

Use: An embrocation stick for relieving muscular aches and pains, containing rubefacients and a salicylate, an aspirin derivative.

Dose: The product should be applied to the affected area as required. It should not be massaged or rubbed in. This treatment is not recommended for children under 16.

RAP-EZE

Use: Antacid tablets for relieving indigestion and heartburn.

Dose: 2 tablets should be chewed or sucked as required. Take a maximum of 16 tablets in 24 hours. Treatment is not recommended for children under 12 years.

REGULAN

Use: A powder treatment for relieving constipation and irritable bowel syndrome. The powders consist of ispaghula husk, a bulk forming laxative.

Dose: Adults should take 1 sachet dissolved in water 1-3 times a day. Children (6-12 years) should be given half to 1 level teaspoonful dissolved in water 1-3 times a day. The powder should be taken with plenty of fluid and not before bedtime. This treatment is not recommended for children under 6 years. The product is also available in other flavours.

REGULOSE

Use: A plum flavoured liquid remedy for relieving constipation, containing lactulose, an osmotic laxative.

Dose: Adults and children over 12 years should take 15-30ml daily for the first 2-3 days, reducing the dose to 10-15ml daily thereafter. Children under 12 years should be given 10-25ml for the first few days, reducing the dose to 5-15ml thereafter.

RELCOFEN

Use: Analgesic tablets for general pain relief, containing either 200mg, or 400mg of ibuprofen.

Dose: 1-2 tablets should be taken 3 times a day. Take a maximum of 6 tablets in 24 hours. This treatment is not recommended for children under 12 years.

REMEGEL ORIGINAL, REMEGEL WIND RELIEF

Use: Square antacid tablets for easing indigestion and heartburn.
Dose: 1-2 squares should be chewed every hour. Take a maximum of 12 squares in 24 hours. This treatment is not recommended for children under 12 years. The product is available in several flavours.

RENNIE DIGESTIF

Use: Antacid tablets for indigestion and heartburn.
Dose: Adults should suck or chew 2 tablets as required. Take a maximum of 16 tablets in 24 hours. Children (6-12 years) should be given 1 tablet as needed, with a maximum of 8 tablets in 24 hours. This treatment is not recommended for children under 6 years.

RINSTEAD PASTILLES

Use: Used for relief of pain associated with mouth ulcers or denture use, containing cetylpyridinium and menthol.
Dose: 1 pastille should be allowed to dissolve in the mouth approximately every 2 hours. This treatment is not recommended for young children.

ROBITUSSIN CHESTY COUGH MEDICINE

Use: A liquid remedy for the treatment of coughs, containing guaiphenesin, an expectorant.
Dose: Adults should take 10 ml 4 times a day. Children (1-12 years) should be 2.5-5 ml, according to age. Read the label for the correct dosage. This treatment is not recommended for children under 1 year.

ROBITUSSIN DRY COUGH

Use: A liquid remedy for the treatment of coughs, containing dextromethorphan, a cough suppressant.
Dose: Adults should take 10 ml 4 times a day. Children (6-12 years) should be given 5 ml 4 times a day. This treatment is not recommended for children under 6 years.

ROBITUSSIN FOR CHESTY COUGHS WITH CONGESTION

Use: A liquid remedy for the treatment of coughs, containing guaiphenesin, an expectorant and pseudoephedrine, a decongestant.

Dose: Adults should take 10 ml 4 times a day. Children (2-12 years) should be given 2.5-5 ml, according to age. Read the label for the correct dosage. This treatment is not recommended for children under 2 years.

RYNACROM ALLERGY

Use: A nasal spray for relieving hayfever symptoms, containing sodium cromoglycate, an anti-inflammatory and xylometszoline, a decongestant.

Dose: 1 spray should be directed into each nostril 2-4 times a day. This treatment is not recommended for children under 5 years.

SALACTOL WART PAINT

Use: A paint for the treatment of corns and calluses, containing salicylic acid.

Dose: The product should be applied to the affected area daily and rubbed down with an emery board.

SALONPAS PLASTERS

Use: A plaster treatment for relieving muscular aches and pains. The plasters contain rubefacients and a salicylate, an aspirin derivative.

Dose: Plaster can be replaced up to 3 times a day for up to 7 days. Not suitable for children under 12 years.

SAVLON ANTISEPTIC CREAM

Use: An antiseptic cream for the treatment of minor wounds and irritations of the skin, containing cetrimide and chlorohexidine gluconate.

Dose: The cream should be applied to the affected part as needed.

SAVLON ANTISEPTIC WOUND WASH

Use: A liquid spray antiseptic for the treatment of minor wounds and skin irritations, containing chlorohexidine gluconate.

Dose: The product should be sprayed onto the wound in order to help wash away any dirt.

SAVLON CONCENTRATED ANTISEPTIC
Use: A liquid antiseptic containing gluconate and cetrimide for the treatment of minor wounds and skin irritations.
Dose: The product should be diluted with water as appropriate for its use.

SAVLON DRY ANTISEPTIC
Use: An antiseptic aerosol powder in the form of a spray for the treatment of minor wounds and skin irritations. The spray contains povidone iodine.
Dose: A light dusting of the powder should be sprayed onto the affected part.

SCHOLL ANTISEPTIC FOOT BALM
Use: A foot balm for relieving sore feet, containing the antiseptic menthyl salicylate and menthol.
Dose: The product should be applied to the affected area morning and evening, or as required.

SCHOLL ATHLETE'S FOOT CREAM
Use: This is a cream for the treatment of athlete's foot, containing tolnaftate, an antifungal ingredient.
Dose: The product should be applied twice a day to the affected area and for a further 2 weeks after the infection has cleared.

SCHOLL CORN AND CALLUS REMOVAL LIQUID
Use: A liquid for the removal of corns and calluses.
Dose: The liquid should be applied to the affected area twice a day, for no longer than 2 weeks. This treatment is not recommended for children under 16 years.

SCHOLL CORN REMOVAL PADS
Use: Medicated pads for the removal of corns, containing salicylic acid.
Dose: A pad should be applied once a day to the affected area until the corn can be removed. This treatment is not recommended for children under 16 years. The product is also available as Scholl Soft Corn Removal Pads.

SCHOLL CORN REMOVAL PLASTERS

Use: Medicated plasters for the removal of corns, containing salicylic acid.

Dose: The medicated plasters should be applied to the affected area once a day until the corn can be removed. This treatment is not recommended for children under 16 years. Waterproof plasters are also available.

SCHOLL POLYMER GEL CORN REMOVERS

Use: A gel for the treatment of corns and calluses, containing salicylic acid.

Dose: A new plaster should be applied each day to the affected area until the corn can be removed. This treatment is not recommended for children under 16 years.

SCHOLL SEAL AND HEAL VERRUCA REMOVAL GEL

Use: A liquid treatment for the removal of verrucae, containing salicylic acid.

Dose: 1-2 drops should be applied onto the affected area once a day and allowed to dry. The treatment should be applied daily until the verruca can be removed. This treatment is not recommended for children under 16 years.

SCHOLL VERRUCA REMOVAL SYSTEM

Use: Medicated plasters for the treatment of verrucae, containing salicylic acid.

Dose: An appropriately sized plaster should be applied to the verruca and left in position for 48 hours before repeating the treatment. The treatment may be continued for up to 12 weeks if necessary. This treatment is not recommended for children under 16 years unless advised otherwise by a doctor.

SEA-LEGS

Use: Tablets for preventing travel sickness, containing meclozine, an antihistamine.

Dose: Adults should take 2 tablets 1 hour before a journey, or on the previous evening. Children over 2 years should be given half to 1 tablet, depending on age. Read the label for the correct dosage. This treatment is not recommended for children under 2 years.

SELSUN
Use: A liquid containing selenium sulphide for the treatment of dandruff.
Dose: The liquid should be applied twice a week as a shampoo for 2 weeks, then once a week for 2 weeks, until the dandruff has cleared. This treatment is not recommended for children under 5 years.

SENOKOT TABLETS
Use: Tablets for relieving constipation, containing senna, a stimulant laxative.
Dose: 2 tablets should be taken at bedtime. This treatment is not recommended for children under 12 years. The product is also available in granular and liquid forms.

SETLERS ANTACID TABLETS
Use: Antacid tablets for relieving indigestion.
Dose: 1-2 tablets should be sucked or chewed as required. Take a maximum of 16 tablets in 24 hours. This treatment is not recommended for children under 12 years. The product is available in several different flavours.

SINUTAB TABLETS
Use: Tablets for relieving the symptoms of colds, flu and sinusitis. Each tablet contains paracetamol and pseudoephedrine, a decongestant.
Dose: Adults should take 2 tablets up to 4 times a day. Take a maximum of 8 tablets in 24 hours. Children (6-12 years) should be given 1 tablet up to 4 times a day, with a maximum of 4 tablets in 24 hours. This treatment is not recommended for children under 6 years.

SOLARCAINE CREAM, SOLARCAINE LOTION, SOLARCAINE GEL, SOLARCAINE SPRAY
Use: A cream for the treatment of bites, stings, minor burns, scalds and sunburn, containing a mild anaesthetic.

Dose: The product should be applied to the affected area 3-4 times a day. Do not inhale. This treatment is not recommended for children under 3 years.

SOLPADEINE PLUS CAPSULES, SOLPADEINE PLUS TABLETS

Use: Analgesic for general pain relief, containing paracetamol, codeine phosphate and caffeine.

Dose: 2 tablets or capsules should be taken 3-4 times a day. Take a maximum of 8 tablets or capsules in 24 hours. This treatment is not recommended for children under 12 years. Preparations are available without caffeine and are called Solpadeine Max.

SOLPAFLEX

Use: Analgesic tablets for general pain relief, containing ibuprofen and codeine phosphate hemihydrate.

Dose: 1-2 tablets should be taken every 4-6 hours as required. Take a maximum of 6 tablets in 24 hours. This treatment is not recommended for children under 12 years. Do not take for more than 3 consecutive days unless otherwise advised by a doctor.

SOMINEX

Use: Tablets for insomnia, containing promethazine, an antihistamine.

Dose: 1 tablet should be taken at bedtime. This treatment is not recommended for children under 16 years.

SOOTHELIP

Use: A cream treatment for cold sores, containing aciclovir, an antiviral.

Dose: The cream should be applied as soon as the tingling of a cold sore is felt and then every 4 hours, 5 times a day for 5 days. Repeat for a further 5 days if necessary.

STUGERON TABLETS

Use: Tablets for the prevention of travel sickness, containing cinnarazine, an antihistamine.

Dose: Adults should take 2 tablets 2 hours before the journey, followed by 1 tablet every 8 hours if required. Children (5-12 years) should be given half the adult dose. Consult doctor before use is suffering from Parkinson's disease. This product is not suitable for children under 5 years.

SUDAFED CONGESTION COLD AND FLU TABLETS

Use: Tablets for easing the symptoms of colds and flu, containing paracetamol and pseudoephedrine, a decongestant.

Dose: Adults should take 1 tablet every 4-6 hours. Take a maximum of 4 tablets in 24 hours. Children (6-12 years) should be given half a tablet every 4-6 hours, with a maximum of 4 doses in 24 hours. This treatment is not recommended for children under 6 years.

SUDAFED EXPECTORANT

Use: A liquid remedy for the treatment of coughs, containing guaiphenesin, an expectorant and pseudoephedrine, a decongestant.

Dose: Adults should take 10 ml 4 times a day. Children (6-12 years) should be given 5 ml. Children (2-5 years) should be given 2.5 ml. This treatment is not recommended for children under 2 years.

SUDAFED LINCTUS

Use: A liquid remedy for coughs, containing dextromethorphan, a cough suppressant, and pseudoephedrine, a decongestant.

Dose: Adults should take 10 ml 4 times a day. Children (6-12 years) should be given 5 ml. Children (2-5 years) should be given 2.5 ml. This treatment is not recommended for children under 2 years.

SUDAFED NASAL SPRAY

Use: A spray for easing nasal congestion caused by colds. The spray contains oxymetazoline, a decongestant.

Dose: 1-2 sprays should be directed into each nostril twice or 3 times a day. A maximum of 3 sprays may be used in 24 hours. This treatment is not recommended for children under 6 years. Do not use for more than a week.

SUDAFED TABLETS

Use: Tablets for relieving cold and flu symptoms, containing pseudoephedrine, a decongestant.

Dose: 1 tablet should be taken every 4-6 hours. Take a maximum of 4 tablets in 24 hours. This treatment is not recommended for children under 12 years.

SUDOCREM

Use: A cream for the treatment of nappy rash, containing zinc oxide, an antiseptic and astringent, and hypoallergenic lanolin.

Dose: The cream should be applied thinly to baby's bottom as required.

SULEO-M LOTION

Use: A lotion for the treatment of lice and scabies, containing malathion and alcohol.

Dose: The lotion should be applied to dry hair and rubbed in well. The hair should be allowed to dry naturally, washed out after 12 hours and then combed through while still wet. This treatment is not recommended for babies under 6 months.

SWARM

Use: A cream for the treatment of insect bites and stings, containing witch hazel and an anti-microbial.

Dose: The product should be applied to the affected area as required. For external use only.

SYNDOL

Use: Analgesic tablets for general pain relief, containing paracetamol, codeine phosphate, caffeine, and doxylamine succinate, an antihistamine.

Dose: 1-2 tablets should be taken every 4-6 hours as required. Take a maximum of 8 in 24 hours. This treatment is not recommended for children under 12 years.

SYNTARIS HAYFEVER

Use: A nasal spray for relieving the symptoms of hayfever, containing flunisolide, a corticosteroid.

Dose: Adults should take 2 sprays into each nostril morning and evening, with a maximum of 4 sprays for each nostril in 24 hours. For children (12-16 years) direct 1 spray into each nostril up to 3 times a day, with a maximum of 3 sprays per nostril in 24 hours. This treatment is not recommended for children under 12 years.

TAGAMET100

Use: Tablets for relieving indigestion, heartburn and general gastric discomfort. They contain cimetidine, a histamine H2 antagonist which reduces the production of stomach acid.

Dose: 2 tablets should be taken when symptoms arise. For indigestion at night, 1 tablet should be taken 1 hour before retiring. Take a maximum of 8 tablets in 24 hours. This treatment is not recommended for children under 16 years. Do not use for longer than 2 weeks. A pharmacist must be consulted before using this medicine.

TCP ANTISEPTIC OINTMENT

Use: An antiseptic ointment for the treatment of minor wounds and skin irritations, containing iodine, methyl salicylate, salicylic acid, sulphur, tannic acid, camphor and TCP liquid antiseptic.

Dose: The product should be applied to the affected area as required.

TCP FIRST AID ANTISEPTIC CREAM

Use: An antiseptic cream for the treatment of minor wounds and irritations of the skin. It contains chloroxylenol, triclosan, sodium salicylate and TCP liquid antiseptic.

Dose: The product should be applied to the affected area as required.

TCP LIQUID

Use: A liquid antiseptic for the treatment of minor wounds and irritations of the skin, containing phenol and halogenated phenols.

Dose: Diluted according to use, or apply neat to spots and mouth ulcers.

TCP SORE THROAT LOZENGES

Use: Lozenges for easing sore throats, containing antibacterial phenols.
Dose: 1 pastille should be sucked or chewed as required. This treatment is not recommended for children under 6 years.

T-GEL

Use: A medicated shampoo for the treatment of dandruff and dry scalp disorders, containing coal tar.
Dose: The product should be massaged into wet hair and scalp and then rinsed. Repeat use once or twice a week.

TIGER BALM RED (REGULAR AND EXTRA STRENGTH)

Use: An ointment for easing muscle pain, containing various rubefacients.
Dose: The balm should be rubbed gently into the affected area 2-3 times a day. This treatment is not recommended for children under 2 years.

TINADERM CREAM

Use: An antifungal cream for the treatment of athlete's foot, containing tolnaftate.
Dose: The cream should be applied twice a day to the affected area.

TIXYLIX CHESTY COUGH

Use: A blackcurrant flavoured liquid remedy for relieving coughs, containing guaiphenesin, an expectorant.
Dose: Children should be given 2.5-10 ml according to age. Read the label for the correct dosage. This treatment is not recommended for babies under 1 year.

TIXYLIX DAYTIME

Use: A liquid remedy for the treatment of coughs, containing pholcodine, a cough suppressant.
Dose: Children should be given 2.5-10 ml every 6 hours, according to age. Read the label for the correct dosage. This treatment is not

recommended for babies under 1 year. A night-time version is also available, containing promethazine, an antihistamine.

TOEPEDO
Use: This is a cream treatment for athlete's foot, containing keratolytics.
Dose: The cream should be applied sparingly to the affected area twice daily until the infection has cleared.

TOPAL
Use: Tablets for easing general digestive discomfort, containing an antacid and an alginate.
Dose: 1-3 tablets should be taken 4 times a day after meals and on retiring. This treatment is not recommended for children under 12 years.

TORBETOL CREAM
Use: A lotion for the treatment of acne and spots, containing cetrimide and chlorhexidine, both anti-microbials.
Dose: The lotion should be applied to the affected area up to 3 times a day. This treatment is not recommended for children under 15 years.

TRANSVASIN HEAT RUB
Use: A cream for easing muscular aches and pains, containing rubefacients and a salicylate, an aspirin derivative.
Dose: The cream should be applied to the affected area up to 3 times a day. This treatment is not recommended for children under 6 years.

TRANSVASIN HEAT SPRAY
Use: A spray for the treatment of various muscular aches and pains, containing rubefacients and a salicylate, an aspirin derivative.
Dose: The product should be sprayed onto the affected area up to 3 times a day. This treatment is not recommended for children under 5 years.

TRAXAM PAIN RELIEF GEL
Use: A gel for relieving muscular aches and pains, containing felbinac, a non-steroidal anti-inflammatory (NSAID).

Dose: The gel should be rubbed into the affected area 2-4 times a day. This treatment is not recommended for children under 12 years.

TUMS
Use: Antacid tablets for relieving indigestion and heartburn.
Dose: 1-2 tablets should be taken as required. Take a maximum of 16 tablets in 24 hours. This treatment is not recommended for children under 12 years.

TYROZETS
Use: Lozenges for relieving sore throats, containing tyrothricin, an antibacterial and benzocaine, an anaesthetic.
Dose: 1 lozenge should be dissolved in the mouth every 3 hours. Take a maximum of 8 in 24 hours. Children (3-11 years) should be given a maximum of 6 lozenges in 24 hours. This treatment is not recommended for children under 3 years.

ULTRABASE
Use: An emollient cream for the relief of eczema and dermatitis, containing a mixture of oils.
Dose: The product should be applied as required.

UNGUENTUM MERCK
Use: An emollient cream for relieving the discomfort of eczema, dermatitis and nappy rash, containing a mixture of various oils.
Dose: The cream should be applied as required.

VASOGEN CREAM
Use: A cream for the treatment of nappy rash, containing zinc oxide, an antiseptic and astringent, and calamine, a soothing ingredient.
Dose: The product should be applied to baby's bottom after washing and drying.

VEGANIN
Use: Analgesic tablets used for general pain relief. Veganin contain

paracetamol, aspirin and codeine phosphate.

Dose: 1-2 tablets should be taken every 3 to 4 hours as required. Take a maximum of 8 tablets in 24 hours. This treatment is not recommended for children under 16 years. The advice of a doctor should be sought if there is no improvement in 3 days.

VENO'S DRY COUGH

Use: A liquid remedy for the treatment of coughs, containing glucose and treacle.

Dose: Adults should take 10ml every 2 to 3 hours. Children (3-12 years) should be given 5ml. This treatment is not recommended for children under 3 years.

VENO'S EXPECTORANT

Use: A liquid remedy for the treatment of coughs, containing guaiphenesin, an expectorant, glucose and treacle.

Dose: Adults should take 10ml every 2-3 hours. Children (3-12 years) should be given 5ml every 2-3 hours. This treatment is not recommended for children under 3 years.

VENO'S TICKLY COUGH

Use: A liquid remedy for the treatment of coughs, containing lemon, glucose and treacle.

Dose: Adults should take 10ml every 2-3 hours. Children (3-12 years) should be given 5ml. This treatment is not recommended for children under 3 years.

VERACUR

Use: A gel for the treatment of verrucae and warts, containing formaldehyde.

Dose: Apply twice a day and remove the dead skin.

VERRUGON COMPLETE

Use: An ointment remedy for the treatment of verrucae, containing salicylic acid.

Dose: The felt ring should be placed on the verruca, and the ointment applied and covered with a plaster. This should be repeated daily. This treatment is not recommended for children under 6 years.

VICKS MEDINITE

Use: A liquid remedy for relieving coughs, containing dextromethorphan, a cough suppressant, ephedrine, a decongestant, doxylamine, an antihistamine and paracetamol.

Dose: Adults should take 30ml at bedtime. Children (10-12 years) should be given 15ml. This treatment is not recommended for children under 10 years.

VICKS SINEX DECONGESTANT NASAL SPRAY

Use: A nasal spray for clearing the congestion caused by colds, flu and sinusitis. It contains oxymetazoline, a decongestant.

Dose: 1-2 sprays should be directed into each nostril every 6-8 hours. This treatment is not recommended for children under 6 years. Do not use for longer than 7 days.

VICKS ULTRA CHLORASEPTIC

Use: A spray for relieving sore throats, containing benzocaine, an anaesthetic.

Dose: Adults should take 3 sprays every 2-3 hours. Children (6-12 years) should be given 1 spray every 2-3 hours. Take a maximum of 8 doses in 24 hours. This treatment is not recommended for children under 6 years and should not be used for more than 3 consecutive days.

VICKS VAPORUB

Use: An inhalant rub for easing congestion caused by colds and flu, containing menthol, eucalyptus and camphor.

Dose: A small amount should be rubbed into the chest, throat and back at bedtime. Alternatively, 2 teaspoons can be added to a bowl of hot water and the vapours inhaled. This treatment is not recommended for babies under 6 months.

VIRASORB

Use: A cream treatment for cold sores, containing aciclovir, an antiviral.

Dose: Should be applied as soon as a cold sore tingling is felt, then every

4 hours, 5 times a day for 5 days. Repeat for a further 5 days if necessary.

VOCALZONE
Use: Pastilles for easing sore throats.
Dose: 1 pastille should be dissolved in the mouth as needed, every 2 hours if necessary. This treatment is not recommended for children under 12 years.

WARTEX OINTMENT
Use: An ointment for the removal of warts, containing salicylic acid.
Dose: The product should be applied to the wart daily until the wart can be removed. This treatment is not recommended for children under 6 years.

WASP-EZE SPRAY
Use: An spray for the treatment of bites and stings, containing an anti-histamine.
Dose: The product should be applied to the affected area immediately and again after 15 minutes if necessary.

WAXSOL EAR DROPS
Use: Ear drops for removing earwax, containing softening ingredients.
Dose: The ears should be filled with the liquid for 2 consecutive nights before syringe treatment.

WITCH DOCTOR GEL, WITCH DOCTOR STICK
Use: An astringent gel for the treatment of bites, stings, minor burns, scalds, sunburn and bruises, containing witch hazel.
Dose: The product should be applied to the area as required.

WOODWARD'S GRIPE WATER
Use: A liquid remedy for relieving infant colic and wind, containing sodium bicarbonate, an antacid and dill oil.
Dose: 5-10 ml (according to age) should be given after or during feeds. Check the label for the correct dosage. Give a maximum of 6 doses in 24 hours. This treatment is not recommended for babies under 1 month.

YEAST-VITE
Use: A tablet remedy for alleviating fatigue, containing caffeine, vitamin B1 and nicontamide.
Dose: 2 tablets should be taken every 3-4 hours as required. Take a maximum of 12 tablets in 24 hours. This treatment is not recommended for children under 16.

ZANPROL
Use: Treatment of the symptoms of heartburn containing omeprazole, a proton pump inhibitor.
Dose: Initially 2 tablets should be taken with some fluid before a meal, for 3-4 days. This can then be reduced to 1 tablet once a day, usually the morning, to control the symptoms. If treatment is needed for longer than 2 weeks then the doctor should be consulted. A pharmacist must be consulted before using this medicine. Any adverse effects should be reported to the pharmacist or doctor.

ZANTAC 75 TABLETS
Use: Tablets for easing digestive discomfort, containing rantidine, a histamine H2 antagonist which helps to reduce the production of stomach acid.
Dose: 1 tablet should be taken initially, followed by 1 more if necessary. Take a maximum of 4 tablets in 24 hours. This treatment is not recommended for children under 16 years. Do not use for more than 2 weeks.

ZIRTEK
Use: A tablet for relieving the symptoms of hayfever and year-round allergic rhinitis, containing cetirizine, an antihistamine.
Dose: 1 tablet should be taken each day. This treatment is not recommended for children under 6 years.

ZOCOR HEART (ZOCOR HEART PRO)
Use: For treatment of moderate coronary heart disease, Zocar Heart contains simvastatin, a cholesterol lowering medicine.
Dose: 1 tablet should be taken each day. Consult a pharmacist before

taking this medicine to ensure it is suitable for the patient. Any sign of muscle or joint pain, or weakness, or skin condition appearing after taking this medicine should be reported to the doctor immediately. If these effects appear the medicine must not be taken.

ZOVIRAX COLD SORE CREAM

Use: A cream treatment for cold sores containing aciclovir, an antiviral.
Dose: The cream should be applied as soon as the tingling of a developing cold sore is felt. Continue to apply every 4 hours, 5 times a day for up to 10 days.

Here are a few medical terms that crop up time and time again, so to help you through the 'medical minefield' we have included descriptions of a few key phrases.

Adjuvant	Additional
Analogue	A chemically similar drug
Antagonist	Interferes with or prevents the normal action
Antipyretic	Reduces fever
Autoimmune	When the person's immune system produces cells that cause inflammation and damage to their own body such as the joints in rheumatoid arthritis
Beta-blocker	Drugs that block the beta-adrenoreceptors in the heart, blood vessels and lungs
Bronchodilator	Increases airflow
Cardiac	Heart related
Catheterisation	Passing a tube into the bladder to allow the person to pass urine
Convulsions	Fits, seizures
Diuretic	Medication which increases the amount of urine passed
Endocrine	Glands that produce hormones such as thyroid, pituitary, pancreas which makes insulin, ovaries, testes.
Flatulence	Passage of gas by mouth or rectum
Gastric	Stomach
G6PD deficiency	An inherited blood condition where infections and certain drugs can cause the patient to become anaemic and jaundiced
Gynaecomastia	Breast enlargement in men
Hypertension	High blood pressure
Hypotension	Low blood pressure
Immunosuppressant	Reduces the ability of the immune system
Impotence	Inability to achieve or maintain penile erection
Insomnia	Inability to sleep
Lactation	Production of breast milk
Lethargy	Tiredness
Libido	Sex drive
Lipids	Fats, mainly cholesterol and triglycerides
Meniere's disease	Condition where sufferers get hearing loss, dizziness, ringing in the ears and a feeling of pressure in the ears
Oesophagus	Throat
Priapism	Painful, prolonged penile erection
Sedation	Sleepiness
Tinnitus	Ringing sound in the ears
Topical	Applied to the skin or other specific area such as the eye
Tremor	Shakiness, generally of the hands
Vasodilator	Increases blood flow